The SMART Gardener's Guide to Growing Vegetables

Dr. Bob Gough

STACKPOLE
BOOKS

To my grandparents, Carmine and Annie,
who with a dime packet of radish seeds
helped raise a horticulturist

Copyright © 1996 by Stackpole Books

Published by
STACKPOLE BOOKS
5067 Ritter Road
Mechanicsburg, PA 17055

Printed in the United States of America

Cover and interior illustrations by Thomas Aubrey
Cover design by Caroline Miller

First Edition

10 9 8 7 6 5 4 3 2 1

Library of Congress Cataloging-in-Publication Data

Gough, Bob.
    The smart gardener's guide to growing vegetables / Bob Gough.—1st ed.
      p. cm.
    Includes index.
    ISBN 0-8117-3087-5
    1. Vegetable gardening. 2. Vegetables. I. Title.
  SB321.G66 1996
  635—dc20
                                         95-44905
                                               CIP

Contents

Speaking of Vegetables

There are many ways to classify vegetables. Botanical classification is used by gardeners worldwide. The taxonomic system, established by Carolus Linnaeus, groups plants into ever more specific categories based on botanical relationships. In this system, related vegetables often have similar cultural requirements (pepper and eggplant), but not always (salsify and lettuce).

The botanical classification of vegetables shows the relationships among species.

Subclass Monocotyledoneae (monocots)
    Amaryllidaceae (amaryllis family)

Allium porrum	Leek
Allium cepa	Shallot, onion
Allium sativum	Garlic
Allium schoenoprasum	Chive

    Gramineae (grass family)

Zea mays var. *everta*	Popcorn
Zea mays var. *saccharata*	Sweet corn

    Liliaceae (Lily family)

Asparagus officinalis	Asparagus

Subclass Dicotyledones (dicots)
    Chenopodiaceae (goosefoot family)

Beta vulgaris	Beet, chard
Spinacia oleracea	Spinach

Compositae (sunflower family)
    Cichorium endivia   Endive, escarole
    Cichorium intybus   Chicory
    Cynara scolymus   Globe artichoke
    Helianthus tuberosus   Jerusalem artichoke
    Lactuca sativa   Lettuce
    Scorzonera hispanica   Scorzonera
    Taraxacum officinale   Dandelion
    Tragopogon porrifolius   Salsify
Convolvulaceae (morning glory family)
    Ipomoea batatas   Sweet potato
Cruciferae (mustard family)
    Armoracia rusticana   Horseradish
    Brassica juncea   Leaf mustard
    Brassica napus   Rutabaga, Siberian kale
    Brassica oleracea (various groups)   Kale, collard,
                                         cauliflower,
                                         cabbage, Brussels
                                         sprouts, kohlrabi,
                                         broccoli
    Brassica rapa (various groups)   Chinese cabbage,
                                         turnip, broccoli raab
    Crambe maritima   Sea kale
    Raphanus sativus   Radish
Cucurbitaceae (gourd family)
    Citrullus lanatus   Watermelon
    Cucumis Melo (various groups)   Melons
    Cucumis sativus   Cucumber
    Cucurbita maxima   Winter squash,
                                         pumpkin
    Cucurbita mixta   Cushaw,
                                         pumpkin
    Cucurbita moschata   Butternut squash,
                                         pumpkin
    Cucurbita pepo var. *pepo*   Pumpkin, acorn
                                         squash, marrow

Cucurbita pepo var. *Melopepo*	Bush summer squash, pumpkin
Leguminosae (pea family)	
Cicer arietinum	Garbanzo (chick-pea)
Glycine max	Soybean
Phaseolus coccineus	Scarlet runner
Phaseolus limensis	Lima bean
Phaseolus vulgaris	Snap bean
Pisum sativum	Pea
Vicia faba	Fava bean
Vigna radiata	Mung bean
Vigna unguiculata	Cowpea
Vigna unguiculata subsp. *cylindrica*	Catjang bean
Vigna unguiculata subsp. *sesquipedalis*	Asparagus bean
Malvaceae (cotton family)	
Abelmoschus esculentus	Okra
Polygonaceae (buckwheat family)	
Rheum rhabarbarum	Rhubarb
Solanaceae (nightshade family)	
Capsicum annuum var. *annuum*	Pepper
Capsicum frutescens	Tabasco pepper
Lycopersicon lycopersicum	Tomato
Lycopersicon lycopersicum var. *cerasiforme*	Cherry tomato
Solanum melongena var. *esculentum*	Eggplant
Solanum tuberosum	Potato
Tetragoniaceae (carpetweed family)	
Tetragonia tetragoniodes	New Zealand spinach
Umbelliferae (parsley family)	
Apium graveolens var. *dulce*	Celery
Apium graveolens var. *rapaceum*	Celeriac
Daucus carota var. *sativus*	Carrot
Pastinaca sativa	Parsnip
Petroselinium crispum	Parsley

The plant division to which all vegetables belong is Spermatophyta, or seed-bearing plants.

The class that contains all vegetables is Angiospermae, plants that bear seeds in an ovary, or fruit.

A few vegetables belong to the subclass Monocotyledoneae, plants that have one seed leaf, or cotyledon, but most are in the subclass Dicotyledoneae, plants that have two seed leaves.

The family is the most general grouping that really means something to the gardener. Vegetables belonging to the same family often share pests and cultural requirements and have similar leaf and fruit shapes.

The genus is more specific than the family. Plants belonging to the same genus have more in common than those merely in the same family. For example, cabbage and broccoli belong to the same genus but share a family with radish.

The species is the fundamental unit of botanical classification. Plants within a species have many characteristics in common. Snap and kidney beans, for example, belong to the same species.

The variety indicates a subgroup within a species that differs in small but important ways from other members of the same species. The variety name is usually preceded by the abbreviation *var.*

Sometimes a variety is stabilized under cultivation and will reproduce true to type. These cultivated varieties are referred to as *cultivars*, and their names usually appear in single quotes.

A strain is a subdivision of a cultivar and differs from the parent cultivar by one or more relatively minor attributes. For example, a certain strain of carrots might develop a darker color, mature earlier, or be more disease resistant than the parent cultivar. Strains are often of local importance; what works in Vermont might not work in Oklahoma.

Here's the botanical classification for one type of carrot:

Division	Spermatophyta
Class	Angiospermae
Subclass	Dicotyledoneae
Family	Umbelliferae (parsley family)
Genu	*Daucus*
Species	*carota*
Variety	*sativus*
Cultivar	'Amsterdam'
Strain	Minicor

Classification of plants by their edible parts—leaf crops, fruit crops, or root crops—is another useful system for gardeners. This system regroups plants of different families and genera, and plants within each grouping have similar cultural requirements. For example, parsnips are grown for their roots, but celery is grown for its leaf stalks, though both are members of the same family. Beets and carrots are also grown for their edible roots but belong to different families.

Gardeners often group vegetable crops according to which part of the plant is eaten.

Mature fruits
> Muskmelons, peppers, pumpkins, shell beans, tomatoes, watermelons, winter squash

Immature fruits
> Cucumbers, eggplant, beans, okra, peas, summer squash, corn, peppers

Immature flower parts
> Broccoli, cauliflower, globe artichokes

Leaves, leaf stalks, leaf buds, and bulbs
> Brussels sprouts, cabbage, celery, chard, chicory, Chinese cabbage, chives, collards, endive, garlic, kale, leeks, lettuce, mustard, New Zealand spinach, onions, parsley, rhubarb, spinach, turnips

Stems and tubers
> Asparagus, Jerusalem artichokes, kohlrabi, potatoes

Roots
> Beets, carrots, celeriac, horseradish, parsnips, radishes, rutabagas, salsify, sweet potatoes, turnips

Classification by temperature requirements helps the gardener know when to plant different crops. *Cool-season crops* grow best in spring and fall. Many will withstand light frosts, and some even tolerate severe freezes. With the exception of peas, most are small, shallow-rooted plants grown for their stems, leaves, immature flower parts, or roots. Peas are an exception. And except for potato, they all store best at around 32 degrees. The cool-season crops can be divided into *hardy* and *half-hardy* vegetables.

Seeds of hardy plants will germinate in cold soil, and the seedlings can tolerate short freezes. Plant them two to four weeks before the date of the last killing frost. Half-hardy plants will tolerate only light freezes. Plant them around the date of the last killing frost.

Group crops by their temperature preferences in order to determine planting sequences.

COOL SEASON		WARM SEASON	
HARDY	HALF-HARDY	TENDER	VERY TENDER
Asparagus	Beets	New Zealand	Cucumbers
Broccoli	Carrots	spinach	Eggplant
Brussels sprouts	Cauliflower	Snap beans	Lima beans
Cabbage	Celery	Sweet corn	Muskmelons
Collards	Chard	Tomatoes	Okra
Garlic	Chinese cabbage		Peppers
Horseradish	Chicory		Pumpkins
Kale	Globe artichokes		Squash
Kohlrabi	Endive		Sweet potatoes
Leeks	Lettuce		Watermelons
Onions	Parsnips		
Parsley	Potatoes		
Peas	Salsify		
Radishes			
Rhubarb			
Rutabagas			
Spinach			
Turnips			

Warm-season crops grow best when air and soil temperatures have reached 65 to 86 degrees. They will not tolerate frosts or grow well in cool weather. Most are larger plants with bigger root systems, and with the exception of New Zealand spinach and sweet potatoes, are grown for their fruit. The vegetables store best at temperatures above 50 degrees and will suffer chilling damage at lower temperatures. Corn is the only exception, storing best at 32 degrees. Plant *tender* plants about one to two weeks after the last killing frost, but wait two to three weeks after the last frost, until the soil has become very warm, to plant *very tender* vegetables.

Knowing whether a crop requires a cool or warm growing season, is transplanted or seeded, and matures slowly or quickly will help you plan for succession cropping.

Cool-season crops
    Transplanted in the garden
        Mature quickly: head lettuce, Cos lettuce, beets, bunching onions
        Mature in early summer: broccoli, cabbage, cauliflower, celery, chard
        Mature in the fall: late cabbage, late cauliflower, late celery, celeriac,
            Brussels sprouts, late broccoli
    Sown in the garden
        Short-season crops:
            Peas
            Spring and fall greens: spinach, mustard, fennel
            Spring salad greens: leaf lettuce, garden cress
            Summer salad greens: parsley, endive, leaf lettuce
            Fall salad greens: endive, Chinese cabbage, head lettuce,
                leaf lettuce, chervil
            Root crops: turnips, radishes, beets, carrots, kohlrabi, turnip-
                rooted chervil
        Long-season crops:
            Potatoes
            Bulb crops: onions, shallots, garlic, leeks
            Summer greens: kale, collards, chard
            Root crops: rutabagas, chicory
        Long-season crops that withstand freezing:
            Root crops: parsnips, scolymus, salsify, scorzonera, horseradish
            Perennials: asparagus, chives, rhubarb, globe artichokes
            Salad greens: chervil, parsley
            Greens: dandelion, sorrel
Warm-season crops
    Transplanted in the garden
        Tomatoes, peppers, eggplant, sweet potatoes
    Usually sown in the garden but may be transplanted
        Cucumbers, lima beans, muskmelons, okra, pumpkins, squash,
        watermelons
    Sown in the garden
        Corn, snap beans, shell beans, New Zealand spinach

Understanding the season of growth of different vegetable plants will help you choose the right kinds for succession planting. Be aware, however, that there can be wide variation in maturing times among cultivars.

Classification by life cycle groups plants according to whether they are annuals, perennials, or biennials. Plant your perennials together out of the way at one end of the garden, and prepare their soil deeply before planting. Many biennials and perennials are grown as annuals in temperate climates. Tomatoes, peppers, eggplants, potatoes, and sweet potatoes are all perennials in their native tropical and subtropical habitats, but they are grown as annuals in the United States. Most biennials are grown as annuals either for their vegetative parts, such as beets, or for their immature flower parts, such as broccoli and cauliflower. Biennials may flower the first year if young plants are exposed to prolonged cold spells.

Knowing the life cycle of your vegetable crop will help you determine its planting location and how to gather its seeds. Biennials and some perennials are grown as annuals in temperate gardens.

PERENNIALS	BIENNIALS	ANNUALS
Asparagus	Beets	Broccoli
Chicory	Brussels sprouts	Cauliflower
Chives	Cabbage	Cucumbers
Dandelion	Carrots	Endive
Eggplant	Celery	Lettuce
Garlic	Chard	Lima beans
Globe artichokes	Chinese cabbage	Muskmelons
Horseradish	Collards	Mustard
Lima beans	Kale	New Zealand spinach
Peppers	Kohlrabi	Okra
Potatoes	Leeks	Peas
Rhubarb	Onions	Pumpkins
Sweet potatoes	Parsley	Snap beans
Tomatoes	Parsnips	Spinach
Watercress	Rutabagas	Squash
	Turnips	Sweet corn
		Watermelons

Classifying vegetables according to their depth of rooting also has some practical advantages, although this is influenced by the soil profile. For example, if you have a water table or hardpan at 2 feet, then roots will penetrate only to that depth. Vegetables with deep root systems are better able to tolerate drought and lax fertilizing practices because they can obtain water and nutrients at greater depths.

The rooting depth of vegetables depends on the soil and water supply, but knowing how deep the roots might go will give you some idea of water needs. Shallow-rooted crops need frequent watering; deeper-rooted crops can obtain water deeper in the soil.

SHALLOW (18–24 in.)	MODERATELY DEEP (36–48 in.)	DEEP (more than 48 in.)
Broccoli	Snap beans	Globe artichokes
Brussels sprouts	Beets	Asparagus
Cabbage	Carrots	Lima beans
Cauliflower	Chard	Parsnips
Celery	Cucumbers	Squash, winter
Chinese cabbage	Eggplant	Pumpkins
Corn	Muskmelons	Sweet potatoes
Endive	Mustard	Tomatoes
Garlic	Peas	Watermelons
Leeks	Peppers	
Lettuce	Rutabagas	
Onions	Squash, summer	
Parsley	Turnips	
Potatoes		
Radishes		
Spinach		

Gardeners along the coast and in the Southwest need to know which vegetables are most salt tolerant. The higher the salt content of the soil, the more difficulty roots have in extracting water, especially under hot, dry conditions. Plants with greater salt tolerance will do better here.

Before you plant vegetables, learn all you can about each crop. Study its soil, water, and fertilizer requirements; the proper cultural practices; and the right time to plant it. Your reward will be your bountiful harvest.

Some vegetables can tolerate salty soils quite well, others not at all. Seaside gardeners and gardeners in the Southwest, take note.

HIGHLY TOLERANT	TOLERANT	SLIGHTLY INTOLERANT	INTOLERANT
Beets	Cabbage	Corn	Radishes
Spinach	Cucumbers	Sweet potatoes	Onions
Tomatoes	Muskmelons	Lettuce	Carrots
Broccoli	Potatoes	Peppers	Beans

2

How Does Your Garden Grow?

In order to get the most from your garden, you have to understand plant growth. Knowing the environmental and cultural factors that govern growth will help you balance these factors to achieve the greatest yield. Any one of these that becomes limiting will decrease productivity.

All green plants manufacture their food from sunlight. Through the biochemical combination of carbon dioxide from the air and water from the soil, they manufacture simple sugar in a process called *photosynthesis*. Through other metabolic processes, they transform sugar into starch, fat, oil, protein, and other compounds. Excess sugar is stored in a variety of forms for later use. The plant breaks down or respires sugars and other compounds to release their energy, which it then uses to build new leaves, shoots, roots, and fruit. It is this energy that provides food for us as well.

If a plant does not get enough sunlight, growth will be weak and often spindly, and the production of fruit and roots poor. Insects and diseases produce similar results by damaging the leaves, thereby decreasing the plants' ability to utilize light.

Sunlight influences other reactions in the plant as well. Photoperiod is the duration of light and dark periods through a twenty-four-hour cycle. This is strongly influenced by the season, latitude, elevation, and amount of shade. Day length influences the amount of sugars the plant can produce and use and regulates the formation of flower buds and storage organs. Spinach will flower and onions will stop producing leaves and begin producing bulbs when the days lengthen. On the other hand, corn begins to silk and potatoes begin to form tubers when the days grow shorter. Some cultivars are more sensitive to photoperiod than others. For

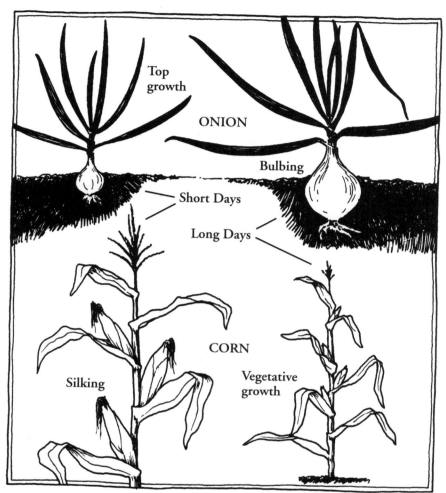

The length of days determines the type of growth some plants make.

example, 'Virginia Savoy' spinach bolts, or produces seed prematurely, when the days lengthen in June, whereas 'Long Standing Bloomsdale' bolts less easily; thus the former is better reserved for fall planting and the latter used for spring planting.

Many of the reactions of photosynthesis and respiration are chemical and influenced by temperature. The higher the temperature, the faster the reactions become. Plants grow faster in warm weather. This isn't always good, as they mature faster and quickly become yellow, woody, and strong flavored. Yields are greatest when days are warm and nights cool, because plants grow mostly at night. The optimum temperatures for a plant depend on that plant's genetic ability to adapt. For example, lima beans grow best in hot weather, broccoli raab in cool, and parsnips aren't fussy. When the plants are grown at temperatures—especially those at night—that are outside their optimum range, yields and quality suffer. Night temperatures that are too low can cause some plants to change phases. For example, biennials and some annuals stop producing leaves and begin producing a seed stalk when exposed to temperatures of 40 to 50 degrees for about six weeks. This is called *bolting,* and it ruins the crop.

Besides sunlight and proper temperature, plants need nutrients from the soil. These are dissolved in water and absorbed by the roots. Most are absorbed by the young root tips, since older root tissue corks over and cannot absorb water. So a plant that is actively growing and has many new roots can absorb more nutrients and remain actively growing. The check in growth often seen after transplanting is largely due to injury to the young roots. Once they have been replaced, growth resumes.

If you fail to water during a prolonged dry period, roots cannot absorb nutrients, and the plant becomes stunted and shows nutrient deficiencies. Water is necessary to dissolve the nutrients for absorption. If you apply a side-dressing, it will do absolutely no good unless it is dissolved

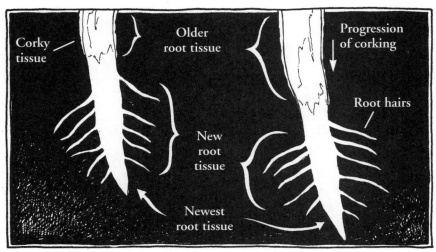

Corky tissue

Older root tissue

Progression of corking

Root hairs

New root tissue

Newest root tissue

Only the tips of new roots can absorb water and nutrients. Older tissue that has corked over cannot absorb these. So the roots must actively grow in order for the rest of the plant to grow.

by rain or watering. Foliar fertilizers work rapidly because they are dissolved in water before application.

Plants lose excess water through pores in their leaves called *stomata*. This process is known as *transpiration*. Because vegetables are mostly water, the moisture lost in transpiration must constantly be replaced to prevent wilting. Watch for signs of moisture stress, particularly during dry, hot, or windy conditions.

When the soil is saturated and all the free water has drained away, it is said to be at *field capacity*. The plants absorb this water easily and make rapid growth. As soil dries, the plants must work harder to absorb the available water.

When the plants wilt at midday and regain turgor at night, this is known as the point of *incipient wilt*. The soil is holding only about half the water available to the plants at

The less soil water there is, the more tightly it is held by soil particles and the less able plants are to absorb it. Roots grow poorly in waterlogged soil because all air spaces are filled with water.

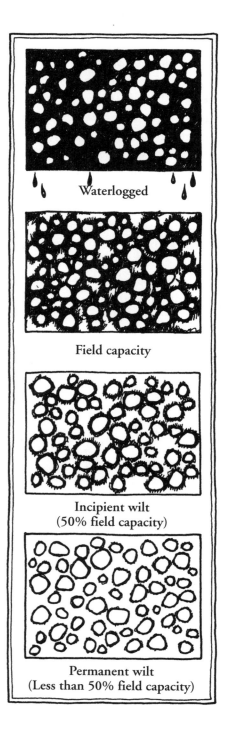

Waterlogged

Field capacity

Incipient wilt
(50% field capacity)

Permanent wilt
(Less than 50% field capacity)

field capacity, and they are struggling to extract soil water. The plants have begun to suffer, growth has been checked, and future yields have already been affected. Vine crops are often the first to show incipient wilt. Water regularly to avoid this situation.

When plants wilt and do not recover at night, soil moisture has been depleted to less than half of field capacity, or to the point of *permanent wilt*, and water must be supplied within a few hours. Even then, your garden will suffer much damage. Many plants will die, and those that do regain their turgor will not grow well. Your yields will be greatly diminished.

For good plant growth, nutrients must be present in the soil in the proper amounts. They may be there naturally, or you may have to add them. Adding too much of a nutrient is just as bad as adding too little. If, for example, a lawn fertilizer high in nitrogen is used on tomato plants, the result is huge plants with many leaves but just a few, small tomatoes that ripen late. Excess nitrogen produces fewer, lower-quality fruits and can be just as damaging as too little nitrogen.

The nutrients' availability to the plants is governed partly by soil pH. A pH that is very high or very low causes chemical reactions in the soil that bind up some nutrients into forms the roots cannot absorb. So even if the soil contains plenty of nutrients, plants may not be able to use them effectively. A slightly acid soil is right for most vegetables.

All vegetable plants go through two phases of growth: vegetative and reproductive. The vegetative phase should be rapid and uninterrupted to establish as many leaves as possible before the plant begins to flower. The more leaves, the better able the plant will be to support high-quality fruit, bulbs, tubers, or roots. The factors that affect vegetative growth include spacing, planting time, soil type, water, light, nutrients, weed growth, pests, and excessively woody mulches. Start with the cultivars best adapted to your area.

Some plants, such as lettuce, spinach, and beets, are harvested before they flower, and the rapid growth will have produced succulent, crisp, tender, high-quality leaves and roots. If you wait until after flowering has begun to harvest such vegetables, the quality declines and they become stringy, strong flavored, and woody.

With other vegetables, we harvest the fruit, seeds, flowers, or storage organs. Healthy leaf growth helps these plants produce huge amounts of sugar, through photosynthesis, that will be stored in the reproductive tissues. Sweet corn and melons are sweeter if the vegetative growth is healthy.

3

Combing the Catalogs

Your crop will not be any better than the seeds you plant. Ten packets for a dollar may not be such a bargain when it results in spotty germination and weak stands. Stay away from deals and go for the best.

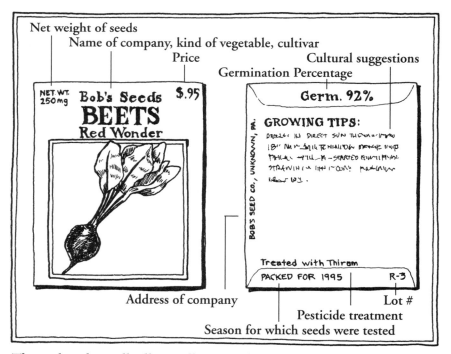

Net weight of seeds
Name of company, kind of vegetable, cultivar
Price
Cultural suggestions
Germination Percentage

NET.WT. 250mg Bob's Seeds $.95   Germ. 92%
BEETS
Red Wonder

GROWING TIPS:

Treated with Thiram
PACKED FOR 1995   R-3

Address of company
Lot #
Pesticide treatment
Season for which seeds were tested

The seed packet will tell you all you need to know about the contents. Read it carefully.

Buy from reputable seed companies. They will sell you seeds that are true to type, are free from foreign material and pest contamination, have high vigor and a high percentage of germination (usually about 85 percent), and are not dormant. They grow good seeds in isolation to ensure that they are pure and their genes are not crossed with those of another cultivar. Every package is labeled with the cultivar name, the lot number or origin, the percentage of germination, the date germination was tested, and the type of pest treatment, if any. Such treatments have been common since the 1960s and usually consist of a dusting of a fungicide dyed a brilliant color, often pink or blue. These protect the seeds from seed-borne and soil-borne diseases and the seedlings from damping-off, a condition caused by fungi in which the plants rot at the soil line and fall over. Purchase seeds that are properly labeled and have been tested for the current season.

Since the first hybrid corn hit the market during the Great Depression, gardeners have been arguing the merits of hybridization. Purists argue that because a plant has been "crossed on purpose" it is therefore man-made and somehow inferior to other plants. That's faulty reasoning. Breeders have just helped nature along a bit.

Hybrid seeds are the results of controlled pollination between two or more inbred lines. For example, let's say that corn cultivar A is selected for its high sugar content and cultivar B for its large ears. Over several years, cultivar A is crossed with itself, called *inbreeding*, and cultivar B with itself. The sweetest and biggest-eared offspring are selected for replanting each time, until the plants consistently produce the same sugar content and the same ear size. This is done in strict isolation to prevent pollination by another cultivar. During inbreeding, the plants decline in vigor and may even look puny. Then, inbred A pollen is manually placed onto inbred B silks. The hybrid seeds produced from this cross will carry the genes for both big ears and high sugar. The plants from these seeds will be highly vigorous. This is known as *hybrid vigor* and is responsible for larger, stronger plants that often produce more and better crops. Other qualities selected for include disease or insect resistance, cold hardiness, and drought tolerance. The production of hybrid seeds is labor intensive and requires many hours for pollination and selection. That makes them more expensive than old-fashioned open-pollinated seeds. And don't be surprised to find only a few hybrid seeds in the packet.

Open-pollinated cultivars are produced by either self- or cross-pollina-

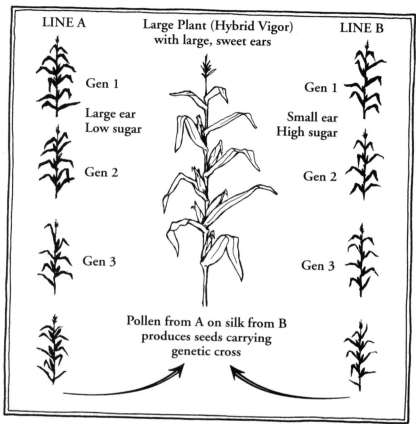

LINE A | Large Plant (Hybrid Vigor) with large, sweet ears | LINE B

Gen 1

Large ear
Low sugar

Gen 2

Gen 3

Gen 1

Small ear
High sugar

Gen 2

Gen 3

Pollen from A on silk from B
produces seeds carrying
genetic cross

Corn plants in line A are crossed with themselves (inbred) for several generations. In each generation, kernels from the largest ears are selected for planting the following season. With each generation, ear size continues to increase, though the plant vigor declines. A similar process is followed in selecting the sweetest ears in line B. After several generations, pollen from line A is dusted onto the silk of line B. Kernels from line B ears carry the genetic cross; when planted, they produce large corn plants showing hybrid vigor and yielding large, sweet ears.

tion. They have been selected over the years from natural crosses and then grown in strict isolation to maintain the purity of the line. Since they require no manual breeding, they are not labor intensive to produce and are therefore less expensive than hybrid seeds. But such plants may not be as pest resistant, cold hardy, or flavorful, and the yields may not be as high.

BUYING SEEDS

There are several factors to consider in selecting the right cultivars for your garden.

First, determine how many growing days you have—the number of days from last spring frost to first fall frost—and get a rough idea of how long your spring and fall are. Do you have a long spring, or does the weather warm rapidly? Since the frost doesn't leave my ground until early May, and I plant nearly all my vegetables in early June, I really only have one month of spring. Then study the catalogs from several seed companies. Carefully consider the cultivar descriptions, but try not to look at the pictures. Your vegetables probably will not look as good as those pictured, so do not use this as a criterion.

Next, consider how many effective growing days you have for a particular crop. Let's look at my garden for an example. My growing season ranges from 90 to 120 days, an average of about 105 days. This is a very short season, but I can still plant parsnips, which require 120 days to mature, because they are not bothered by fall frosts. I can use some other cool-season crops because light frosts don't bother them. But celery is a 120-day cool-season crop and is bothered by frosts, so it won't make it here. With a 105-day season, I should be able to plant a 95-day tomato, right? Wrong! Tomatoes need lots of warm temperatures. Though I may not have a frost in June, the weather is cool and often rainy. Because tomatoes don't grow well until the temperatures get into the sixties and higher, my season for them is effectively reduced to about 70 days. In order to grow tomatoes, I have to select a cultivar that matures in less than 70 days, such as 'Early Girl'.

Some vegetables also respond to photoperiod. For example, some onion cultivars form bulbs under short days. These are adapted to the South, where they are grown as a late fall, winter, or early spring crop. If you grow them in summer in the North, they won't bulb properly. There you need a long-day cultivar instead.

To help you in choosing cultivars, ask your neighbors what grows well for them. Get a list of cultivars recommended for your area from your cooperative extension office. Deal with local or regional seed companies as much as possible. In my case, a company in the northeastern United States is more likely to carry cultivars adapted to my area than one located in the Southwest. Each year, keep a detailed record on the performance of each cultivar in your garden. Refer to this when you select the next year's seeds.

Have a little fun with your garden. I know a lot of boring gardeners who plant the same thing every year—five 'Marglobe' tomato plants, three 'Milano' zucchini plants, and three 'Straight Eight' cucumber plants. Try something new. Plant one new cultivar or new kind of vegetable every year. Plant only a little at first to see if you like it, and expand the planting the next year if you do. This will add a little spice to your vegetables.

SAVING SEEDS

If you've bought too many seeds, you can save most of them for planting the next year. Seeds of some vegetables, however, such as onions and parsnips, retain their viability for only a year or so. Discard them and purchase fresh seeds each year. But you can save seeds of other vegetables for up to five years if you store them properly in a cool place, such as your refrigerator.

Some gardeners really have fun and save seeds from their own plants every year. Seed saving was widely practiced up until the end of World

Some seeds can be stored for several years under the right conditions and remain viable.

| | | YEARS | | |
1	2	3	4	5
Corn	Leeks	Asparagus	Beets	Celery
Onions	Okra	Beans	Brussels sprouts	Cucumbers
Parsnips	Parsley	Carrots	Cabbage	Eggplant
Salsify		Celeriac	Cauliflower	Endive
		Chinese cabbage	Chard	Lettuce
		Kohlrabi	Chicory	Muskmelons
		New Zealand spinach	Kale	Watermelons
		Peas		
		Peppers		
		Tomatoes		

War II. But then good, inexpensive seeds became widely available, hybrids became more common and popular, gardeners got lazy, and the practice fell by the wayside. Saving your own seeds is fun and rewarding, as long as you remember a few rules.

Don't try to save seeds of hybrid cultivars. When planted the next year, they won't come true and usually produce inferior crops. And it may be illegal to boot. Save only seeds from the best open-pollinated cultivars. Collect them from plants that are vigorous and produce good leaves, fruit, and roots; have less disease and fewer insects; and produce crops uniform in color, size, and shape. For carrots or beets, select from plants that produce small-cored roots with little zoning, which is the red and white bands that appear in the roots.

Take care that little crossing has taken place. You can save seeds from plants that are self-pollinated with little worry. Cultivars of plants that

If you want to save your own seed, cultivars of crops that are wind pollinated must be planted at least a mile apart, and those that are insect pollinated, a half mile apart. Self-pollinated crops may be planted together.

SELF-POLLINATED	WIND POLLINATED	INSECT POLLINATED	
Beans	Beets	Asparagus	Brassica group
Chicory	Chard	Carrots	(Chinese cabbage,
Endive	Corn	Celeriac	radishes, mustard,
Lettuce	Spinach	Celery	turnips, rutabagas)
Tomatoes		Cucumbers	Melon group
		Eggplant	(muskmelons,
		Onions	Persian, water-
		Parsley	melons, casaba,
		Peppers	crenshaw, honey-
		Pumpkins	dew)
		Squash	
		Cabbage group	
		(broccoli, kale,	
		Brussels sprouts,	
		cabbage, collards,	
		kohlrabi)	

are wind pollinated should be isolated from each other by at least a mile. For example, 'Detroit Dark Red' and 'Early Wonder' beets will cross if not isolated. Their seeds will carry the cross and when planted the next year will produce plants with various characteristics. The same is true, but a little trickier, with plants that are insect pollinated. With this population, cultivars of the same kind of vegetable should be isolated from each other by at least a half mile. Also, cultivars belonging to certain groups of vegetables will cross as well and must be isolated. For example,

It's easy to save seeds of fleshy fruit. (A) Cut fruit into small pieces and place in a jar. (B) Crush gently. (C) Add water and cover with cheesecloth or nylon stocking to keep fruit flies away. (D) Let ferment several days, then pour off liquid and floating seeds. (E) Wash remaining seeds with clear water. (F) Spread on paper towel to dry. (G) Seal dried seeds in envelope. (H) Label.

you cannot plant broccoli within a half mile of any member of its group, including collards and kohlrabi, or they will all intercross.

Use the following procedures to collect the seeds. Dry all seeds in the shade.

If the seeds are produced in pods, like beans or peas, let them ripen fully on the plant, then dry them in paper bags stored in a cool, dry place.

Harvest moist seed-bearing fruits when they are fully ripe. For tomatoes or cucumbers, crush the fruit in a glass jar, being careful not to injure the seeds, add some water, and cover the mouth with cheesecloth or a nylon stocking. Allow the mixture to ferment for several days; during this time the good seeds will sink to the bottom. Pour off the floaters, liquid, and pulp carefully, and wash the good seeds with clean water. Spread them on a paper towel to dry before storing them. With peppers, melons, pumpkins, or squash, simply scrape out the seeds and spread them onto a paper towel to dry.

With plants that produce seeds in flower heads, such as lettuce, endive, or dill, rub the seeds from the dried heads. Some of these might lose seeds before you've harvested them, so cover the ripening heads with muslin bags or nylon stockings to catch the seeds. Store them in paper bags until fully dried.

Some plants, mostly biennials, must be exposed to cold before they will flower. If your plants haven't flowered by the end of the growing season, leave them in the garden over the winter.

Cool temperatures hasten flowering:
> Broccoli, cauliflower, chicory (early cultivars), Chinese cabbage, endive (early cultivars), kohlrabi, lettuce, peas (late cultivars), radishes, spinach, turnips

Cool temperatures required for flowering:
> Beets, Brussels sprouts, cabbage, carrots, celery, chard, chicory (late cultivars), collards, endive (late cultivars), kale, leeks, onions, parsnips, parsley, rutabagas

Cool temperatures do not affect flowering:
> Asparagus, beans, corn, cucumbers, eggplant, melons, peas (early cultivars), peppers, potatoes, pumpkins, squash, sweet potatoes, tomatoes

---

The seeds of biennial plants are borne in the second season following a cold period, so leave the plants in the ground over the winter. With root crops, however, carefully dig them up in the fall, and select those that are the largest and have the best characteristics. Remove their tops and replant them right away just as they were growing in the garden. The following spring, they'll produce new tops and a seed stalk from which you can collect seeds. If you have very cold winters, store the roots in a root cellar and plant them in the garden very early in the spring.

Seeds of the cole crops can carry diseases that will infect your garden. After harvest, soak seeds of cabbage in 122-degree water for 25 minutes. Soak seeds of broccoli, Brussels sprouts, and cauliflower for 18 minutes. Be sure the time and temperature are exact. After treatment, dry and store the seeds.

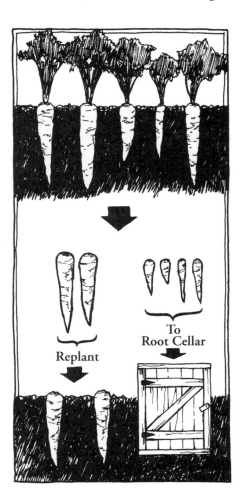

To select the best root crops from which to save the seed, dig in the fall and discard the tops. Replant the best roots immediately, and use the rest in the kitchen. The following spring, the replanted roots form seed stalks. Remove the foliage carefully so as not to injure the tops of the roots.

Planting on Paper

Start to plan your garden on paper right after Christmas. If you're starting a new plot, begin the summer before so that you can prepare the soil in the fall.

Plant only what will grow well, what you will eat, and what you have room for. It makes no sense to plant two hundred feet of kohlrabi if no one in your family likes kohlrabi. If you're tight on space, grow those vegetables that taste the best when eaten fresh from the garden, such as tomatoes and peas. Corn, pumpkins, and potatoes take up a lot of space for the amount of produce you get from them.

Some crops, such as rhubarb, do poorly in southern gardens; others, such as okra and sweet potatoes, are difficult to grow in the North. Don't waste your time on such crops if you live in a marginal area.

Draw your plan on paper. Include the cultivars, crop succession, the amount of space for each crop, the row lengths and spacings, and the earliest and latest planting dates for each. Group plants with similar cultural requirements and pest problems—for example, plant all crucifers together, all root crops together, and all vine crops together. Plant your perennial vegetables, such as asparagus and Jerusalem artichokes, at one end of the garden so that they won't interfere with the cultivation of the rest of the garden. Plant crops that remain in the garden for the entire season, such as peppers, melons, parsnips, and tomatoes, on one side of the garden, and short-season crops, such as beets, carrots, and leaf lettuce, on the other.

Plan to sow very fast maturing crops, such as radishes and leaf lettuce, at fourteen-day intervals through the spring and fall. That way you

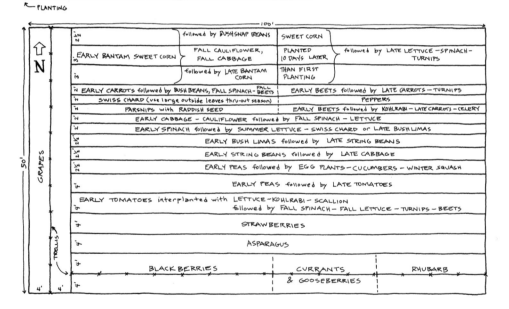

Draw a plan for your garden arrangement before you plant. Make use of intercropping and succession plantings to get the most from your space. These are discussed in more detail in chapter 15.

won't wind up with 15 bushels of radishes all at once. Intercrop, or plant together, small, fast-growing crops with those that take a longer season. For example, you can grow leaf lettuce between rows of tomatoes before the tomatoes are large enough to need the room. Plant tall crops, such as corn, on the north side of the garden so that they won't shade smaller crops. Be sure to plant corn in several short rows; long, single rows may not receive sufficient pollination.

Idle ground is a welcome mat for weeds. When a spring crop is done, either plant another crop, called a *succession crop*, in that area, or turn the soil under and plant buckwheat for the summer. This wonderful plant makes a thick foliage cover that prevents weeds and adds valuable nutrients to the soil. Turn it under before it sets seeds, unless you want another crop of buckwheat next year.

HOW BIG?

Don't let your enthusiasm lead you into making your garden so large that it becomes a burden. And don't think that you can give away all the extra produce to your neighbors. I tried that once and wound up having to pick and deliver it myself. I even offered to cook the stuff if only my neighbors would take it. Think about it. If they're too lazy to have a garden, they're probably too lazy to harvest one.

A quarter-acre plot (10,000 square feet, or 100 feet by 100 feet) will feed a family of five all year long. If this sounds good, think again. Who's going to do all the work? If you have only limited time in the evenings for gardening, then a plot

A trellis made with a wooden frame and poultry fencing and set at a 45-degree angle is a great way to vertical-crop melons and other vine crops. A trellis made of heavy twine strung between wooden posts makes a great prop for pole peas.

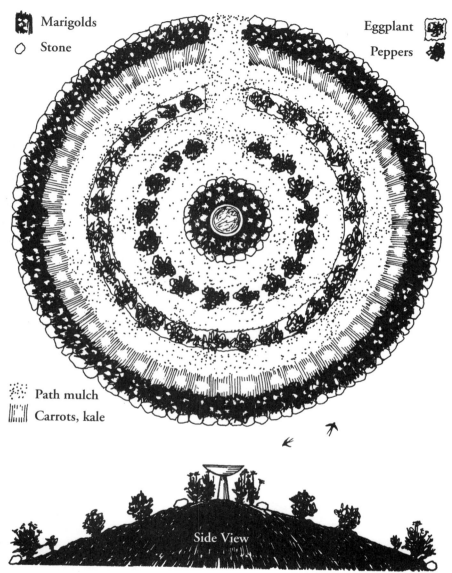

Marigolds

Stone

Eggplant

Peppers

Path mulch

Carrots, kale

Side View

Keep gardens for the front yard simple. A raised bed encircling a flagpole or birdbath is popular. Plant only small plants; avoid vine crops, which will sprawl and make lawn mowing difficult. Good plants for planting out front are kale and peppers, which have nice-looking foliage, and eggplant, which has attractive flowers. A small rock border and colorful flowers define the garden edge. Walkways are made of wood chips underlaid with black plastic to reduce weed problems.

50 feet by 50 feet is about all you'll be able to handle. Allowing time for recreational activities will make a plot 25 feet by 25 feet sound even more reasonable. And that's probably the most common size vegetable garden today. For a garden this small, consider only those vegetables that are the most efficient producers: beans, beets, broccoli, cabbage, carrots, leaf lettuce, onions, peas, radishes, spinach, chard, tomatoes, and turnips. If you can't live without cucumbers or winter squash, train them onto vertical or sloped trellises to save space, or manipulate the vines to grow out into the lawn or border area. You won't be able to cut the grass, but you'll save some garden space.

WHAT SHAPE?

Most gardens are square or rectangular, because it's easier to plant and to figure area that way, and because most of us are not very creative. But vegetables grow just as well in circular, triangular, or fan-shaped plots. These can be very attractive if you must plant on the front lawn.

WHERE?

Site selection is one of the most important aspects of successful gardening. Once you have a well-thought-out plan on paper, choose an appropriate location for the garden. Look for a spot that receives full sun, is handy to the water spigot and kitchen, and is unobtrusive and protected, lest your ripe melons walk away at night. Locate the garden away from large trees; their leaves and branches block sunlight, and their roots often extend half again as far from the trunk as the branches and rob your plants of water and nutrients. If you have no choice but to plant near a tree, dig a trench 2 feet deep between it and your garden, severing all roots to that depth. Then line one side of the trench with a double layer of plastic sheeting before refilling it. That will prevent roots from getting to your garden for several years. Keep the garden away from plantings of mint and bamboo, both of which have intrusive and aggressive root systems that will infiltrate your growing space.

Exposure to full sun is very important. Be sure your garden receives at least six hours of sun daily. A southern exposure is best. It's the warmest and will produce the earliest crops, but the soil dries faster than soil on other exposures. Warm-season crops planted near the south side of a building will benefit from heat radiated from the walls. Western exposures are fine and are warmer than eastern exposures, but your plants

Dripline

Shade

Severed roots decay

Refill

Left. *Plants too close to a tree are stunted by shade and root competition. Plants outside the shade but still in the root system perimeter are stunted by root competition. Sever roots at the dripline—beneath the outside tips of the branches—by digging a trench 2 feet deep between the tree and garden. Line one side of the trench with double plastic and refill.*

Below. *Locate your garden where it will receive full sun.*

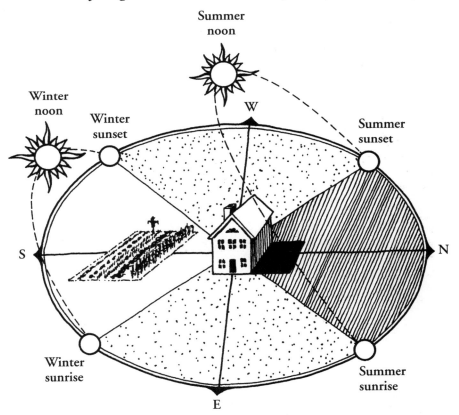

may be exposed to strong winds. Avoid northern exposures. Don't plant within 10 feet of the north side of a one-story building, because your plants won't get enough sun. Plant even farther away from tall buildings.

If part of your garden is lightly shaded or the entire garden receives dappled shade most of the day, select crops that tolerate light shade. They'll grow, but they won't do their best under those conditions.

These vegetables will grow fairly well and produce reasonable crops in light shade.

Beets	Leeks	Raab
Cabbage	Lettuce	Radishes
Carrots	Mustard	Spinach
Chives	Green onions	Swiss chard
Kale	Parsley	Turnips

A gentle slope is a fine asset. Slopes of 1 percent (a drop of 1 inch in 8 feet) or less allow cold air to drain away from the garden so that your plants will be less apt to suffer damage from late spring or early fall frosts, yet they're not so steep as to make tilling difficult. They also allow for air

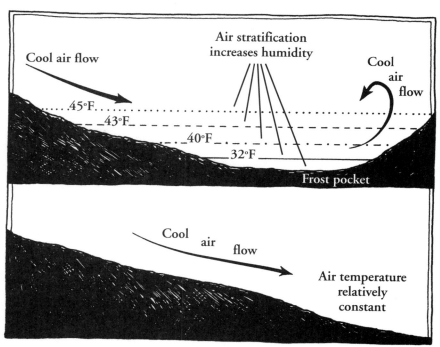

Plant on a gentle slope to allow cool air drainage. (A) Frost pockets occur where flow is blocked by a rising slope, trees, or a fence. (B) Where flow is unimpeded, high humidity and occurrence of frost are reduced.

circulation. This keeps the humidity near your plants down and reduces disease problems. If you're planting on a steep slope, run your rows across the slope to reduce soil erosion. Don't plant near a building, stockade fence, or hedge that will reduce air circulation. Don't plant in a low area; this will be a frost pocket in spring and fall and will probably have poor soil drainage as well.

If you've chosen a spot that is now in lawn, you must kill the grass or remove it completely before planting. Killing it is easier than digging it

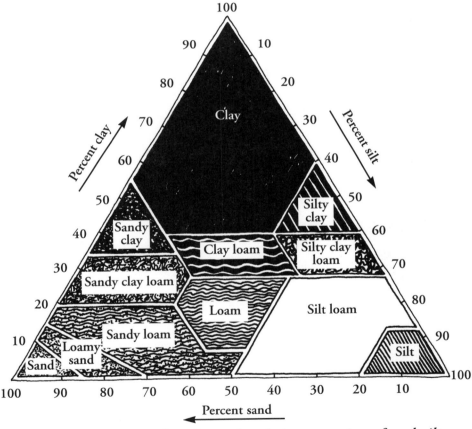

USDA soil texture triangle indicates the relative proportions of sand, silt, and clay in different soils. Clays compact excessively, sands dry too rapidly, and silts hold too much moisture. The best garden soils are the loams, which contain roughly equal proportions of sand, silt, and clay.

out, and turning under the dead grass will add organic matter to the soil. Prepare the site the spring before planting. Cover the area of the future garden with black plastic. Weight it down with stones or boards, and leave it until late fall. When you remove it, all vegetation will be dead and partially rotted, and you can fall plow to prepare the soil for spring planting. An alternative is to spray the entire area with glyphosate herbicide in the early fall. Vegetation will die within a few weeks, and you can prepare the soil for spring planting. Follow label directions.

Sandy loams and silt loams are the best garden soils. Sandy soils warm faster in spring but can dry quickly in summer and allow nutrients to leach. Heavy soils warm more slowly in spring but retain their moisture during summer. There is little leaching, but they will compact and crust, causing poor drainage and aeration. The best soils have an organic matter content of 3 to 5 percent. The soil in most yards will need to be amended with sand and organic matter for the best crops. If your soil is very heavy, planting on raised beds will improve drainage.

5

Mind Your pH

The pH of the soil—its alkalinity or acidity—determines the availability of nutrients to plants. Even if the total amount of a nutrient is not altered, the nutrient will become more or less soluble and available to the plant according to how acid the soil is.

The pH scale runs from 0 to 14, with 7 being neutral. Numbers below 7 indicate acid reactions; those above 7, alkaline. Because the scale is logarithmic, there is a difference of a factor of ten between the numbers; that is, a pH of 5 is ten times more acidic than a pH of 6.

Most vegetables grow best when the soil pH is between 5.5 and 7. Some gardeners grow potatoes at pH 5 because the fungus that causes potato scab doesn't grow well in soil with such a low pH, although the growth of the potatoes won't be affected.

Soils east of the Mississippi and in other humid areas are naturally acid because of the loss of calcium through crop removal and leaching, the decomposition of organic matter, and the bacterial conversion of ammonium-nitrogen to nitrate-nitrogen, which releases hydrogen ions into the soil solution to make it acid. The low pH also reduces microbial activity, slowing the decomposition of organic matter and creating poor soil texture. Acid soils below pH 6 may be deficient in potassium, calcium, and magnesium and may hold phosphorus so tightly that plants cannot absorb it. The low pH also makes aluminum, boron, zinc, iron, and manganese highly soluble, and these can become toxic to plants.

Soils west of the Mississippi and in other dry areas are naturally alkaline because of little leaching of calcium, magnesium, potassium, and

pH

| 4.0 | 4.5 | 5.0 | 5.5 | 6.0 | 6.5 | 7.0 | 7.5 | 8.0 | 8.5 | 9.0 | 9.5 | 10.0 |

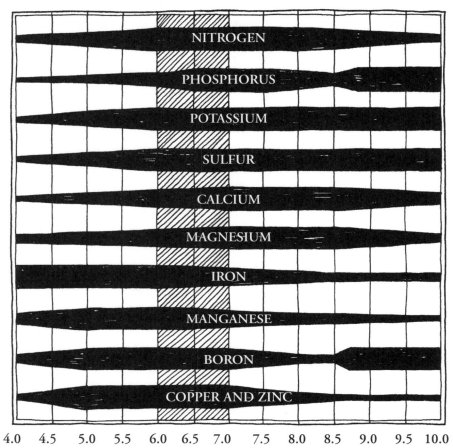

| 4.0 | 4.5 | 5.0 | 5.5 | 6.0 | 6.5 | 7.0 | 7.5 | 8.0 | 8.5 | 9.0 | 9.5 | 10.0 |

Soil pH influences the availability of soil nutrients. A pH range of 6 to 7 ensures that most nutrients will be widely available for absorption by the plant.

other alkaline-forming materials. In soils with pH higher than 7.4, manganese, iron, and boron can become unavailable. If the soil pH exceeds 9, sodium can become available in toxic amounts.

Test your soil in the fall before planting, and adjust the pH to within suggested limits for vegetables. If the soil is too acid, raise the pH by applying a liming material or wood ashes; if it's too alkaline, apply sulfur to lower the pH.

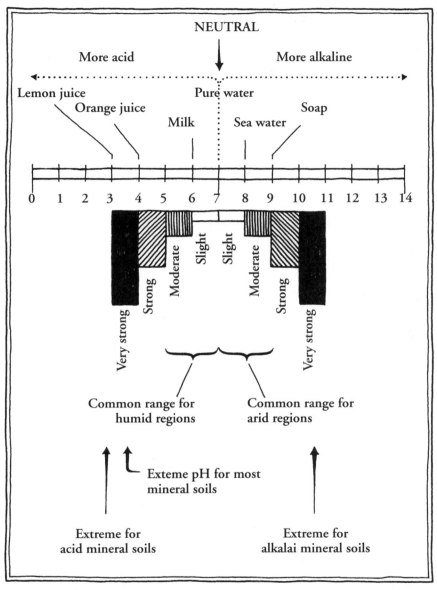

NEUTRAL

More acid   More alkaline

Lemon juice   Pure water
    Orange juice   Soap
                  Milk   Sea water

0 1 2 3 4 5 6 7 8 9 10 11 12 13 14

Very strong — Strong — Moderate — Slight — Slight — Moderate — Strong — Very strong

Common range for   Common range for
humid regions   arid regions

Exteme pH for most
mineral soils

Extreme for   Extreme for
acid mineral soils   alkalai mineral soils

The pH scale is a handy way to express the acidity and alkalinity of the soil. It is a logarithmic scale in which each higher number represents ten times less acidity than the preceding number.

The best soil pH range for some common vegetables.

pH RANGE	VEGETABLE
6.0–8.0	Asparagus
6.0–7.5	Beets, cabbage, muskmelons, peas, spinach, summer squash
6.0–7.0	Celery, chives, endive, horseradish, lettuce, onions, radishes, cauliflower
5.5–7.5	Corn, tomatoes, pumpkins
5.5–7.0	Beans, carrots, cucumbers, parsnips, peppers, rutabagas, Hubbard squash
5.5–6.5	Eggplant, watermelons
4.5–6.5	Irish potatoes

Apply lime in the fall to raise soil pH to 6.5.

	POUNDS OF LIME PER 1,000 SQUARE FEET		
SOIL pH	SANDY SOIL	LOAMY SOIL	CLAY SOIL
6.0	25 lbs.	50 lbs.	60 lbs.
5.5	48	93	115
5.0	65	128	165
4.5	80	160	210
4.0	95	193	250

LIME

Lime supplies calcium and magnesium and neutralizes acidity. The amount necessary to adjust your soil pH depends on the soil type, the amount of organic matter it contains, the type of lime you use, and how much you must alter the pH. Heavy soils and those that are highly acid need more lime than light soils and those that are only slightly acid. Never apply more than 200 pounds of lime per 1,000 square feet at one time. It will cake up and become difficult to incorporate. Most limes do not alter pH immediately; apply them in the fall to allow time for the pH to rise before spring planting. Most soils will require liming only

There are many kinds of liming materials you can use to raise the garden soil pH.

MATERIAL	NUTRIENTS	EQUIVALENT TO 100 POUNDS GROUND LIMESTONE
Hydrated lime	Calcium, magnesium	82 lbs.
Dolomitic lime	Calcium, magnesium	86
Lime	Calcium	100
Marl	Calcium	100
Oyster shells	Calcium	100
Wood ashes	Calcium, potassium	300

every couple of years to maintain the proper pH. Liming every year can be harmful to the soil.

There are several liming materials for gardeners. Calcitic lime (limestone, agricultural lime, or ground lime) raises soil pH and adds calcium as well. Dolomitic lime adds both calcium and magnesium to the soil. Use dolomitic limestone when your soil is low in magnesium. Some gardeners use hydrated lime, which adds calcium and some magnesium and adjusts the pH rapidly. Stay away from it, however, as it's dusty and can burn plants and irritate the skin. Use a finely ground calcitic or dolomitic limestone; the finer the grind, the faster the lime will neutralize the soil acidity.

WOOD ASHES
Hardwood ashes contain about 6 percent potash and 2 percent phosphorus. Their neutralizing effect on soil is about one-third that of lime. In addition to significant quantities of potassium, ashes also supply some calcium and trace elements. Be careful not to use too much, though. Overuse will raise the soil pH excessively high, make some nutrients unavailable for plant use, and interfere with the plant's ability to take up sufficient calcium, and it could lead to a buildup of heavy metals. Apply the ash as you would limestone, at the rate of 20 pounds (one 5-gallon

bucketful) per 1,000 square feet per season. This is the amount of ash you would obtain from a cord of wood. It would be equivalent to applying 6 pounds of limestone per 1,000 square feet and is considered a safe level for repeat applications year after year. For a one-time application, to be repeated only after several years, you can apply 100 pounds per 1,000 square feet. This can raise the soil pH close to a whole unit.

SULFUR

If you live west of the Mississippi, or if you got carried away with the wood ashes, you'll probably have to lower your soil pH. Do this with sulfur. Garden sulfur forms weak sulfuric acid in the soil solution and lowers the pH rapidly. Apply it well before planting, and don't let it touch young plants.

If your soil pH is too high, add garden sulfur (wettable sulfur) before planting to lower it to 6.5. Flowers of sulfur is difficult to wet and is not recommended. Don't let sulfur touch young plants.

	POUNDS OF SULFUR PER 1,000 SQUARE FEET		
SOIL pH	SANDY SOIL	LOAMY SOIL	CLAY SOIL
8.5	50 lbs.	63 lbs.	75 lbs.
8.0	30	38	50
7.5	13	20	25
7.0	3	4	8

6

Organic Matter

Organic matter is the partly decomposed remains of plants and animals. It's a very important component of garden soil and reduces erosion and nutrient leaching. It also fluffs or granulates the soil, improving its structure, and buffers the soil, making it resistant to chemical change. It increases the porosity of heavy soils, enabling them to absorb more air, water, and nutrients. The increased aeration promotes bacterial growth, which in turn liberates more nutrients from the decomposing organic matter. It prevents sandy soil from becoming too porous, and its dark color warms the soil faster in the spring.

Too much organic matter is just as bad as not enough, however. Fresh manure applied too close to planting time can burn the plants through the release of ammonia. Compacted layers of organic matter can block infiltration of water and air into the soil. Organic matter ties up some of the soil nitrogen during bacterial decomposition and can interfere with tilling and seeding. Some types of organic matter, such as a mat of green grass clippings, can ferment to form toxic compounds.

Soils across the United States vary in their amounts of organic matter. Gardens in the arid West may have soil with only 1 percent organic matter; soils in the damp Northeast may have as much as 8 percent. Commonly, though, most garden soils contain 2 to 4 percent organic matter. This is broken down over time by bacterial decomposition, a process speeded up by cultivation, which aerates the soil and makes bacteria proliferate.

You must build up and maintain the organic matter in your soil if

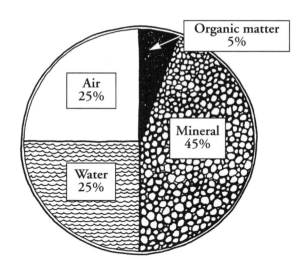

Organic matter
5%

Air
25%

Mineral
45%

Water
25%

An ideal garden soil should contain about 25 percent air, 25 percent water, and 45 percent minerals. The remaining 5 percent is organic matter.

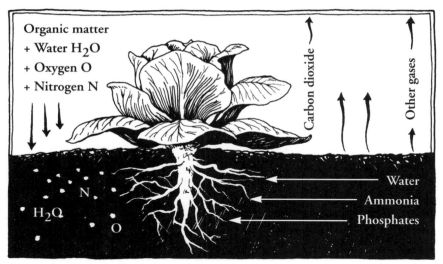

Organic matter
+ Water H_2O
+ Oxygen O
+ Nitrogen N

Carbon dioxide

Other gases

N

H_2O

O

Water

Ammonia

Phosphates

Soil organic matter is broken down by soil microorganisms in the presence of water and oxygen. The organisms use some nitrogen for energy. Breakdown products are released into the atmosphere or are used for plant growth. The more the soil is tilled, the more it becomes oxygenated and the faster organic matter decays.

you are serious about having a good garden. You can do this incidentally by using organic mulches, or add organic materials directly.

MANURE

Manure is an excellent soil builder. Fresh manure adds more nutrients, beneficial bacteria, and buffering capacity to the soil than rotted manure but adds more weed seeds as well. It can also burn the plants if used too close to planting time. If you apply fresh manure, do so in the fall and plow it under. You'll be better off, however, using rotted or composted manure, which is nonburning, has a more uniform texture, and does not interfere with cultivation. Also, the nitrogen and phosphorus contents

What's the best manure and how much should you use? Here are the approximate percentages of primary nutrients in animal manures, plus the suggested number of pounds to use per 1,000 square feet of garden. One bushel of manure weighs about 50 pounds. Do not use pet manures, as they may transmit disease. Nutrients in sheep and chicken manure are rapidly available for plant use and can cause excessive growth. When using fresh manure, apply an additional 2 pounds of phosphorus (10 pounds of 10–20–0 or 15 pounds of steamed bone meal) per 1,000 square feet.

MANURE	N	P	K	AMOUNT
Cattle, fresh	0.5	0.2	0.5	500 lbs.
Cattle, dried	1.5	2.0	2.3	200
Goat, dried	1.4	1.0	3.0	200
Horse, fresh	0.7	0.3	0.5	500
Pig, fresh	0.7	0.6	0.7	500
Sheep, fresh	1.4	0.7	1.5	300
Sheep, dried	4.2	2.5	6.0	100
Chicken, fresh	1.5	1.0	0.5	300
Chicken, dried	4.5	3.5	2.0	100
Rabbit, fresh	2.0	1.3	1.2	150

are more balanced, since some of the nitrogen is lost during decomposition. Composting also destroys most weed seeds. The nutrient content of manure varies according to the animal species, the feed, and how the manure was handled and stored.

COVER CROPS AND GREEN MANURE CROPS

Cover crops and green manure crops both add nutrients and organic matter to the soil when plowed under. Cover crops are grown in the off season to prevent soil erosion; green manure crops are grown in the same season as the vegetables on a section of the garden not in a crop. They will rot faster and be less of a drain on soil nitrogen supplies if turned under while still green.

Buckwheat, Japanese millet, and sweet clover make excellent green manure crops. The buckwheat especially makes rank growth that smothers any weed seeds that might germinate. Winter rye is almost universally used as a winter cover crop. Be sure to turn it under the following spring before it gets more than 8 inches tall. If you wait longer, it may dry the soil excessively and you'll have trouble turning it under.

How much cover crop seed should you sow per 1,000 square feet?

Crop	Amount
Buckwheat	2 lbs.
Japanese millet	1
Sweet clover	0.1
Winter rye	3

COMPOST

Compost is simply decomposed organic matter. It improves the soil in the same manner as other organic materials, but because it is already decomposed, it's less of a drain on soil nitrogen supplies.

You can use almost any organic plant material to make compost. Do not compost dairy products, large bones, fat, grease, meat, or eggs; these will smell and attract flies and vermin. Do not compost pet manures, as they can carry diseases that could be transmitted to humans. Do not

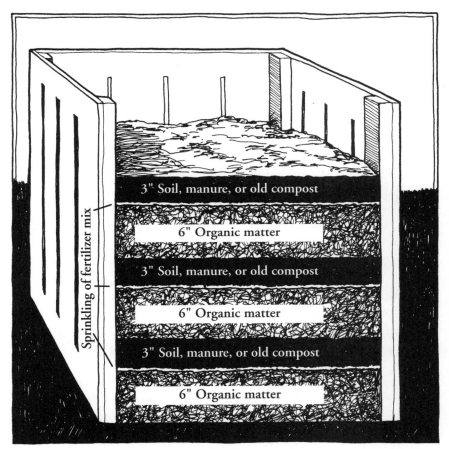

In the illustration, from top to bottom:

3" Soil, manure, or old compost

6" Organic matter

Sprinkling of fertilizer mix

3" Soil, manure, or old compost

6" Organic matter

3" Soil, manure, or old compost

6" Organic matter

Compost piles make good use of refuse. The pile is constructed in layers. It should be encompassed by spaced boards, fencing, or snow fence to allow for plenty of aeration all around.

compost glass, metal, plastic, or Styrofoam. Walnut leaves contain a substance that interferes with plant growth. Keep them, clippings from lawns treated with herbicides, and obviously diseased plant parts out of your compost heap.

Build a compost pile in a handy spot. Enclose it with wire or use a wooden bin with plenty of holes in the side for aeration. Put a 6-inch layer of organic material in the bottom, and sprinkle over it some fertilizer mix (described below). Add a 3-inch layer of soil, old compost, or manure, moisten, and repeat the layering process until the bin is full. You don't need special composting enzymes or other products.

Keep the top of the pile flat or slightly concave and moist. After forty-five days, turn the pile so that the material at the edges and top are now in the center. The center of a good working pile will heat to 138 degrees F. or more. This kills many weed seeds and pathogens that could otherwise infest the garden. Material that remains on the edge of the pile won't heat as much and will retain viable weed seeds and pathogens.

The compost is ready to use when the organic matter has broken down so that its original form is unrecognizable and it has become dark and rich looking. This can take a year to a year and a half, depending on the size of the material, the amount of fertilizer you've added, and the length of your summers.

Three factors determine the speed of decomposition: the fineness of the material, the supply of lime and nitrogen, and the ratio of carbon to nitrogen (C:N) in the green material. The finer the material, the faster it decomposes. Grass clippings decompose rapidly, whereas wood chips take a long time. Try to shred the material with a rotary lawn mower before you put it into the pile. The layer of old compost, soil, or manure

The carbon-to-nitrogen ratios of some common materials.

Material	C:N Ratio	Material	C:N Ratio
Corncobs	420:1	Composted manure	20:1
Sawdust	400:1	Seaweed	19:1
Wood chips	400:1	Buckwheat	19:1
Paper	175:1	Sheep manure	15:1
Strawy manure	80:1	Alfalfa hay	12:1
Straw	75:1	Apple pomace	12:1
Leaves	70:1	Normal soil	12:1
Corn stalks	60:1	Vegetable waste	12:1
Peat moss	58:1	Clover hay	12:1
Green rye	36:1	Liquid manure	10:1
Horse manure	35:1	Chicken manure	7:1
Kitchen scraps	30:1	Blood meal	4:1
Sweet clover (mature)	24:1		

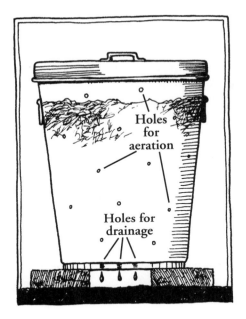

To compost in a garbage can, punch small holes in the sides for aeration and the bottom for drainage, place the can on blocks, fill with fine material such as grass clippings, wet, and cover.

Holes for aeration

Holes for drainage

you add provides the microorganisms to decompose the organic material. They use nitrogen to break down the material, however, and the process is acid forming. To keep all reactions going smoothly, you must supply some nitrogen to feed the bacteria and lime to neutralize the acid. That's where the fertilizer mix comes in.

Mix 25 pounds of 10–10–10 fertilizer and 10 pounds of limestone, and add 1 pound of this mixture to every 40 pounds of green material. If you want to garden organically, mix 15 pounds of wood ashes, 7 pounds of dried blood, and 4 pounds of steamed bone meal, and add 3 pounds of this mixture to every 40 pounds of green material.

How long will your organic matter last?

| | RATE OF DECAY | |
RAPID	SLOW	SLOWEST
Manure	Leaf mold	Corncobs
Grass clippings	Compost	Bark
		Sawdust

These rates are average. The actual amount needed is determined by the C:N ratio of the material to be composted. All organic materials supply some carbon and some nitrogen. If the C:N ratio of the material you use is less than 30:1 (see table on page 46), you don't have to add any fertilizer to the pile. You must still add a sprinkling of lime, however. The higher the ratio, the woodier the material and the longer it will take to decompose.

If you don't want a big compost pile near your garden, you can compost in a garbage can. Punch a half dozen holes in the bottom and several more in the sides for aeration, set it on blocks about a foot off the ground for drainage and aeration, and fill the can with fine material, such as grass clippings and chopped leaves. Water the material until the water drips from the bottom of the can, then cover. Within three days, the temperature inside the can will reach 138 degrees F., and in one and a half to two weeks, the compost will be done.

There are several other ways to make compost, but those are two of the more common methods.

7

The Nutrients Plants Need

There are sixteen elements essential for plant growth. About 90 percent of the plant's dry weight is cellulose and sugars made from the carbon, hydrogen, and oxygen obtained from air and water, and much of the plant's fresh weight is water used to transport nutrients, for chemical reactions, and for cooling plant tissues.

The plant gets the other thirteen elements from the soil. These can be divided into the major nutrients, or macronutrients, and minor nutrients, or micronutrients. The macronutrients are not more important, but they are used in greater amounts. Nitrogen (N), phosphorus (P), potassium (K), calcium (Ca), magnesium (Mg), and sulfur (S) are the macronutrients. They are further subdivided into the primary (nitrogen, phosphorus, and potassium) and the secondary (calcium, magnesium, and sulfur) nutrients. The primary nutrients are the ones most often lacking in garden soils. The secondary nutrients are found in plants in smaller quantities than the primary nutrients but are just as essential. The micronutrients are manganese (Mn), iron (Fe), zinc (Zn), boron (B), molybdenum (Mo), copper (Cu), and chlorine (Cl).

NITROGEN (N)

Nitrogen is the nutrient most responsible for increases in plant growth and strongly promotes the growth of leaves, stems, and roots. Leafy crops, such as spinach, lettuce, and kale, need large amounts of this nutrient. Atmospheric nitrogen, which makes up about 80 percent of the air we breathe, cannot be used by plants directly, but must first be

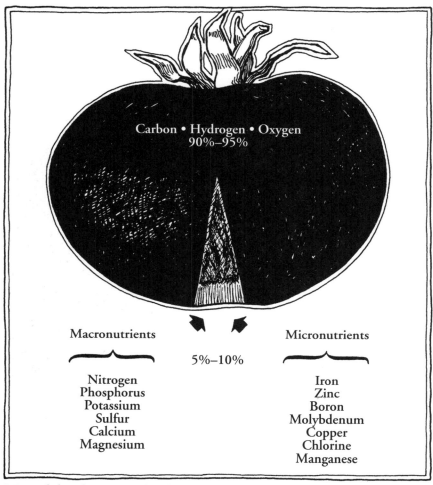

Carbon • Hydrogen • Oxygen
90%–95%

Macronutrients	5%–10%	Micronutrients
Nitrogen		Iron
Phosphorus		Zinc
Potassium		Boron
Sulfur		Molybdenum
Calcium		Copper
Magnesium		Chlorine
		Manganese

Most of the plant is made of nutrients from the air and water. But the small amount that comes from the soil is just as important.

converted by microorganisms or fertilizers into nitrate and ammonium forms. The nitrogen compounds in organic fertilizers also must be broken down into these simpler forms before plants can use them.

The ammonium form is volatile but doesn't leach readily. Bacteria convert it into the nonvolatile nitrate form, which leaches easily, especially in sandy soils. This bacterial conversion is rapid in warm soil. When soil is compacted and poorly aerated, bacteria convert nitrates back into atmospheric nitrogen, making it unavailable for plant use.

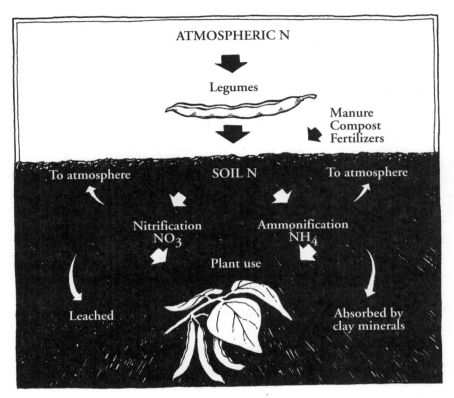

Nitrogen is constantly being lost from the soil and must periodically be replenished. Bacteria in the roots of legumes fix nitrogen in the atmosphere and make it available for plant growth; as the roots die and decay, the nitrogen is released into the soil. There, nitrogen is turned into either the nitrate form or the ammonium form, both of which can be used by the plants or lost from the root zone by volatilization into the atmosphere or by leaching.

Bacteria use nitrogen to break down soil organic matter. The more organic matter you put into the garden, the more nitrogen will be used to help it decay, which means that what is perhaps the most useful plant nutrient is rapidly lost. In fact, about 50 percent of the nitrogen in manure volatilizes and is lost before plants can use it. And 30 to 60 percent of the nitrogen applied in commercial fertilizers is used by soil microorganisms to decompose soil organic matter. This means that only about half the nitrogen you apply to your garden is available for use by the plants.

Bacteria living in nodules on the roots of legumes turn atmospheric nitrogen into a form plants can use.

Plants in the legume family actually add nitrogen to the soil. Nitrogen-fixing bacteria live in tiny nodules on the roots of these plants and convert atmospheric nitrogen into forms useful to the plant. Peas can actually fix about 72 pounds of nitrogen per acre, beans 40 pounds, soybeans 58 pounds, and peanuts 42 pounds. For this reason, these crops do not need to be heavily fertilized with nitrogen.

Some nitrogen is also added to the soil by other organisms, lightning, and rain, but the amounts are negligible.

Plants deficient in nitrogen are stunted with stiff, fibrous stems and small, yellowed leaves. The discoloration appears first on the older bottom leaves of the plant, then moves to progressively younger leaves.

PHOSPHORUS (P)

Phosphorus promotes the growth and development of roots, flowers, fruit, and seeds, and stiffens the stems of plants. Much of the phosphorus in the soil is not available to the plant, and phosphorus that is applied sometimes becomes quickly bound and unavailable for plant use. Phosphorus is most available at a soil pH between 5 and 7. Because phosphorus does not move readily in the soil, it must be applied in the root zone, where it can be quickly taken up by the plant.

Phosphorus deficiency delays plant growth and maturity and causes the stems to become thin and short. A purple-pink color develops on the undersides of the leaves, then progresses through the entire leaf.

POTASSIUM (K)

Potassium is soluble and leaches unless held for plant use by soil organic matter. This nutrient stimulates the vigor and general health of the plant and promotes root growth. For that reason, root crops, such as beets and carrots, need more potassium than other crops.

Plants deficient in potassium develop gray or buff-colored areas near the margins of older leaves. In time, the entire leaf margin becomes scorched, and light yellow areas may develop throughout the leaf.

CALCIUM (Ca)
Calcium is used to make strong cell walls. This nutrient is seldom deficient, because garden lime contains calcium, and it is also added along with the phosphorus in fertilizer, in the form of dicalcium phosphate. Under water stress conditions, however, some plants may have difficulty absorbing and transporting it to all parts, resulting in blossom end rot in tomatoes and peppers, cavity spot in parsnips, cabbage tipburn, black heart in celery, and internal browning in Brussels sprouts.

MAGNESIUM (Mg)
Magnesium is used in the production of chlorophyll. It is added to the soil in the form of dolomitic lime or epsom salts. Although magnesium is soluble, it is held in place for plant use by soil organic matter and clay particles. A deficiency might occur in acid, sandy soils or if too much lime or potassium is added to the soil. These elements interfere with the plant's ability to absorb soil magnesium.

Magnesium deficiency causes yellowing between the veins of older leaves. This discoloration then moves to younger leaves, and the older leaves fall prematurely.

SULFUR (S)
Sulfur deficiency is rare, thanks to air pollution. Rainfall provides between 1 and 100 pounds per acre of this nutrient every year. Plants need this nutrient, in about the same amount as phosphorus, to make certain proteins. These compounds give radishes and the crucifers their pungency and odor.

MICRONUTRIENTS
Micronutrients are seldom limited in most gardens if you take care of the soil. Deficiencies may occur in soils very low or very high in organic matter, coarse-textured or strongly weathered soils, or soils with very high

pH. Of these, pH is the most important factor. Manganese, iron, boron, copper, and zinc all become less available as the pH increases, so keep the soil pH between 6 and 6.5.

Boron is the micronutrient most often deficient. Beets, turnips, celery, broccoli, and cauliflower are most susceptible to boron deficiency, which usually shows up as a blackened sunken spot with internal or external dead or water-soaked areas. Fruits are rough and spotted, and flowering is reduced. Stems of some plants, particularly the crucifers and celery, are brittle, hollow, or cracked.

With micronutrients, there is a thin line between too little and too much. Excessive amounts of some, especially boron and manganese, can damage sensitive crops, such as cucumbers. Do not add micronutrients to your garden unless you have had a deficiency positively identified by a specialist. Then, carefully, follow the label directions and recommended rates of application.

Feeding Your Vegetables

Every time you pick a cucumber, you remove nutrients that came from the soil. Unless you use fertilizers to replace those nutrients, your soil will gradually become depleted and your garden less productive.

All materials that supply nutrients to growing plants are fertilizers, though they may differ in the amounts of nutrients they carry. Fertilizers are labeled with their grade, or analysis, which expresses the percentage of the major nutrients in the material. The first number always represents the percentage of nitrogen; the second, phosphorus; and the third, potassium. Thus, a bag of 5–10–10 fertilizer contains 5 percent nitrogen, 10 percent phosphorus, and 10 percent potassium.

Usually, the higher the analysis, the less expensive the material. A 50-pound bag of 5–10–10 might cost $5 and a 50-pound bag of 10–20–20 $8. You're getting twice the nutrients in the bag of 10–20–20 for less than twice the cost. The higher-analysis fertilizers are more concentrated salts, however, so you must apply smaller amounts to your plants or you'll burn them.

The fertilizer ratio expresses the proportion of one nutrient to another. For example, 5–10–10 and 10–20–20 have different analyses but the same ratio, 1–2–2.

Fertilizers come in two types: commercial and organic. Many people call the former chemical fertilizers, some with the idea that all chemicals are bad. This is silly, since organic fertilizers are made of chemicals, too, as are the plants. In fact, a bag of organic fertilizer has hundreds more

When you harvest your garden, you remove nitrogen, phosphorus, and potassium. These must be replaced to keep your garden growing well year after year.

| Yield per 100 Square Feet | | Ounces removed per 100 Square Feet | | |
Crop		N	P	K
Asparagus	9 lbs.	.80 oz.	.16 oz.	.32 oz.
Beans	9	.48	.16	.48
Beet root	45	1.76	.80	3.04
Cabbage	45	2.24	.48	2.08
Carrots	58	2.24	.96	5.44
Cauliflower	42	2.24	.80	1.76
Corn	14	.96	.16	.32
Cucumbers	43	.80	.32	1.76
Eggplant	26	.80	.32	1.76
Lettuce	27	1.44	.16	.80
Muskmelons	15	.48	.16	.96
Onions, bulb	45	1.60	.08	.80
Parsnips	57	2.24	1.60	8.00
Peppers	24	.96	.16	.80
Pumpkins	58	2.24	.96	6.24
Spinach	14	1.12	.16	2.08
Squash, summer	46	.80	.16	1.44
Squash, winter	58	2.24	.96	6.24
Tomatoes	57	1.76	.48	2.72
Turnips	51	1.76	.80	2.24
Watermelons	23	.32	.112	.48

chemicals in it than a bag of commercial fertilizer. Both types of fertilizers contribute different things to the vegetable garden. Neither is all good or all bad; each has its good points and bad.

Commercial fertilizers are made of mineral salts mined from the earth. Some are treated chemically to concentrate their nutrients and make them more available to plants. The nitrogen is often a by-product of the oil industry. All the components come from the earth, then, and are no more man-made than cow manure. They're just refined and concentrated. Because of this, you need much smaller amounts of them than of organic fertilizers. They are inexpensive, dry, easy to handle, and odorless, and their nutrients are more or less readily available for plant use. If they're used improperly, however, their high salt concentration can burn plants and their rapid availability of nutrients can stimulate excessive plant growth at the expense of productivity. Tomatoes fertilized too heavily will grow tall and luxuriant but produce few mature fruit. Commercial fertilizers supply no soil-building organic matter and can speed the breakdown of soil organic matter already present.

Organic fertilizers are natural refuse products from plants and animals. They're not concentrated, so you'll need more of them to do the

Organic fertilizers have smaller amounts of nitrogen, phosphorus, and potassium but add beneficial organic matter to the soil. Mix feather meal with manure from the same species to speed its breakdown. The phosphorus in rock phosphate is nearly unavailable in soils above pH 6.0 (most garden soils). Only less than 5 percent of the phosphorus is ever available to plants.

| | % DRY WEIGHT | | | |
	N	P	K	
Bat guano	10	1.8	1.7	Expensive, odor
Blood (dried)	13	0.9	0.8	Expensive
Bone meal (raw)	3.0	6.0	—	Difficult to spread, odor
Bone meal (steamed)	2.0	12.0	—	Expensive
Cattle manure (dry)	1.5	2.0	1.2	Compost raw manure
Chicken manure (dry)	3.5	2.0	2.6	Compost raw manure
Compost	2.0	1.0	1.0	Apply 4 inches deep
Cottonseed meal	6.0	1.3	0.8	Expensive
Fish meal	10.0	3.8	—	N and P slowly available
Seaweed	0.2	0.1	0.6	
Wood ashes	—	1.0	5.0	23% Ca, raises pH
Granite meal	—	—	3.0	K not readily available
Greensand	—	1.0	7.0	K slowly available
Feather meal	12.0	—	—	N slowly available
Rock phosphate	—	30.0	—	Dusty, 33% Ca

job. They're often bulky and inconvenient to handle, like manure, and have strong odors, like blood meal and fish meal. These odors will sometimes attract pests, such as dogs and raccoons, to the garden. Organic fertilizers add varying quantities of beneficial organic matter to the soil. Because they are not concentrated, their salts are not likely to burn plants, although poultry manure can burn young plants because it liberates large amounts of ammonia.

The nutrients in organic fertilizers are bound up in large molecules that must be broken down by soil microbes before they are available for plant growth. This is done over time, and the liberation of nutrients from organic materials is difficult to control. This slow release has its advantages and disadvantages. Long-season crops will receive nutrients throughout the season, but short-season crops won't be able to make use of all the nutrients. Also, you may not want some plants, such as tomatoes, to receive so many nutrients after midseason.

I use both commercial and organic fertilizers in my garden— the commercial to supply the bulk of the nutrients quickly, and the organic to help maintain soil organic matter and supply smaller amounts of nutrients throughout the season. Studies have shown that this practice will produce bigger and better crops.

TESTING THE SOIL

Fertilizer application rates and timing depend on what you're growing and how fertile your soil is. Test your soil to determine its fertility. In the fall, take several cups of soil from different parts of your garden, and mix them in a bucket. Take your samples from 2 to 5 inches below the surface, as surface soil may not be representative of that in the root zone. Dry a cup of the composite mix in a sunny window, then submit it to your cooperative extension service for testing. The cost is modest and the information reliable.

The standard soil test indicates the amounts of phosphorus, potassium, and sometimes nitrogen in the soil, as well as the soil texture and pH. Note that soil pH may be slightly lower in the fall than in the spring. The tests for nitrogen are highly variable and unreliable, so don't put too much faith in that number. Most soil-testing services supply a fertilizer recommendation with the test results.

50 ft.

20 ft.

2"-5"

5 cups

Soil
mix

1
cup

Composite
mix

Base your fertilizer needs on a soil test. For a 1,000-square-foot garden, collect 1 cup of soil from 2 to 5 inches below the surface at each of five locations. Combine the samples in a plastic bucket, and mix thoroughly. Use 1 cup of the mixed soil for testing. Garden areas that are radically different should be tested separately, however.

Amount of organic fertilizers to use for your vegetable garden.

MATERIAL	POUNDS TO APPLY PER 1,000 SQUARE FEET
Blood, dried	10 lbs.
Fish meal	15
Cottonseed meal	20
Soybean meal	20
Steamed bone meal	15
Rock phosphate	150–300
Greensand	150–300
Wood ashes	20

If you do not wish to take a soil test, broadcast and turn under about 20 pounds of 5–10–10 fertilizer per 1,000 square feet before you plant. This will be adequate to get most plants off to a good start.

APPLYING FERTILIZERS

Fertilizer can be applied by broadcasting or side-dressing. With *broadcasting*, fertilizer is scattered on the soil and tilled under. Do this just before planting; if you do it too far ahead of time, some of the nitrogen and potassium may leach out of the root zone, particularly in sandy soil. If you're applying fresh manure, work it into the soil in the fall before planting. Broadcast rotted manure a few weeks before spring planting, in a layer 2 to 3 inches deep, and work it into the soil.

Side-dressing is applying fertilizer in a broad band 6 to 10 inches from the base of the plants. This is done during the growing season. Encircle individual larger plants, such as cabbage. A half handful of fertilizer around each transplant should be sufficient. With row crops, like carrots, apply fertilizer along both sides of the row; sprinkle enough fertilizer so that it looks like a very light dusting of snow. Five pounds of 10–10–10 per 100 square feet, or a handful per 10 feet of row, is just about right.

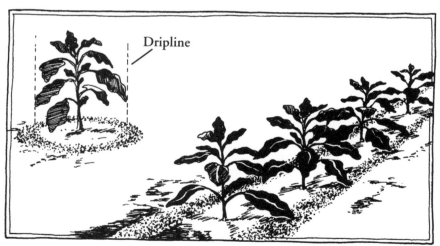

When side-dressing individual plants, spread the fertilizer in a broad band beneath the dripline of the plants and completely around them. When side-dressing rows, spread the fertilizer in a broad band about 8 inches from the plants.

(One cup of fertilizer weighs about a half pound.) Scratch the fertilizer lightly into the soil with a rake. If you've applied organic mulch, rain will wash the fertilizer through the mulch into the soil. Side-dressings supply additional nutrients during the second half of the season, when most growth is made. They also resupply some of the nitrogen and potassium that may have leached from the root zone since earlier broadcasting.

Starter solutions are high-analysis, rapidly available, water-soluble and liquid fertilizers that are used to water in plants during transplanting. They are particularly high in phosphorus, which stimulates root growth. Some common analyses are 16–32–16, 20–20–20, and 10–52–8. Organic growers use manure tea. There are several formulas for manure tea. I put a bushel of manure in a 55-gallon barrel and then fill it with water. After stirring the contents, I let it sit for a week. Most of the manure will settle to the bottom. The water component is the tea.

Foliar fertilizers are most useful for supplying micronutrients to the plant. These are needed only in small amounts that can be absorbed directly through the leaves. Don't try to use these fertilizers to supply the major nutrients; so much would have to be applied that the foliage would burn. Some companies advocate the use of foliar fertilizers on a regular weekly basis to supply all the nutrient needs of the plant. This may be counterproductive, however, producing huge, viney tomato plants with no fruit, or large, succulent pepper plants that break in the wind. Don't waste your money on products that seem too good to be true. Instead, follow a sensible fertilizer program.

9

Tools of the Trade

One of the most important steps in having a good vegetable garden is breaking the soil and preparing it for planting, and you need a few tools to do it right. The only hand tools you really need are a hoe, a steel garden rake, a garden line with sharp stakes at each end, a measuring tape or wooden measuring stick, and a spade or spading fork. A putty knife and a trowel are handy to have if you grow your own transplants. For a large garden, consider investing in a rotary tiller. Take care to buy good-quality tools.

There are many types of hoes. Besides their use for weeding, hoes are handy for opening furrows and transplanting hills, covering seeds, and loosening the soil. Hoes are meant to cut, not chop, so keep their edges sharp; a dull hoe is almost useless. Purchase a hoe that is not too heavy and has a handle long enough that you can stand nearly straight when you use it. Wheel hoes are very good for larger plots. Buy one with sharp, thin blades. Those fitted with cultivator tines don't do nearly as good a job, are harder to push, and disturb the vegetable roots a bit more.

A steel garden rake with strong, straight teeth is great for smoothing the soil and covering very small seeds. You can also use it to root out small weeds.

A garden line helps you keep the rows straight, and a measuring tape or stick enables you to space them properly. I like to use a wooden measuring stick instead of a tape because it's easier for one person to manage. Rip a scrap of 1-inch pine 1 inch wide and 8 feet long. Then mark it with an indelible marker at 6 inches, 1 foot, 18 inches, 2 feet, 3 feet, and

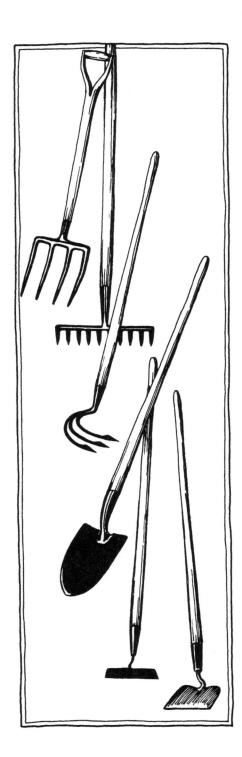

The home gardener needs only a few hand tools. **Left to right:** *spading fork, steel garden rake, hand cultivator, spade, onion hoe, garden hoe.*

so forth. (I use it again in the fall for measuring my stacked stovewood.)

A flat-tined spading fork is handy for turning small plots. It requires less effort than a spade and breaks clods more easily. Be sure to get a flat-tined fork, since those with round tines are not meant for turning soil.

A good trowel is strong and narrow, with a strong shank. Don't waste your money on a cheap one with thin metal that will bend. A trowel comes in handy for lifting transplants from flats and making transplant holes.

A narrow, strong-bladed putty knife is useful for blocking plants for hardening and for lifting transplants from flats. It's also helpful in removing caked soil from tool blades. Keep your putty knife sharp.

A rotary tiller is almost a must for a big garden. Those with rear-mounted tines are sometimes easier to handle,

A wheel hoe is handy for cultivating both sides of a row at once.

A rotary tiller is a handy tool. Be sure to till in both directions for fine soil preparation.

particularly over hard ground, than those with front-mounted tines. They're often more expensive, too. Tillers with 3-horsepower engines are fine for tilling clean ground that has been worked in previous years. But if you're turning new ground or turning under a cover crop or other refuse, you'll be better off with an engine of at least 5 horsepower.

TOOL CARE

Take care of your tools, and they'll last a lifetime. Keep wooden handles smooth with fine sandpaper or steel wool. Those that have been varnished or polyurethaned will give you blisters in no time. Sand off the finish and rub the handle down with a couple of coats of boiled linseed oil.

Keep the edge of your hoe sharp. File to a short taper, then finish with a whetstone. Remove the beaded edge with a few downward strokes of the stone or file. Don't sharpen to a long taper—it'll dull too quickly. Slightly sharpen the edges of spades to aid their cutting action. Too sharp an edge may become badly nicked.

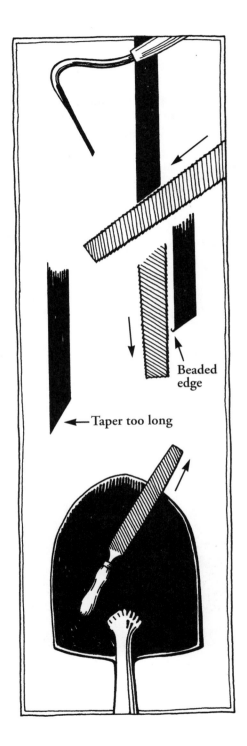

Beaded edge

Taper too long

Resand and recoat the handles each year before putting the tools up for the winter.

Remove paint or varnish from metal parts, and brighten them with emery cloth. Keep cutting tools like hoes and putty knives very sharp. Keep digging tools, like spades, slightly duller, since they my become badly nicked if too sharp. Rough out the blades with an 8- to 10-inch flat file, then finish with a medium-sized whetstone or scythestone with both coarse and fine sides. Avoid putting the blades onto an emery wheel. If used incorrectly, it can take the temper out of the steel.

Clean your tools after each use, and store them in a dry place. Scrape the soil from the metal, and wipe it clean with an oiled rag. If your tools have rusted, soak them in kerosene for a few hours, then use a wire brush or emery cloth to remove the rust. Give the metal a good coating of motor oil before storing the tools for the winter.

Remove, sharpen, and oil the blades of your rotary tiller each fall. Let the engine run until all the gasoline has burned, then remove the spark plug and put a teaspoon of light oil (10 W) into the cylinder. Turn the engine over a few times to distribute the oil. Drain the old oil from the crankcase, and replace it with new. Store the tiller in a dry place.

Whipping the Weeds

A weed is a plant out of place. Volunteer squash is a weed if it's growing in your turnip patch. Another way to look at it is that a weed is a plant that is unsightly, reduces yield, or causes harmful effects. Most important, though, a weed is a plant, and any measure you take to kill it can also kill your vegetables if you're not careful.

Weeds compete with vegetable plants for sunlight, water, and nutrients. They also harbor insects and diseases that can attack your crops. If you do not control weeds, they will reduce the productivity of your garden.

Herbicides have few uses in the home garden, so stay away from them. Tilling before planting, cultivating during the growing season, and mulching are the methods most commonly used in the home garden to control weeds.

TILLING

Plowing and tilling the soil in the autumn turns under trash and buries weed seeds deeply so they won't germinate. It also exposes some long-buried seeds to winter conditions, which can kill them.

Tilling in the fall can cause winter soil erosion in some southern gardens but is useful in the North where there are hard freezes. The freezing and thawing of the soil breaks clods and improves the soil texture. Fall tilling also allows you to turn under organic matter for decomposition, kills some burrowing insects by exposing them to harsh winter conditions, and allows the soil to dry earlier in the spring. This means you can plant earlier.

Spade by turning soil of one row over and into the trench from the previous row. Note the refuse placed into the furrow for burying.

If you don't till in the fall, grow a winter cover crop and till in the spring. Tilling in the spring turns under any weeds that might have germinated and destroys their root systems. Recent studies have shown that tilling at night discourages weed seeds from germinating. Try it: Choose a moonlit night for tilling the garden and see whether it makes a difference.

Don't plow your soil when it's too wet. To check this, press a handful of soil into a ball. Then touch the ball lightly. If it breaks apart easily, it's fine for turning. If the ball holds together, it's too wet. Working wet soil will ruin its structure and cause it to cake and crust. When gardening books recommend planting "as soon as the ground can be worked," their authors mean as soon as the soil is dry enough, not as soon as the frost is out of it.

Complete spring tilling about two weeks before planting. If you plow too early, the soil may harden and weeds germinate before you plant. If you plant too soon after tilling, the soil will bury fine seeds as it settles.

Till the soil about 6 to 8 inches deep. After you've turned the soil, wait a day until the clods have dried, then rake the surface as smooth as possible, removing stones and debris. This makes planting small seeds easier.

CULTIVATING

After planting, cultivation with tillers or hoes destroys weeds, loosens the soil, breaks the soil crust, and aerates vegetable roots. Aeration encourages microbial activity in the soil that releases nutrients to plant roots. By

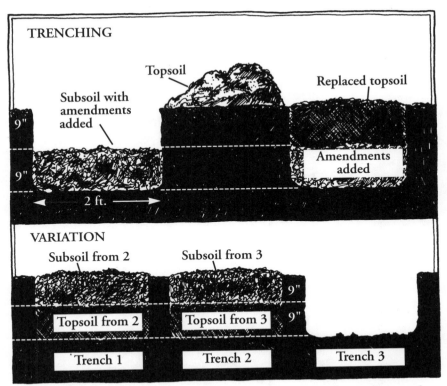

TRENCHING

Subsoil with amendments added

Topsoil

Replaced topsoil

Amendments added

9"

9"

2 ft.

VARIATION

Subsoil from 2

Subsoil from 3

9"

Topsoil from 2

Topsoil from 3

9"

Trench 1

Trench 2

Trench 3

Trenching is done every five years, or a fifth of the garden is done each year. Step 1. Remove the topsoil from a trench 2 feet wide. Step 2. Turn the subsoil, adding lime, phosphorus, and organic matter. Step 3. Replace the topsoil. A variation is to remove 2 feet of soil in each of two trenches. Place the topsoil from the second trench in the bottom of the first trench; the subsoil of the second trench becomes the topsoil of the first. These systems are practical only where the garden soil is a very deep loam.

destroying weeds, cultivation conserves soil moisture, and by loosening the soil, it decreases runoff and slows the migration of moisture from deeper soil layers to the surface. Also, because compact soil is a better heat conductor, cultivating lowers the soil temperature slightly. All of these benefits are incidental. The main reason for cultivating is to control weeds.

The key to good cultivation is *shallow*. Don't disturb more than the top inch or so of soil. Going deeper will damage the vegetables' root systems. Do it just as the weeds are breaking through the soil surface, cut-

The correct way to cultivate is to merely scrape the surface of the soil around the plant. Digging deeper will damage the root system.

If your weeds become too big, their roots will intertwine with those of your vegetables. Then, if you pull the weed, you'll damage the vegetables' root systems. It's better to cut the weed at the soil line and leave the roots intact. Better still, don't let the weeds get so big.

ting them off at the soil line. Gardeners usually cultivate soon after a rain, because that's when weed seeds germinate. But never cultivate wet soil. That destroys its texture and causes it to compact and crust when it dries. Instead, cultivate when the soil is dry enough to crumble, but not so dry as to break into clumps. For every day you let a weed grow, you add an hour to your weeding time, and as the weeds grow and the hours mount, you will be tempted to pull them to get them out of your cabbage. Don't! Pulling weeds whose roots are intertwined with those of your vegetables will damage the vegetable plants. Better to cut the weeds off at the soil surface and leave their roots intact. But you'll have to cut them every few days for the rest of the season to keep them down. I know a gardener who had to mow his garden to find his cabbage. And he bragged about it! If your garden gets that bad, it's time to go fishing.

The hoe is the gardener's best friend. Keep it sharp, and use it to cut weeds at the soil line. There are several types of hoes for different purposes. An onion hoe works best for getting into tight places. A wheel hoe allows you to hoe both sides of the row at one time.

A cultivator, either hand-held or on a wheel, disturbs and aerates the soil and uproots weeds. Small weeds can pass between its tines, however.

Some gardeners cultivate with a rotary tiller. Set the tines so that they will cultivate no more than 1 inch deep. Cultivating 6 or 8 inches deep will ruin vegetable plants' fibrous root systems and subject them to greater nutrient and water stress. It will also bring long-buried weed seeds to the surface.

A lawn tractor is fine for spring or fall plowing, but I don't recommend it for regular cultivating. It may compact the soil too much, and you'll have to space your rows widely enough to accommodate the width of the tractor, which wastes space. You'll still have to hand hoe to get weeds out of tight places.

MULCHING

Mulch reduces fruit rots by keeping ripening fruit off the soil, conserves soil moisture by 10 to 50 percent over bare soil, and can increase the rate of water absorption into the soil. Depending on the type of mulch, it can also cool or warm the soil, increase its organic matter content, and smother weed seedlings. Remove all weeds, however, before you apply any mulch. Mulch will not control most grasses, perennial weeds, and established annual weeds. The soil should be moist, but not wet, before you mulch. Mulching dry soil can prevent rain from soaking in, and mulching sopping wet soil can keep it from drying out and warming up. Either way, plant growth will be slowed.

Organic mulches generally cool the soil and add organic matter to it when they rot. They prevent crusting and compaction, and the roots of vegetables will grow through the lower layers, forming a dense root system. The soil microbes that break down the organic mulch use some of the soil nitrogen for their activity, however, and you'll have to add nitrogen to compensate. Apply 2 pounds of 5–10–5, 5–10–10, or equivalent fertilizer to every 100 square feet of mulch surface to feed the microbes that eat the mulch. You'll need 4 to 6 inches of organic mulch around your plants for effective weed control.

If you use straw, be sure it's loose, fluffy, and clean. Good straw will keep the soil cool and moist, so apply it only when the soil has warmed. Putting it on too soon will keep the soil cold and reduce yields. Oat straw is softer and makes a better mulch than rye or wheat straw. Barley straw is good too, but the barbs will irritate your skin. A 1,000-square-foot garden requires about 1 ton of mulching straw. Don't smoke while standing on straw mulch.

Legume hay is okay provided it's seed free. It breaks down rapidly and generally requires no additional nitrogen. Because it releases its nutrients fairly quickly, use it particularly on slow-growing plants, such as peppers and eggplant. Salt or marsh hay makes an excellent mulch but takes several years to break down; it's best for large perennials. Don't use hay that contains seed heads and leaves.

Leaves make a great mulch, though some weeds will grow through them. Chop large leaves with a rotary mower to prevent matting.

Grass clippings make a good mulch, particularly for slow-growing plants that benefit from their nutrients. Let the grass dry for a day before you rake the clippings for mulch, because fresh clippings tend to mat and can ferment and injure young plants. Never use clippings from lawns that have been treated with herbicides.

Compost is weed-free and makes an excellent mulch, as does well-rotted manure. Never use fresh manure or chicken manure in any form for a mulch. The former will host a great crop of weeds; the latter can burn young plants.

Peat moss makes an excellent mulch but can crust if allowed to dry, making it impermeable to water and air. It's also too expensive to use in a large garden.

Newspaper makes an excellent mulch if it is shredded in a rotary mower. Unshredded papers laid flat in layers can mat and restrict air and water penetration into the soil. Sometimes even shredded papers can mat if the season is particularly wet. I used to worry about using newsprint, especially colored, as a mulch, for fear that heavy metals would leach into the soil. Recent research has shown, however, that the heavy metal content of newsprint is well within safe limits for use as mulch. So put those papers to good use. Be sure to soak them in water before you use them, or they'll blow away.

Wood chips take a long time to break down. They interfere with cultivation and usually cause a nitrogen deficiency to develop. Use them on perennials and landscape plants, but keep them out of the vegetable garden. Wood shavings blow away too easily; like sawdust, they are best composted first.

Bagasse, or dried, shredded sugarcane, is a good general-purpose mulch. It conserves moisture very well, but the fibers may stick to ripening strawberry fruit wet with dew and to sweaty arms and legs.

Inorganic mulches are being used more and more. They are handy to apply and easy to remove.

Black polyethylene plastic is inexpensive and well suited for mulching. It's sold by thickness measured in mils (thousandths of an inch). Three-mil poly is commonly used in the vegetable garden. The black plastic blocks sunlight from hitting the soil and stops germinating weed seeds cold while making the soil surface 10 to 15 degrees *warmer* than bare soil. This heat, along with the soil moisture conserved by the plastic, strongly promotes root growth, and your crops will mature up to ten days earlier than they would on bare soil. Black plastic mulch is especially good for cucumbers,

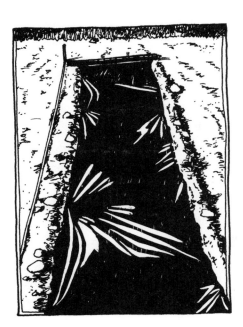

Black polyethylene mulch is fine for warm-season crops. Unroll the plastic, and cover the edges with soil and small stones to hold the mulch in place.

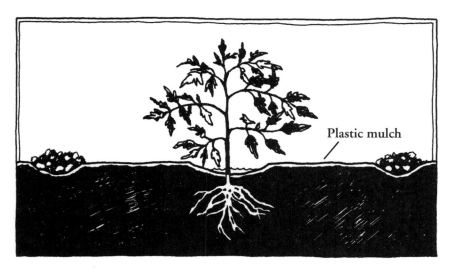

Plastic mulch

Punch holes through the plastic mulch, and set your plants. The pressure of punching the holes will create small depressions, which will encourage water to drain into the planting holes. Place the edges of the mulch in a furrow and cover with stones and soil to hold the mulch in place.

squash, early corn, and melons in northern gardens where temperatures ordinarily remain cool.

Aluminum foil mulch keeps the soil up to 10 degrees *cooler* than bare soil. It reflects sunlight that missed the plant on the way down back onto the leaves, thereby increasing plant growth and yields. The reflected light also confuses and repels aphids. Wait for the soil to warm before you apply the foil.

COVER CROPS AND CROP ROTATION

Nature abhors a vacuum. When a crop has been harvested and the soil is bare, plant a cover crop. Buckwheat makes a fine summer cover crop; its lush growth shades the soil surface and smothers any weeds that emerge. Put in a cover crop of winter rye in late summer or fall to block any weeds that might germinate during the fall and winter. Plowed down, cover crops add valuable moisture and organic matter to the soil.

You can also control weeds somewhat by practicing a good rotation plan. Vine crops are particularly helpful in smothering the weeds that overran your carrot patch last year.

11

Watering

Vegetable plants need a lot of water. Water is not only important for carrying soil nutrients into the plants, but its atoms enter into plant structure, and most vegetables are about 90 percent water.

The amount of water a crop requires depends on the crop, soil type, climate, garden management practices, and plant spacing, among other things. Mature plants need more water than young plants, and those with shallow root systems need more frequent watering than those with deep roots. Insufficient water leads to stunting, stress, poor tip fill in corn, and flower abortion in tomatoes. Too much water delays maturity, attracts pests, can result in a poor stand of germinating seeds, and causes fruit to crack.

WHEN TO WATER

Early crops get most of their water from rainfall and snowmelt. But during dry periods we must supplement natural rainfall for best production, particularly during critical periods of water use by the plant. A lack of water at these times could spell disaster for summer and fall crops.

Examine the soil every few days. Keep it wet to a depth of 1 to 2 feet at all times, and don't let more than 1 inch of the surface soil dry out. If it does, shallow-rooted crops will suffer. Feel the soil. If it forms a loose ball when squeezed, you're probably okay. To be safe, you may want to purchase an inexpensive soil water meter. Calibrate it, then plunge it into the soil to root depth. If it indicates that the soil is at 50 percent or less of field capacity, water immediately.

Your crops need water throughout the growing season, but it becomes particularly critical during certain stages of crop development. The solanaceous crops need even watering throughout their growth.

CROP	STAGES WHEN WATERING IS CRITICAL
Cabbage, broccoli, cauliflower, lettuce	Head development
Carrots, beets, turnips, radishes rutabagas	Root enlargement
Onions, garlic	Bulb enlargement
Potatoes	Tuber enlargement
Corn	Tasseling, ear development
Asparagus	Fern development
Beans, peas	Flowering, pod development
Tomatoes, cucumbers, eggplant, peppers, melons, squash	Flowering, fruit set, fruit development
All crops, but especially those planted in summer and fall	Germination

Invest in an inexpensive rain gauge. If rainfall exceeds 1 inch per week, preferably in a gentle, slow, soaking rain, you may not have to water. Water from violent, heavy rains runs off the garden before soaking in. Showers supplying less than 1/4 inch of rain are useless, since much of the water evaporates before it reaches the root zone. And just how much water is 1 inch? Watering a 1,000-square-foot garden with 1 inch per week requires about 623 gallons.

HOW TO WATER

My grandfather faithfully watered the garden with a hose every other night after supper. As I watched him standing there swishing the water stream back and forth over the peppers, I thought how faithful he was to his garden. He was faithful, but he wasn't smart. Not only was he watering at the wrong time, but he was sprinkling.

Water in the morning, not at night. Plants going into the evening with wet foliage are a welcoming committee for diseases.

Water well. A light sprinkling does nothing but waste water and

MOISTURE AVAILABLE	SAND (Gritty When Wet)	SANDY LOAM (Gritty When Wet, Dirties Fingers)	CLAY LOAM (Sticky When Wet)	CLAY (Like Modeling Clay When Wet)
0%	Dry, loose, flows through fingers	Dry, loose, flows through fingers	Dry clods break into powder	Hard, cracked, clods hard to break
Less than 50% (irrigate)	Dry, will not form ball	Dry, will not form ball	Crumbly, forms loose ball	Pliable, forms loose ball
50%–75% (okay)	Same as 50%	Forms loose ball	Forms ball; feels slick under pressure	Forms ball; ribbons between thumb and fore-finger
75% to field capacity (okay)	Sticks together, forms very weak ball	Forms loose ball; does not feel slick	Forms pliable ball; may feel slick	Easily ribbons between fingers
Field capacity (saturated)	No free water upon squeezing; hand moist	Same as sand	Same as sand	Same as sand
Above field capacity (waterlogged)	Free water appears when soil is bounced in hand	Free water appears when soil is kneaded	Squeeze out free water	Puddles and free water on surface

time. Instead, water once a week, and apply at least 1 inch of water every time. If the weather has been hot, dry, and windy, you may have to supply 2 to 4 inches every week. Soak the soil to a depth of 1 to 2 feet. Deep watering encourages better plant growth. To monitor my watering, I

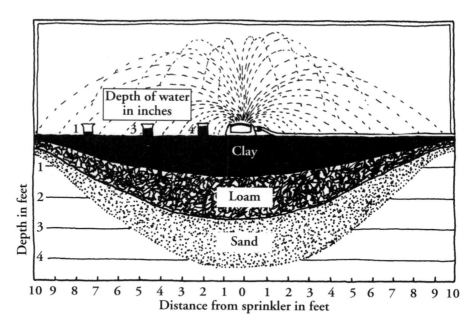

Garden sprinklers distribute water unevenly. Move them around the garden, and be sure their spray patterns overlap. Otherwise, soil at the outer edges of the spray will receive too little water and that near the center will become waterlogged. Water penetrates deeper and faster in sandy soil than in clay soil.

place several empty tunafish cans around the garden and water until the cans contain at least 1 inch. Placing them randomly helps me determine the evenness of water distribution.

Most gardeners use a hose-end sprinkler for watering. They do a good job, but they distribute water unevenly, dropping more in the center of the stream than at the edges. Monitor your watering with tunafish cans, and move the sprinkler around to water all places evenly. Because much of the water from sprinklers evaporates before it reaches the soil, particularly on hot and windy days, you may want to try a more efficient system. Soaker hoses are more expensive than sprinklers, but they distribute water evenly to the roots, don't wet vacant areas of the garden to encourage weeds, and use less water because evaporation is much less than with sprinklers. You can monitor water flow by sinking a tunafish can into the soil to its rim and running the hose over it.

12

Starting from Seeds

High-quality seeds are always a good buy, regardless of price. Purchase them from a reputable company and well ahead of planting time.

Some gardeners *prime*, or *osmocondition*, their seeds by soaking them for 24 hours before planting. This allows the seeds to soak up plenty of water and sets the early stages of germination in motion. It is particularly helpful if the soil is hot and dry. If, however, you presoak seeds for planting in soil that is cold and wet, the seeds may then rot.

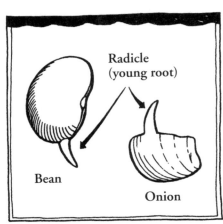

Some gardeners soak their seeds in water before planting. Priming is soaking the seeds for a day. The seed will swell, but the young root will not be apparent. Chitting is soaking the seed until the root has emerged and the seed has germinated.

Chitting, an English term, involves soaking seeds until they start to germinate and the small root, or radicle, begins to emerge. When planted, they will grow into seedlings much more quickly, and the chances of seed rot and damping-off are lessened. As with priming, however, the

From the Nursery

Unless you are growing a great number of transplants, it's probably less expensive to purchase plants from a nursery. Look for sets that are stocky and 6 to 8 inches tall. Lack of uniform size may indicate that the plants were crowded on the bench. Sets should be free from insect and disease damage and have no yellow leaves. The stem should be pencil thick and may show some pink coloration if plants have been hardened. No set should have open flowers or fruit. The presence of flower buds or, more important, open flowers and fruit suppresses root initiation and reduces the production of new roots.

The success you have with your transplants depends on many factors. Younger sets survive transplanting better than older ones. Some old-timers recommend pruning the tops of sets at transplanting to decrease water loss through the leaves. Now we know that removal of any portion of the top decreases the speed of root regeneration. Don't do it. Do, however, pick off any flowers or fruit before transplanting.

The tomato sets on the left are too tall and lanky. The ones on the right are just right. If you must purchase plants like those on the left, plant them deep.

These cucumber sets are too lanky. Also, since they were grown in a flat, their roots will be disturbed during transplanting, which will set them back substantially.

This tomato set has flowers and small fruits. The crop will be restricted if you try to plant such a set in the garden. A plant setting flowers and fruits is putting much energy into reproduction, with little left over for new roots and shoots. But unless new roots and shoots are produced, there will be little food for fruit growth and flowering. It's a no-win situation. Simply pinching off the flowers may not help all that much.

seeds are more prone to rot under poor soil conditions. Chitted seeds require careful handling to avoid damaging the roots.

Small seeds, like those of carrots and lettuce, are difficult to plant at proper spacings, and the young plants require thinning. This takes time, and you'll waste a lot of seeds. Using seeds that are coated with clay, or *pelleted*, to make them larger enables you to space them properly and avoid having to thin the crop, although such seeds are expensive. Pesticides are sometimes included in the coating. As an alternative, try mixing small seeds with fine sand before you sow. This will help you disperse them more thinly.

Decortication is a relatively new procedure. Seeds of some vegetables, such as beets and Swiss chard, are encased in the dried fruits. The crinkled balls you find in the seed packet are not the seeds, but the dried fruits, with several seeds contained inside. When you plant one, several seedlings emerge, and you'll have to thin to get the best crop. Again, this is time-consuming and wasteful. Decorticated seed has the fruit removed so that you can plant the individual seeds. Some of these are pelleted to make handling easier.

The use of pelleted or decorticated seeds is a bit more costly and not absolutely necessary, but it can save you time later on.

GERMINATION

Botanically, *germination* refers to the emergence of the root, or radicle, from the seed. To the horticulturist and gardener, a seed has germinated when the seedling has emerged from the soil. Water, oxygen, temperature, and, sometimes, light are factors involved in germination.

The seed is a dormant, dry receptacle containing an embryo. When it soaks up water, its metabolism increases and the cells begin to divide and elongate. The tissue swells and cracks the seed coat.

Oxygen enters through the cracked seed coat and allows the proper reactions to occur for growth. Waterlogged or heavy soils are low in oxygen and will cause the seed to rot. Light, fluffy soils are high in oxygen and promote rapid germination if they are kept moist.

Even if the seeds have adequate water and oxygen for germination, the process will not proceed if the temperature is incorrect. Although seeds of most cool-season crops germinate at soil temperatures near 32

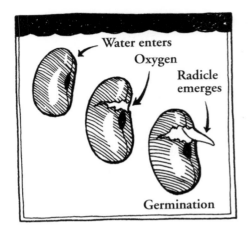

Water enters

Oxygen

Radicle emerges

Germination

Seed germination follows a sequence of events. The seed absorbs water and swells, and the seed coat cracks. This allows oxygen to enter, and active metabolism begins. Germination occurs when the young root, or radicle, emerges from the seed. Soil temperature must be warm enough for proper metabolism. Some seeds require light to germinate; others don't.

degrees F. and those of warm-season crops at temperatures above 59 degrees F., both do so much better at higher temperatures. The optimum temperature depends on the species. The seeds of some plants will become dormant if exposed to soil temperatures that are too high. This is called *thermodormancy* and is a natural defense against the seeds' germinating when temperatures are too high to sustain plant growth. Be sure the soil has reached the proper temperature for your crop before planting seeds outdoors.

Light is sometimes necessary for germination. Some celery and lettuce seeds, for example, will not germinate if they are planted so deeply that all light is excluded. This is not really a problem in practice, however, since you would never plant small seeds so deeply.

GETTING SET FOR SETS

Growing your own transplants lets you choose cultivars not available in your local nursery and get the greatest number of usable plants from expensive seeds. You can get a jump on the season by starting them for planting earlier. You can easily control germinating and growing conditions—soil depth and texture, temperature, moisture, light. And you can take care to grow the healthiest plants for your garden.

Growing your own transplants, or *sets,* as they are often called, is easy provided you follow three rules: Use sterile or pasteurized media; supply the seedlings with adequate warmth, light, moisture, and space; and harden the plants properly before you set them out.

Containers

You can use almost anything to hold the plants and growing medium—tin cans, paper cups, milk cartons—as long as you punch holes in the bottom for drainage. Two common containers designed specifically for this purpose are flats and peat pots.

Flats are long, wide trays used for starting plants. They come in various sizes but usually measure about 24 inches long by 16 inches wide by 3 or 4 inches deep. They were formerly made of a rot-resistant wood such as cedar or redwood, but most are now made of plastic. The old wooden flats had slatted bottoms for drainage. The gardener would place a layer of newspaper on the bottom of the flat before filling it with the medium. The paper prevented the medium from falling through the cracks but allowed excess water to drain. Some of the newer plastic flats are too shallow and have no drainage holes, which can cause waterlogging problems. If you can find some old wooden flats, buy them. If you can't, make them.

Flats are reusable from year to year and thus are less expensive than peat pots. Fill them to the top with medium and drop them gently on the bench once or twice to settle the medium before planting. Two drawbacks: Because the seeds are usually sown in small rows, you'll have to thin the seedlings, and because the plants must be lifted out of the flats before planting, you can't help but disturb their root systems. Nevertheless, they're great for growing most transplants, except the cucurbits—squash, pumpkins, melons, and cucumbers—which will not transplant well if their roots are disturbed. When you're done with them for the season, wash them in a 1-to-9-part mixture of bleach and water and stack them in a dry, unheated area.

Peat pots come in several sizes and are made from compressed peat. They're packed in a flat or some other container before use, filled to overflowing, and covered completely with medium. This is important to prevent moisture from being wicked upward through the sides and evaporated from the rim of the pot. Planting only one or two seeds in each pot eliminates the need to thin seedlings, and since the entire pot is placed in the garden, you do not disturb the plant's root system. This makes peat pots particularly useful for growing cucurbits.

The peat pellet is a refinement of the peat pot. The pellets are small cylinders of compressed peat wrapped in a thin mesh for support. Place them in warm water for a few minutes, and they swell into small, solid

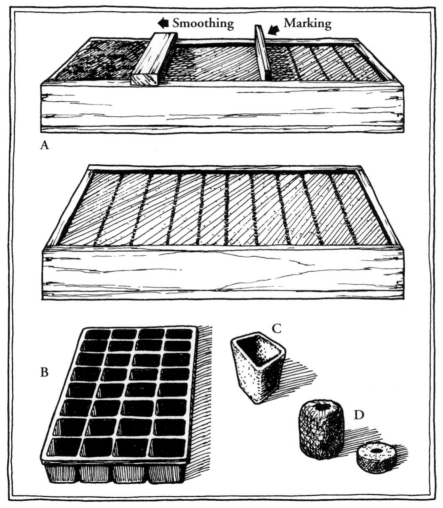

There are many types of starting containers. The wooden flat (A), standard for many years, has been replaced by the plastic tray. This may be opened or sectioned (B). The peat pot (C) and the peat pellet (D) are made of compressed peat moss and can be planted along with the plant. The latter expands when wet, and the seed is planted at the top. Cut the mesh before planting.

peat cylinders. They are used in the same way as peat pots, but you save the expense of having to purchase medium. Slice through the webbing in one or two places on the pellet before planting so that the roots can grow into the soil unrestricted.

Media

A medium can be plain garden soil, but such soil contains weeds and pathogens that make growing healthy seedlings difficult. Good media are sterile, fine and uniformly textured, light, well aerated, and well drained. Most garden-supply stores offer many brands of sterile, soilless mixes for starting plants. Use these and you won't go wrong. To make your own, begin with composted soil (high in organic matter) and add vermiculite, perlite, sand, or peat to lighten the soil and increase its water-holding capacity. Here are some good proportions:

1 part composted soil:1 part peat:1 part sand
1 part composted soil:1 part perlite:1 part peat
2 parts composted soil:1 part peat:1 part sand

Mix the medium well, spread it in a shallow baking pan, and bake it in your kitchen oven at 350 degrees F. for 45 minutes. That should kill most of the harmful pathogens and weed seeds. Take care not to over-cook your medium, because that may cause the release of toxic elements and kill many of the good soil organisms.

Making your own medium is time-consuming and can strain marital relations. But baking medium doesn't smell that bad—sort of like Aunt Angeline's brown bread.

SOWING INSIDE

When to sow your seeds depends on when the plants should be set in the garden and how old they should be when you do it. Some species trans-plant better at a younger age than others.

Smaller seeds are sown thickly and the plants thinned when their first true leaves appear. Larger seeds, like those of tomato and cucumber, can be sown one or two at a time and spaced far enough apart that thinning will be unnecessary. Cover the seeds with vermiculite or sand to prevent crusting and excessive drying of the medium and to decrease the inci-dence of damping-off. This disease is caused by any of several pathogens living in the moist surface soil and attacks young seedlings at the soil line, causing the stems to blacken and shrivel and the plants to fall over.

Fungicide seed treatments help control the problem. Because the pathogen needs moisture to be destructive, sand or vermiculite placed over the seeds at planting keeps the surface dry enough to prevent an outbreak.

Next, lay a sheet of newspaper over the top of the medium and sprinkle with water. The newspaper breaks the fall of the water so that the seeds are not disturbed. The damp paper also prevents the medium from drying out too rapidly. Remove the paper once seedlings have emerged. Some gardeners instead cover the flat with clear plastic after watering to form a minigreenhouse. This not only keeps the atmosphere inside the flat moist, but also helps hold the temperature to acceptable levels.

Light

I don't care what other books say, the kitchen window just doesn't provide enough light in late winter to start healthy seedlings. Try it and you'll see that the plants are spindly and weak. In the house, you'll need to supplement natural sunlight with artificial light to get the best growth.

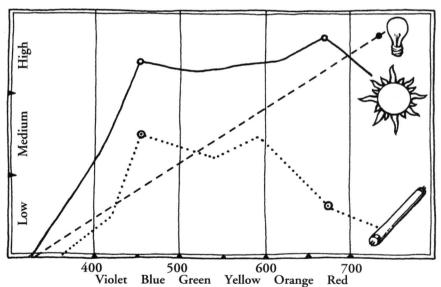

Sunlight contains all colors of the rainbow but is particularly high in blue and red light. Incandescent light has little blue light but much red. Cool white fluorescent light has a fair amount of blue light but little red. A combination of cool white fluorescent and incandescent lamps will mimic sunlight in the colors most important for plant growth.

Sunlight contains all colors of the rainbow. Of all these colors, plants use the reds and the blues most. Special grow lights are available on the market that mimic the light spectrum of sunlight. These are usually more expensive than normal light bulbs and shine with a purple glow that some people dislike. They work well, but you can save money and mimic sunlight with a combination of cool white fluorescent and incandescent bulbs. Fluorescent bulbs are especially high in blue light but low in red light. Incandescent bulbs are high in red light but low in blue. By combining the two, you can provide the plants with light of the proper wavelengths for the best growth. Use one or two 40-watt incandescent bulbs along with four or five 40-watt fluorescent bulbs. Keep them on for about 12 hours each day, and keep them 6 to 8 inches above the plants at all times. Incandescent bulbs also emit much heat, so keep a thermometer at plant level to monitor the temperature, and turn on a fan when it gets too hot.

Temperature
Starting plants in cold frames or hotbeds usually provides them with enough light, but temperature often becomes the limiting factor since

Here are the best temperatures at which to germinate and grow your vegetable plants.

| | | BEST FOR GROWING | |
CROP	BEST FOR GERMINATION	DAY	NIGHT
Broccoli	70–80°F	60–70°F	50–60°F
Brussels sprouts	70–80	60–70	50–60
Cabbage	70–80	60–70	50–60
Cauliflower	70–80	60–70	55–60
Cucumbers	70–95	70–80	60–70
Eggplant	75–85	70–80	65–70
Lettuce	60–70	55–75	45–55
Muskmelons	75–95	70–80	60–70
Onions	65–80	60–70	45–55
Peppers	75–85	65–80	60–70
Tomatoes	75–80	60–75	60–65
Watermelons	70–95	70–80	60–70

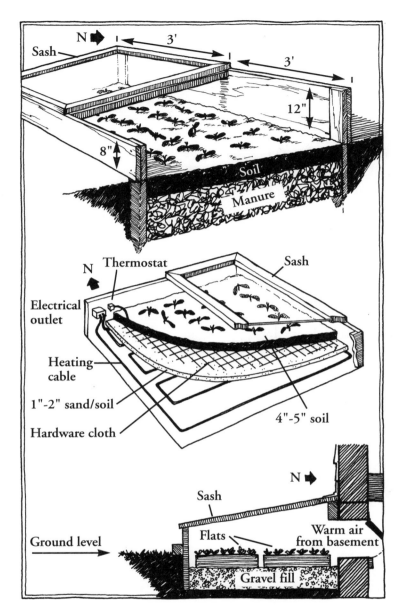

A hotbed is a great way to start plants. Top. *An old-fashioned hotbed heated by fermenting horse manure.* Middle. *A modern hotbed heated with electric heating cables positioned below the soil.* Bottom. *A hotbed placed against a basement window to take advantage of residual warm air.*

A cold frame is a hotbed with no source of heat other than the sun. Position the frames so that they slope to the south. Insulate their north sides with mounded soil, hay bales, or bags of leaves, or abut them against a building.

these structures are outside. Each species has its own temperature limits below or above which it will not grow. Too high a temperature will cause the plants to become spindly, especially if light is insufficient. Too low a temperature retards growth and can cause bolting in cabbage and cauliflower. The first fruit of tomato plants grown under excessively cool temperatures will be rough and unattractive. Most plants grow better if night temperatures are 5 to 10 degrees cooler than day temperatures.

Water

Water your plants only when necessary, and then do it thoroughly. Light sprinkling does nothing but waste time and water. Use a fine spray so as not to disturb the young seedlings, and water only in the morning to give the plants enough time to dry before nightfall. Don't water too much. Overwatering prevents the development of a good root system, causes overly lush growth that usually falls over, and increases the incidence of damping-off. Plants grown under cooler temperatures and less light require less water than those grown under higher temperatures and light intensities. When the medium feels dry, water.

Nutrients

Seedling media usually contain few nutrients, so you'll have to fertilize periodically. This is the job of starter fertilizers. These have high analyses and are mixed with water and sprinkled over the plants with the regular watering. Organic starter fertilizers have lower analyses. Always follow the directions on the label; they usually are mixed at the rate of 1 tablespoon of fertilizer per gallon of water and applied once a week for the first two to three weeks. After three weeks, you can increase the concentration to 2 tablespoons per gallon. Sprinkle the foliage with clear water after fertilizing to wash off any remaining salts.

Thinning

Try as you might to space your seeds, you'll have some plants growing too close to each other in the flat. These will be spindly, weak, and yellow and will produce a poor crop. Outside, if your garden soil is loose and friable, some plants may be able to push out of each other's way and mature reasonably well without thinning. But seedlings in a flat can't do

Tolerance of crops to transplanting and frost and the time needed to grow them to transplant maturity. Some crops transplant well, others poorly, depending on the plant's ability to regenerate a full root system rapidly. Allow enough time to produce good transplants ready to set in the garden at the proper time.

CROP	TOLERANCE TO TRANSPLANTING	WEEKS TO GROW	FROST SUSCEPTIBILITY
Broccoli	Good	5–7	Tolerant
Brussels sprouts	Good	5–7	Tolerant
Cabbage	Good	5–7	Tolerant
Cauliflower	Good	5–7	Tolerant
Celeriac	Good	8–10	Tolerant
Celery	Requires care	8–10	Very susceptible
Cucumbers	Sow in container	3–4	Very susceptible
Eggplant	Requires care	6–8	Very susceptible
Endive	Good	3–4	Tolerant
Kale	Good	5–7	Tolerant
Lettuce	Good	3–4	Moderately tolerant
Muskmelons	Sow in container	3–4	Very susceptible
Onions	Good	8–10	Tolerant
Parsley	Good	5–7	Tolerant
Peppers	Requires care	6–8	Susceptible
Pumpkins	Sow in container	4–6	Very susceptible
Squash	Sow in container	4–6	Very susceptible
Tomatoes	Good	4–7	Susceptible
Watermelons	Sow in container	5–7	Susceptible

that. Take the time to hand thin to the proper spacings, and you'll be better satisfied with your garden.

If you sow in peat pots, space the pots so that the leaves of one plant will not touch those of another. If you sow in flats, thin the young seedlings to stand at least $^1/_2$ inch apart. Thin them repeatedly as they grow so that the plants are a couple inches apart by the time they are ready for planting in the garden.

Some thinnings, such as those of young beet and kale, can be transplanted. Their stems are delicate and easily crushed, so hold them by the leaves when you transfer them. They'll probably wilt a bit after transplanting, so keep them moist for a few days until they take (regain their rigidity). Plants that do not transplant well, such as spinach, are great in salads.

Minimize root damage when you transplant. Younger plants take transplanting better than older ones, and some species transplant better than others. The cucurbits will not transplant well if their roots are disturbed.

13

Hardening Off and Planting Out

Plants grown in a warm, moist environment, provided with all the water and nutrients they need, and sheltered from pests and wind often won't survive the shock of direct transplanting into the harsh garden environment. Sets first need to be hardened off or gradually acclimated to the outside environment. There are several ways to harden off plants, all of which involve a forced reduction in growth rate and a toughening of plant tissues and require about two weeks to complete.

Slowly lower the temperature from the optimum in which the plants were growing to the real temperatures they will experience outside. With hotbeds or cold frames, gradually increase the ventilation until the sash is removed completely, day and night, and no artificial source of heat is used. With plants grown indoors,

Before transplanting in the garden, block plants in the flat by severing the root systems on all sides. Lift the plants with a putty knife.

A well-hardened plant is blocky and deep green. Veins along the undersides of the leaves are pink-purple, as are portions of the stems. Blocked roots have proliferated into many side roots that increase the plant's capacity to absorb water.

move them outside during the day at first, then leave them outside day and night the week before transplanting.

Decrease the watering, letting the medium dry somewhat between waterings. Provide only enough water to keep the plants from wilting.

If you've grown your transplants in flats, cut the medium with a knife into small blocks, each containing one plant. This is called *blocking*. By so doing, you reduce the total number of roots, restricting the amount of water and nutrients the plant can absorb. This slows growth and forces branch roots to form. In time, this will increase the amount of root surface and will help the root system to remain in a soil ball during transplanting.

Do not shade the plants during hardening. Give them all the sunlight you can to keep photosynthesis going at optimum levels. During hardening, the plant will continue to make carbohydrates but, because of lower temperatures, will not use all of them in respiration. Some of the excess is stored for later use in red pigments known as anthocyanins. These cause the stems and veins of well-hardened plants to appear pink or purple. The stored carbohydrates are used for growth in the garden and promote rapid production of new roots to replace those lost in transplanting.

Withholding water causes the plant to thicken the waxy layer, or cuticle, on its leaves to conserve the water it has. The heavy cuticle will help keep the plant from drying out in the lower humidity and wind it will experience in the garden.

Withholding nutrients causes the plant to become stocky and a little woody, with smaller, dark green leaves rich in the chlorophyll necessary for photosynthesis. The stocky plants better survive wind whipping, and the chlorophyll-rich leaves can make the best use of filtered sunlight on cloudy days. With its restricted root system, the plant easily suffers from lack of water until it takes. Plant in the early evening when the relative humidity of the air is higher and the temperature cool. Water the plants well with either a starter solution or clear water immediately after setting them in the garden. Starter solutions provide a quick boost to get the plant off to a good start. Those high in phosphorus also stimulate early root growth.

TOUGH LOVE

There are different degrees of hardening, and some species suffer from any hardening at all. Use the following guidelines for hardening off your plants.

Broccoli

Harden to withstand frost, but repeated chilling of young plants to temperatures below 50 degrees F. for more than two weeks can cause the plants to bolt.

Brussels Sprouts

Harden to withstand frost, but crowding and inadequate watering will stunt the plants, causing the stems to become woody and the buds poor. Grow in individual containers.

Cabbage

Harden to withstand frost, but repeated chilling of young plants to temperatures below 50 degrees F. for more than two weeks can cause the plants to bolt.

Cauliflower

Harden to tolerate frost, but the plants are delicate. Crowding in the flat and inadequate watering will stunt the plants and cause the stems to become woody, resulting in poor head development. Best grown in individual containers.

Cucurbits

Melons, squash, pumpkins, and cucumbers for transplanting should be started in individual containers and transplanted in the garden at a young age. Do not disturb the roots, and do not harden the plants. If you need to thin plants in individual pots, pinch some of them, but don't pull them out.

Eggplant

Do not harden these plants. Any reduction in growth will result in poor fruit quality.

Lettuce

Easy to grow and can be hardened to tolerate a light frost.

Onions

Easy to grow and can be hardened to tolerate a light frost.

Peppers

Harden only slightly, keeping temperatures above 50 degrees F. at all times.

Tomatoes

Container-grown plants usually produce an earlier crop than those grown in flats. Plants for transplanting to the garden should be hardened slightly at temperatures above 50 degrees F. and have the first flower cluster visible, but not opened. Overhardening causes a delay in establishment and rough fruit on the first two clusters.

CROP PROTECTORS

Small devices placed over or around the young sets will protect them from strong winds, drying conditions, and cool temperatures.

Row covers resemble miniature greenhouses and are made from clear polyethylene, polypropylene, or polyester. The material is supported over

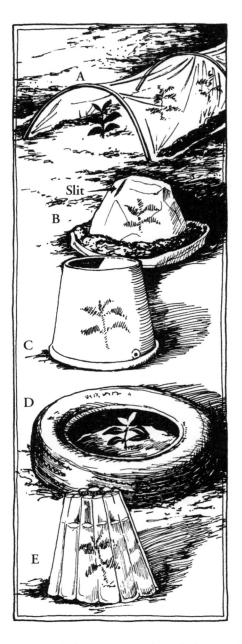

Crop protectors come in various forms. (A) Leave the ends of row tunnels open, and slit or lift the plastic at the sides as temperatures warm. (B) The paper hot cap is thimble-shaped and turned up at the edges to hold soil. Slit it near the top on the leeward side for ventilation. (C) A 5-gallon plastic bucket, with or without a portion of the bottom removed, can be used to provide protection. Wash it thoroughly before using. (D) An old tire, with or without a plastic covering, releases the sun's heat slowly at night. (E) Water jackets are great plant protectors.

the plants by wire hoops stuck into the soil about 5 feet apart. These row tunnels enhance early growth and maturity by increasing the temperature and humidity and provide the plants with protection from wind, frost, and insects. Perforate tunnels made of solid, clear film so that temperatures do not get too high for good growth. Some of the new spunbonded materials are lightweight enough to be placed directly on the crops without hoops for support. These floating row covers work best on crops with leaf canopies of even height, such as vine crops, since they tend to sag between tomato or pepper plants. They are well ventilated but can blow away in strong winds.

A cloche is a tunnellike plant protector made of plastic or glass. The row tunnels are, in a sense, cloches. If you use a cloche or tunnel, be sure the ends are open. You may have to cut slits in the top when temperatures get too high.

Individual plant protectors once were made of inverted flowerpots, bell jars, and whiskey barrels. They gave moderate protection from frost, but some severely restricted light penetration to the plant. A modern counterpart is the hot cap, a small cone usually made of waxed paper that is placed over the plant. The bottom edge forms a turned-up lip that is filled with soil to hold the cap in place. Cut a slit near the top of the cap for ventilation. These are inexpensive and work well where wind is not strong. In my garden, however, they last for about fifteen seconds before being blown away.

A homemade alternative to commercial hot caps are plastic gallon milk jugs. Cut out the bottoms, remove the caps, and place the jugs over the plants. Polyethylene lets heat out and is no good for frost protection, but it will hold slightly warmer air during the day and so might speed plant growth somewhat. For larger plants, use inverted 5-gallon plastic buckets, each with half its bottom removed.

I like to use four-sided wooden boxes and cover one open side with clear plastic. Placed over the plants, this provides ample room for growth

A bottomless wooden box covered with plastic is fine for protecting small plants. Remove the box when the plants get large.

and doesn't blow away. An alternative is to surround the plant with an old automobile tire with clear plastic stretched over the open top. The black tire absorbs the heat and liberates it slowly at night. As the weather warms, remove the plastic from the tire or box.

Water jackets are a fairly new product on the market. They resemble double-walled clear plastic cones. Fill them with water and place them over the plant. Sunlight can penetrate the walls, but the water holds the heat of the sun and liberates it slowly through the night, keeping the air surrounding the plant fairly warm. With this jacket, as with the rubber tire, only the portion of the plant below the top of the device is protected from frost.

Plant protectors do not increase earliness over the long run in many gardens, especially in those where winters are severe. A plant not under a hot cap or water jacket will be smaller than a protected plant at first but will catch up and ripen its crop at about the same time, provided it was not injured by frost or wind.

Direct Seeding

It's most economical to sow seeds directly in the garden, provided conditions are right for growth. Here are some points to consider before you plant.

1. *Prepare the seedbed properly.* Till or spade deeply and thoroughly, incorporating all organic matter, and rake the bed smooth and level. The soil will work up better if you rake a day or so after plowing or spading. Remove weeds or stones, and bring the soil surface to a fine texture. Overworking the soil or working it when it is wet destroys its texture, leading to crusting and compaction and interfering with plant growth.

2. *Some seeds produce weak seedlings.* Carrot, parsnip, and onion seeds produce weak seedlings that are very susceptible to weed competition and soil crusting. Cover the seeds with vermiculite or sand and keep the bed weedfree.

3. *Some plants won't tolerate high salts.* Legumes will not tolerate high salts in the soil. Be careful how you fertilize, and plant on the sides of furrow ridges if your soil is naturally high in salts.

4. *Heavy soils are cold.* Heavy soils hold water and are slower to warm in the spring. Germination and plant growth are slower. Wait until the soil has warmed sufficiently before planting in these soils.

5. *Proper row orientation helps.* To get early-spring crops off to a slightly faster start, orient your rows east to west, although row orientation does not matter greatly. If you plant on raised beds, slope them slightly to the south. The soil of these beds can be as much as 10 degrees warmer than that of flat beds.

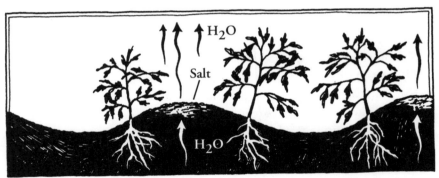

Many plants, particularly legumes, will not tolerate high soil salts. If you have this problem, plant on the sides of garden ridges. As water moves up through the soil, it carries the salts with it. When it evaporates, it will leave them as a crust on the top of the ridge, away from the plants' root zones.

Soil in raised beds sloped gently to the south will warm faster in spring than soil in a flat garden.

PLANTING DATES

The time to plant depends on the hardiness of the crop, its tolerance to cold and warmth, the length of the season, the time required to mature the crop, and geographic location. As a rule of thumb, the growing season is one week later for every 100 miles farther north you are. Large bodies of water and mountains modify this somewhat.

Plants mature faster in warm temperatures, but this is not always welcomed. High temperatures result in a rapid loss of quality in cool-season crops and will cause staggered plantings to ripen at the same time. Hot, wet conditions result in soft, watery fruits that are disease prone, low in sugar, and poor keepers. Insect damage is greater under hot, dry conditions, but much less under cool, dry conditions. Try to time your planting so that the crop will mature under the most favorable weather conditions.

Cool-season crops tolerate light frost, and some even tolerate hard winter freezing. Their seeds germinate in cold soil, so plant them in the early spring to mature before temperatures get too warm, or in the sum-

How soon can you plant? Here are the approximate earliest planting dates of some spring crops. These dates are only suggestions, however; go by how the season "feels."

VERY HARDY (4-6 weeks before last frost)	HARDY (2-3 weeks before last frost)	TENDER (just after last frost)	VERY TENDER (2 weeks after last frost)
Kale	Beets	Snap beans	Lima beans
Lettuce	Carrots	New Zealand spinach	Cucumbers
Collards	Chard	Summer squash	Muskmelons
Kohlrabi	Mustard	Corn	Okra
Peas	Parsnips	Tomato plants	Pumpkins
Onions	Radishes		Black-eyed peas
Rutabagas	Cauliflower plants		Winter squash
Turnips	Chinese cabbage plants		Watermelons
Salsify			Eggplant plants
Spinach			Pepper plants
Asparagus			Sweet potatoes
Broccoli			
Cabbage			

How late can you plant and still get a good crop? The latest dates you can plant are handy to know when you are planning succession crops.

Moderately Heat Tolerant (do well in summer plantings)	Fall Crops (plant 6-8 weeks before first frost)
Beans, chard, squash, corn, New Zealand spinach	Beets, Brussels sprouts, collards, kale, lettuce, mustard, spinach, turnips

mer to mature during the cool fall. Plants in this group have small, shallow root systems and must be weeded, watered, and fertilized more than warm-season crops. Some of the biennials in this group—beets, carrots, cabbage, and celery— will bolt if exposed to temperatures below 50 degrees F. for two weeks or more. Don't plant them too early while the temperatures are too cold for good growth. The cool-season crops are highly nutritious and are not subject to chilling injury at temperatures below 50 degrees F. The edible portion of cool-season crops is usually the leaf, stem, root, or flower; in warm-season crops it is the fruit or seeds.

Warm-season crops will not tolerate frost and will germinate and grow only in soil above about 60 degrees F. These plants are larger than cool-season crops and are grown mostly for fruit. Time your plantings so that these crops make most of their growth and mature during the warm summer months.

You have to know your local climate to know precisely when to plant. Books and calendar dates can only give you rough guidelines. Some regions of the country have an extended spring that allows planting over several months. But in northern Maine, we only have two seasons: this winter and next winter. Frost doesn't come out of the ground in my garden until the middle of May, and all the vegetables—corn, peas, tomatoes, and parsnips—are planted on June 1. The season is so compressed that we don't have the luxury of planting over an extended period. So plant by how the season is warming and by using common sense. After a few years, you'll get the hang of it.

Earliest dates for safe spring planting.

PLANTING DATES

	AVERAGE DATE OF LAST FROST					
	Jan. 30	Feb. 8	Feb. 18	Feb. 28	Mar. 10	Mar. 20
Asparagus	———	———	———	———	1/1-3/1	2/1-3/10
Beans, lima	2/1-4/15	2/10-5/1	3/1-5/1	3/15-6/1	3/20-6/1	4/1-6/15
Beans, snap	2/1-4/1	2/1-5/1	3/1-5/1	3/10-5/15	3/15-5/15	3/15-5/25
Beets	1/1-3/15	1/10-3/15	1/20-4/1	2/1-4/15	2/15-6/1	2/15-5/15
Broccoli plants	1/1-1/30	1/1-1/30	1/15-2/15	2/1-3/1	2/15-3/15	2/15-3/15
Brussels sprouts plants	1/1-1/30	1/1-1/30	1/15-2/15	2/1-3/1	2/15-3/15	2/15-3/15
Cabbage plants	1/1-1/15	1/1-2/10	1/1-2/25	1/15-2/25	1/25-3/1	2/1-3/1
Cabbage, Chinese			Generally fall planted			
Carrots	1/1-3/1	1/1-3/1	1/15-3/1	2/1-3/1	2/10-3/15	2/15-3/20
Cauliflower plants	1/1-2/1	1/1-2/1	1/10-2/10	1/20-2/20	2/1-3/1	2/10-3/10
Celery and celeriac	1/1-2/1	1/10-2/10	1/20-2/20	2/1-3/1	2/20-3/20	3/1-4/1
Chard	1/1-4/1	1/10-4/1	1/20-4/15	2/1-5/1	2/15-5/15	2/20-5/15
Chervil and chives	1/1-2/1	1/1-2/1	1/1-2/1	1/15-2/15	2/1-3/1	2/10-3/10
Chicory	———	———	———	———	6/1-7/1	6/1-7/1
Collard plants	1/1-2/15	1/1-2/15	1/1-3/15	1/15-3/15	2/1-4/1	2/15-5/1
Corn salad	1/1-2/15	1/1-2/15	1/1-3/15	1/1-3/15	1/1-3/15	1/1-3/15
Corn, sweet	2/1-3/15	2/10-4/1	2/20-4/15	3/1-4/15	3/10-4/15	3/15-5/1
Cress, upland	1/1-2/1	1/1-2/15	1/15-2/15	2/1-3/1	2/10-3/15	2/20-3/15
Cucumbers	2/15-3/15	2/15-4/1	2/15-4/15	3/1-4/15	3/15-4/15	4/1-5/1
Eggplant plants	2/1-3/1	2/10-3/15	2/20-4/1	3/10-4/15	3/15-4/15	4/1-5/1
Endive	1/1-3/1	1/1-3/1	1/15-3/1	2/1-3/1	2/15-3/15	3/1-4/1
Fennel, Florence	1/1-3/1	1/1-3/1	1/15-3/1	2/1-3/1	2/15-3/15	3/1-4/1
Garlic			Generally fall planted			2/1-3/1
Horseradish	———	———	———	———	———	———
Kale	1/1-2/1	1/10-2/1	1/20-2/10	2/1-2/20	2/10-3/1	2/20-3/10
Kohlrabi	1/1-2/2	1/10-2/1	1/20-2/10	2/1-2/10	2/10-3/1	2/20-3/10
Leeks	1/1-2/1	1/1-2/1	1/1-2/15	1/15-2/15	1/25-3/1	2/1-3/1
Lettuce, head	1/1-2/1	1/1-2/1	1/1-2/1	1/15-2/15	2/1-2/20	2/15-3/10
Lettuce, leaf	1/1-2/1	1/1-2/1	1/1-3/15	1/1-3/15	1/15-4/1	2/1-4/1

PLANTING DATES

			AVERAGE DATE OF LAST FROST				
Mar. 30	Apr. 10	Apr. 20	Apr. 30	May 10	May 20	May 30	June 10
2/15-3/20	3/10-4/10	3/15-4/15	3/20-4/15	3/10-4/30	4/20-5/15	5/1-6/1	5/15-6/1
4/15-6/20	4/1-6/30	5/1-6/20	5/15-6/15	5/25-6/15	———	———	———
4/1-6/1	4/10-6/30	4/25-6/30	5/10-6/30	5/10-6/30	5/15-6/30	5/25-6/15	———
3/1-6/1	3/10-6/1	3/20-6/1	4/1-6/15	4/15-6/15	4/25-6/15	5/1-6/15	5/15-6/15
3/1-3/20	3/15-4/15	3/25-4/20	4/1-5/1	4/15-6/1	5/1-6/15	5/10-6/10	5/20-6/10
3/1-3/20	3/15-4/15	3/25-4/20	4/1-5/1	4/15-6/1	5/1-6/15	5/10-6/10	5/20-6/10
2/15-3/10	3/1-4/1	3/10-4/1	3/15-4/10	4/1-5/15	5/1-6/15	5/10-6/15	5/20-6/1
	Generally fall planted			4/1-5/15	5/1-6/15	5/10-6/15	5/20-6/1
3/1-4/10	3/10-4/20	4/1-5/15	4/10-6/1	4/20-6/15	5/1-6/1	5/10-6/1	5/20-6/1
2/20-3/20	3/1-3/20	3/15-4/20	4/10-5/10	4/15-5/15	5/10-6/15	5/20-6/1	6/1-6/15
3/15-4/15	4/1-4/20	4/10-5/1	4/15-5/1	4/20-6/15	5/10-6/15	5/20-6/1	6/1-6/15
3/1-5/25	3/15-6/15	4/1-6/15	4/15-6/15	4/20-6/15	5/10-6/15	5/20-6/1	6/1-6/15
2/15-3/15	3/1-4/1	3/10-4/10	3/20-4/20	4/1-5/1	4/15-5/15	5/1-6/1	5/15-6/1
6/1-7/1	6/10-7/1	6/15-7/1	6/15-7/1	6/1-6/20	6/1-6/15	6/1-6/15	6/1-6/15
3/1-6/1	3/1-6/1	3/10-6/1	4/1-6/1	4/15-6/1	5/1-6/1	5/10-6/1	5/20-6/1
1/15-3/15	2/1-4/1	2/15-4/15	3/1-5/1	4/1-6/1	4/15-6/1	5/1-6/15	5/15-6/15
3/25-5/15	4/10-6/1	4/25-6/15	5/10-6/15	5/10-6/1	5/15-6/1	5/20-6/1	———
3/1-4/1	3/10-4/15	3/20-5/1	4/10-5/10	4/20-5/20	5/1-6/1	5/15-6/1	5/15-6/15
4/10-5/15	4/20-6/1	5/1-6/15	5/15-6/15	5/20-6/15	6/1-6/15	———	———
4/15-5/15	5/1-6/1	5/10-6/1	5/15-6/10	5/20-6/15	6/1-6/15	———	———
3/10-4/10	3/15-5/15	3/25-4/15	4/1-5/1	4/15-5/15	5/1-5/30	5/1-5/30	5/15-6/1
3/10-4/10	3/15-4/15	3/25-4/15	4/1-5/1	4/15-5/15	5/1-5/30	5/1-5/30	5/15-6/1
2/10-3/10	2/20-3/20	3/10-4/1	3/15-4/15	4/1-5/1	4/15-5/15	5/1-5/30	5/15-6/1
3/1-4/1	3/10-4/10	3/20-4/20	4/1-4/30	4/14-5/15	4/20-5/20	5/1-5/30	5/15-6/1
3/1-3/20	3/10-4/1	3/20-4/10	4/1-4/20	4/10-5/1	4/20-5/10	5/1-5/30	5/15-6/1
3/1-4/1	3/10-4/10	3/20-5/1	4/1-5/10	4/10-5/15	4/20-5/20	5/1-5/30	5/15-6/1
2/15-3/15	3/1-4/1	3/15-4/15	4/1-5/1	4/15-5/15	5/1-5/20	5/1-5/15	5/1-5/15
3/1-3/20	3/10-4/1	3/20-4/15	4/1-5/1	4/15-5/15	5/1-6/30	5/10-6/30	5/20-6/30
2/15-4/15	3/15-5/15	3/20-5/15	4/1-6/1	4/15-6/15	5/1-6/30	5/10-6/30	5/20-6/30

| | AVERAGE DATE OF LAST FROST | | | | | |
	Jan. 30	Feb. 8	Feb. 18	Feb. 28	Mar. 10	Mar. 20
Muskmelons	2/15-3/15	2/15-4/1	2/15-4/15	3/1-4/15	3/15-4/15	4/1-5/1
Mustard	1/1-3/1	1/1-3/1	2/15-4/15	2/1-3/1	2/10-3/15	2/20-4/1
Okra	2/15-4/1	2/15-4/15	3/1-6/1	3/10-6/1	3/20-6/1	4/1-6/15
Onion plants	1/1-1/15	1/1-1/15	1/1-1/15	1/1-2/1	1/15-2/15	2/10-3/10
Onion seeds	1/1-1/15	1/1-1/15	1/1-1/15	1/1-2/15	2/1-3/1	2/10-3/10
Onion sets	1/1-1/15	1/1-1/15	1/1-1/15	1/1-3/1	1/15-3/10	2/1-3/20
Parsley	1/1-1/30	1/1-1/30	1/1-1/30	1/15-3/1	2/1-3/10	2/15-3/15
Parsnips	———	———	1/1-2/1	1/15-2/15	1/15-3/1	2/15-3/15
Peas	1/1-2/15	1/1-2/15	1/1-3/1	1/15-3/1	1/15-3/15	2/1-3/15
Peas, black-eyed	2/15-5/1	2/15-5/15	3/1-6/15	3/10-6/20	3/15-7/1	4/1-7/1
Pepper plants	2/1-4/1	2/15/4/15	3/1-5/1	3/15-5/1	4/1-6/1	4/10-6/1
Potatoes	1/1-2/15	1/1-2/15	1/15-3/1	1/15-3/1	2/1-3/1	2/10-3/15
Radishes	1/1-4/1	1/1-4/1	1/1-4/1	1/1-4/1	1/1-4/15	1/20-5/1
Rhubarb	———	———	———	———	———	———
Rutabagas	———	———	———	1/1-2/1	1/15-2/15	1/15-3/1
Salsify	1/1-2/1	1/10-2/10	1/15-2/20	1/15-3/1	2/1-3/1	2/15-3/1
Shallots	1/1-2/1	1/1-2/10	1/1-2/20	1/1-3/1	1/15-3/1	2/1-3/10
Sorrel	1/1-3/1	1/1-3/1	1/15-3/1	2/1-3/10	2/10-3/15	2/10-3/20
Soybeans	3/1-6/30	3/1-6/30	3/10-6/30	3/20-6/30	4/10-6/30	4/10-6/30
Spinach	1/1-2/15	1/1-2/15	1/3-3/1	1/1-3/1	1/15-3/10	1/15-3/15
Spinach, New Zealand	2/1-4/15	2/15-3/15	3/1-4/15	3/15-5/15	3/20-5/15	4/1-5/15
Squash, summer	2/1-4/15	2/15-4/15	3/1-4/15	3/15-5/15	3/15-5/1	4/1-5/15
Sweet potatoes	2/15-5/15	3/1-5/15	3/20-6/1	3/20-6/1	4/1-6/1	4/10-6/1
Tomatoes	2/1-4/1	2/20-4/10	3/1-4/20	3/10-5/1	3/20-5/10	4/1-5/20
Turnips	1/1-3/1	1/1-3/1	1/10-3/1	1/20-3/1	2/1-3/1	2/10-3/10
Watermelons	2/15-3/15	2/15-4/1	2/15-4/15	3/1-4/15	3/15-4/15	4/1-5/1

PLANTING DATES

Average Date of Last Frost							
Mar. 30	Apr. 10	Apr. 20	Apr. 30	May 10	May 20	May 30	June 10
4/10-5/15	4/20-6/1	5/1-6/15	5/15-6/15	6/1-6/15	———	———	———
3/1-4/15	3/10-4/20	3/20-5/1	4/1-5/10	4/15-6/1	5/1-6/30	5/10-6/30	5/20-6/30
4/10-6/15	4/20-6/15	5/1-6/1	5/10-6/1	5/20-6/10	6/1-6/20	———	———
2/15-3/15	3/1-4/1	3/15-4/10	4/1-5/1	4/10-5/1	4/20-5/15	5/1-5/30	5/10-6/10
2/20-3/15	3/1-4/1	3/15-4/1	3/15-4/15	4/1-5/1	4/20-5/15	5/1-5/30	5/10-6/10
2/15-3/20	3/1-4/1	3/10-4/1	3/10-4/10	4/10-5/1	4/20-5/15	5/1-5/30	5/10-6/10
3/1-4/1	3/10-4/10	3/20-4/20	4/1-5/1	4/15-5/15	5/1-5/20	5/10-6/1	5/20-6/10
3/1-4/1	3/10-4/10	3/20-4/20	4/1-5/1	4/15-5/15	5/1-5/20	5/10-6/1	5/20-6/10
2/10-3/20	2/20-3/20	3/10-4/10	3/20-5/1	4/1-5/15	4/15-6/1	5/1-6/15	5/10-6/15
4/15-7/1	5/1-6/1	5/10-6/15	5/15-6/1	———	———	———	———
4/15-6/1	5/1-6/1	5/10-6/1	5/15-6/10	5/20-6/10	5/25-6/15	6/1-6/15	———
2/20-3/20	3/10-4/1	3/15-4/10	3/20-5/10	4/1-6/1	4/15-6/15	5/1-6/15	5/15-6/1
2/15-5/1	3/1-5/1	3/10-5/10	3/20-5/10	4/1-6/1	4/15-6/15	5/1-6/15	5/15-6/1
———	3/1-4/1	3/10-4/10	3/20-4/15	4/1-5/1	4/15-5/10	5/1-5/20	5/15-6/1
2/1-3/1	———	———	5/1-6/1	5/1-6/1	5/1-5/20	5/10-5/20	5/20-6/1
3/1-3/15	3/10-4/15	3/20-5/1	4/1-5/15	4/15-6/1	5/10-6/1	5/10-6/1	5/20-6/1
2/15-3/15	3/1-4/1	3/15-4/15	4/1-5/1	4/10-5/1	4/20-5/10	5/1-6/1	5/10-6/1
2/20-4/1	3/1-4/15	3/15-5/1	4/1-5/15	4/15-6/1	5/1-6/1	5/10-6/10	5/20-6/10
4/20-6/30	5/1-6/30	5/10-6/20	5/15-6/15	5/25-6/10	———	———	———
2/1-3/20	2/15-4/1	3/1-4/15	3/20-4/20	4/1-6/15	4/10-6/15	4/20-6/15	5/1-6/15
4/10-6/1	4/20-6/1	5/1-6/15	5/1-6/15	5/10-6/15	5/20-6/15	6/1-6/16	———
4/10-6/1	4/20-6/1	5/1-6/15	5/1-5/30	5/10-6/10	5/20-6/15	6/1-6/20	6/10-6/20
4/20-6/1	5/1-6/1	5/10-6/10	5/20-6/10	———	———	———	———
4/10-6/1	4/20-6/1	5/5-6/10	5/10-6/15	5/15-6/10	5/25-6/15	6/5-6/20	6/15-6/30
2/20-3/20	3/1-4/1	3/10-4/1	3/20-5/1	4/1-6/1	4/15-6/1	5/1-6/15	5/15-6/15
4/10-5/15	4/20-6/1	5/1-6/15	5/15-6/15	6/1-6/15	6/15-7/1	———	———

Latest dates for safe fall planting.

PLANTING DATES

	AVERAGE DATE OF FIRST FROST				
	Aug. 30	Sept. 10	Sept. 20	Sept. 30	Oct. 10
Asparagus	——	——	——	——	10/20-11/15
Beans, lima	——	——	——	6/1-6/15	6/1-6/15
Beans, snap	——	5/15-6/15	6/1-7/1	6/1-7/10	6/15-7/20
Beets	5/15-6/15	5/15-6/15	6/1-7/1	6/1-7/10	6/15-7/25
Broccoli	5/1-6/1	5/1-6/1	5/1-6/15	6/1-6/30	6/15-7/15
Brussels sprouts	5/1-6/1	5/1-6/1	5/1-6/15	6/1-6/30	6/15-7/15
Cabbage plants	5/1-6/1	5/1-6/1	5/1-6/15	6/1-7/10	6/1-7/15
Cabbage, Chinese	5/15-6/15	5/15-6/15	6/1-7/1	6/1-7/15	6/15-8/1
Carrots	5/15-6/15	5/15-6/15	6/1-7/1	6/1-7/10	6/1-7/20
Cauliflower plants	5/1-6/1	5/1-7/1	5/1-7/1	5/10-7/15	6/1-7/25
Celery and celeriac	5/1-6/1	5/15-6/15	5/15-7/1	6/1-7/5	6/1-7/15
Chard	5/15-6/15	5/15-7/1	6/1-7/1	6/1-7/5	6/1-7/20
Chervil and chives	5/10-6/10	5/1-6/15	5/15-6/15	Generally spring planted	
Chicory	5/15-6/15	5/15-6/15	5/15-6/15	6/1-7/1	6/1-7/1
Collard plants	5/15-6/15	5/15-6/15	5/15-6/15	6/15-7/15	7/1-8/1
Corn salad	5/15-6/15	5/15-7/1	6/15-8/1	7/15-9/1	8/15-9/15
Corn, sweet	——	——	6/1-7/1	6/1-7/1	6/1-7/10
Cress, upland	5/15-6/15	5/15-7/1	6/15-8/1	7/15-9/1	8/15-9/15
Cucumbers	——	——	6/1-6/15	6/1-7/1	6/1-7/1
Eggplant plants	——	——	——	5/20-6/10	5/15-6/15
Endive	6/1-7/1	6/1-7/1	6/15-7/15	6/15-8/1	7/1-8/15
Fennel, Florence	5/15-6/15	5/15-7/15	6/1-7/1	6/1-7/1	6/15-7/15
Garlic			Generally spring planted		
Horseradish			Generally spring planted		
Kale	5/15-6/15	5/15-6/15	6/1-7/1	6/15-7/15	7/1-8/1
Kohlrabi	5/15-6/15	6/1-7/1	6/1-7/15	6/15-7/15	7/1-8/1
Leeks	5/1-6/1	5/1-6/1	——	——	——

PLANTING DATES

		Average Date of First Frost				
Oct. 20	Oct. 30	Nov. 10	Nov. 20	Nov. 30	Dec. 10	Dec. 20
11/1-12/15	11/15-1/1	12/1-1/1	——	——	——	9/1-10/1
6/15-6/30	7/1-8/1	7/1-8/15	7/15-9/1	8/1-9/15	9/1-9/30	9/1-11/1
7/1-8/1	7/1-8/15	7/1-9/1	7/1-9/10	8/15-9/20	9/1-9/30	9/1-1/1
7/1-8/5	8/1-9/1	8/1-10/1	9/1-12/1	9/1-12/15	9/1-12/31	9/1-1/1
7/1-8/1	7/1-8/15	8/1-9/1	8/1-9/15	8/1-10/1	8/1-11/1	9/1-1/1
7/1-8/1	7/1-8/15	8/1-9/1	8/1-9/15	8/1-10/1	8/1-11/1	9/1-1/1
7/1-7/20	8/1-9/1	9/1-9/15	9/1-12/1	9/1-12/31	9/1-12/31	9/1-12/1
7/15-8/15	8/1-9/15	8/15-10/1	9/1-10/15	9/1-11/1	9/1-11/15	9/15-12/1
6/15-8/1	7/1-8/15	8/1-9/1	9/1-11/1	9/15-12/1	9/15-12/1	9/15-11/1
7/1-8/5	7/15-8/15	8/1-9/1	8/1-9/15	8/15-10/10	9/1-10/20	10/1-1/1
6/1-8/1	6/15-8/15	7/1-8/15	7/15-9/1	8/1-12/1	9/1-12/31	6/1-1/1
6/1-8/1	6/1-9/10	6/1-9/15	6/1-10/1	6/1-11/1	6/1-12/1	11/1-1/1
Generally spring planted			11/1-1/1	11/1-1/1	11/1-1/1	8/15-10/15
6/15-7/15	7/1-8/10	7/10-8/20	7/20-9/1	8/15-9/30	8/15-10/15	9/1-1/1
7/15-8/15	8/1-9/15	8/15-10/1	8/25-11/1	9/1-12/1	9/1-12/31	10/1-1/1
9/1-10/15	9/15-11/1	10/1-12/1	10/1-12/1	10/1-1/1	10/1-1/1	——
6/1-7/20	6/1-8/1	6/1-8/15	6/1-9/1	——	——	10/1-1/1
9/1-10/15	9/15-11/1	10/1-12/1	10/1-12/1	10/1-1/1	10/1-1/1	8/15-10/1
6/1-7/15	6/1-8/1	6/1-8/15	6/1-8/15	7/15-9/15	8/15-10/1	8/1-9/30
6/1-7/1	6/1-7/1	6/1-7/15	6/1-8/1	7/1-9/1	8/1-9/30	9/1-1/1
7/15-9/1	7/15-8/15	8/1-9/1	9/1-10/1	9/1-11/15	9/1-12/31	9/1-12/1
6/15-8/1	7/1-8/1	7/15-8/15	8/15-9/15	9/1-11/15	9/1-12/1	9/15-11/15
Generally spring planted		8/1-10/1	8/15-10/1	9/1-11/15	9/15-11/15	——
		Generally spring planted				9/1-1/1
7/15-8/15	7/15-9/1	8/1-9/15	8/15-10/15	9/1-12/1	9/1-1/1	9/1-1/1
7/15-8/15	8/1-9/1	8/15-9/15	9/1-10/15	9/1-12/1	9/15-1/1	9/15-11/1
——	——	——	9/1-11/1	9/1-11/1	9/1-11/1	9/15-1/1

PLANTING DATES

	AVERAGE DATE OF FIRST FROST				
	Aug. 30	Sept. 10	Sept. 20	Sept. 30	Oct. 10
Lettuce, head plants	5/15-7/1	5/15-7/1	6/1-7/15	6/15-8/1	7/15-8/15
Lettuce, leaf	5/15-7/15	5/15-7/15	6/1-8/1	6/1-8/1	7/15-9/1
Muskmelons	——	——	5/1-6/15	5/15-6/1	6/1-6/15
Mustard	5/15-7/15	5/15-7/15	6/1-8/1	6/15-8/1	7/15-8/15
Okra	——	——	6/1-6/20	6/1-7/1	6/1-7/15
Onion plants	5/1-6/10	5/1-6/10	Generally spring planted		
Onion seeds	5/1-6/1	5/1-6/10	Generally spring planted		
Onion sets	5/1-6/1	5/1-6/10	Generally spring planted		
Parsley	5/15-6/15	5/1-6/15	6/1-7/1	6/1-7/15	6/15-8/1
Parsnips	5/15-6/1	5/1-6/15	5/15-6/15	6/1-7/1	6/1-7/10
Peas	5/10-6/15	5/1-7/1	6/1-7/15	6/1-8/1	Generally spring
Peas, black-eyed	——	——	——	——	6/1-7/1
Pepper plants	——	——	6/1-6/20	6/1-7/1	6/1-7/1
Potatoes	5/15-6/1	5/1-6/15	5/1-6/15	5/1-6/15	5/15-6/15
Radishes	5/1-7/15	5/1-8/1	6/1-8/15	7/1-9/1	7/15-9/15
Rhubarb	9/1-10/1	9/15-10/15	9/15-11/1	10/1-11/1	10/15-11/15
Rutabagas	5/15-6/15	5/1-6/15	6/1-7/1	6/1-7/1	6/15-7/15
Salsify	5/15-6/1	5/10-6/10	5/20-6/20	6/1-6/20	6/1-7/1
Shallots	Generally spring planted				
Sorrel	5/15-6/15	5/1-6/15	6/1-7/1	6/1-7/15	7/1-8/1
Soybeans	——	——	——	5/25-6/10	6/1-6/25
Spinach	5/15-7/1	6/1-7/15	6/1-8/1	7/1-8/15	8/1-9/1
Spinach, New Zealand	——	——	——	5/15-7/1	6/1-7/15
Squash, summer	6/10-6/20	6/1-6/20	5/15-7/1	6/1-7/1	6/1-7/15
Squash, winter	——	——	5/20-6/10	6/1-6/15	6/1-7/1
Sweet potatoes	——	——	——	——	5/20-6/10
Tomatoes	6/20-6/30	6/10-6/20	6/1-6/20	6/1-6/20	6/1-6/20
Turnips	5/15-6/15	6/1-7/1	6/1-7/15	6/1-8/1	7/1-8/1
Watermelons	——	——	5/1-6/15	5/15-6/1	6/1-6/15

PLANTING DATES

AVERAGE DATE OF FIRST FROST						
Oct. 20	Oct. 30	Nov. 10	Nov. 20	Nov. 30	Dec. 10	Dec. 20
8/1-8/30	8/1-9/15	8/15-10/15	9/1-11/1	9/1-12/1	9/15-1/1	9/15-1/1
7/15-9/1	8/15-10/1	8/25-10/1	9/1-11/1	9/1-12/1	9/15-1/1	——
6/15-7/20	7/1-7/15	7/15-7/30	——	——	——	9/15-12/1
8/1-9/1	8/15-10/15	——	8/15-11/1	9/1-12/1	9/1-12/1	——
6/1-8/1	6/1-8/10	6/1-8/20	6/1-9/10	6/1-9/20	8/1-10/1	10/15-12/1
Generally spring planted		9/1-9/15	10/1-1/1	10/1-1/1	10/1-1/1	8/1-10/1
Generally spring planted			9/1-11/1	9/1-11/1	9/1-11/1	10/1-1/1
Generally spring planted		10/1-12/1	11/1-1/1	11/1-1/1	11/1-1/1	9/15-11/1
7/15-8/15	8/1-9/15	9/1-11/15	9/1-1/1	9/1-1/1	9/1-1/1	11/1-1/1
Generally spring planted			8/1-9/1	9/1-11/15	9/1-12/1	10/1-1/1
planted	8/1-9/15	9/1-11/1	10/1-12/1	10/1-1/1	10/1-1/1	9/1-12/1
6/1-7/1	6/1-8/1	6/15-8/15	7/1-9/1	7/1-9/10	7/1-9/20	10/1-1/1
6/1-7/10	6/1-7/20	6/1-8/1	6/1-8/15	6/15-9/1	8/15-10/1	7/1-9/20
6/15-7/15	7/20-8/10	7/25-8/20	8/10-9/15	8/1-9/15	8/1-9/15	8/15-10/1
8/1-10/1	8/15-10/15	9/1-11/15	9/1-12/1	9/1-1/1	8/1-9/15	8/1-9/15
10/15-12/1	11/1-12/1	——	——	——	——	10/1-1/1
7/10-7/20	7/15-8/1	7/15-8/15	8/1-9/1	9/1-11/15	10/1-11/15	——
6/1-7/1	6/1-7/10	6/15-7/20	7/15-8/15	8/15-9/30	8/15-10/15	10/15-11/15
Generally spring planted		8/1-10/1	8/15-10/1	8/15-10/15	9/15-11/1	9/1-10/31
7/15-8/15	8/1-9/15	8/15-10/1	8/15-10/15	9/1-11/15	9/1-12/15	9/15-11/1
6/1-7/5	6/1-7/15	6/1-7/25	6/1-7/30	6/1-7/30	6/1-7/30	9/1-1/1
8/20-9/10	9/1-10/1	9/15-11/1	10/1-12/1	10/1-1/1	10/1-1/1	6/1-7/30
6/1-8/1	6/1-8/1	6/1-8/15	6/1-8/15	——	——	10/1-1/1
6/1-7/20	6/1-8/1	6/1-8/10	6/1-8/20	6/1-9/1	6/1-9/15	——
6/1-7/1	6/10-7/10	6/20-7/20	7/1-8/1	7/15-8/15	8/1-9/1	6/1-10/1
6/1-6/15	6/1-6/15	6/1-7/1	6/1-7/1	6/1-7/1	6/1-7/1	8/1-9/1
6/1-7/1	6/1-7/1	6/1-7/15	6/1-8/1	8/1-9/1	8/15-10/1	6/1-7/1
7/15-8/15	8/1-9/15	9/1-10/15	9/1-11/15	9/1-11/15	10/1-12/1	9/1-11/1
6/15-7/20	7/1-7/15	7/15-7/30	——	——	——	10/1-1/1

METHODS OF SEEDING

Most home gardeners plant by hand. String a line between two stakes to keep the rows neat and tidy. For large seeds, use a hoe to make a furrow of even depth. For smaller seeds, use the hoe handle.

A relatively new technique for planting seeds in the home garden is the use of seed tapes. Seeds are properly spaced and enclosed in a tape that is sold in rolls. Gardeners simply lay the tape down, cover it with soil, and wait for it to disintegrate. The seedlings emerge at the correct spacings, and you don't have to thin.

There are vast tables that give planting depths for seeds, but you don't need them. What good does it do to know that you must plant celery seed $1/8$ inch deep? How are you going to measure that? All you need to know is to plant seeds no deeper than twice their largest diameter. A bean seed half an inch long should be

Use a taut line to keep your rows straight.

planted no deeper than 1 inch; the tiny celery seed should be sprinkled on the soil surface and lightly raked in and tamped. The only nutrients the seedling has to live on before it emerges from the soil are what it carries in the seed. If you plant too deep, it'll run out of food before it gets to the soil surface. Planting too shallow, on the other hand, can cause the seed to dry out and prevent germination and early seedling growth.

Use the handle of a hoe to make a shallow furrow for planting small seeds.

Modify planting depth by following two rules. In heavy soils, which are cold in the spring, plant a little less deep to take advantage of the warm surface layer. In light soils, which warm faster but don't hold water as well, plant a bit deeper to take advantage of the greater moisture in the layers just below the surface.

Some gardeners use planters—machines that are wheeled through the garden and open the furrows, drop the seeds at the proper spacings, and cover them with soil all in a single operation. They're handy, but they're not necessary.

15

Cropping Systems

Practice good cropping systems to make the most use of your garden area. Use one or more of the following in your garden every year. Fill that postharvest vacuum with a crop before nature fills it with weeds.

COMPANION PLANTING

Companion planting means two things. One is to plant repellent plants along with your main crop to control pests. This really doesn't work for major garden pests, however. The other is to place together vegetables that need similar types of care. For example, plant all your crucifers together because their nutrient and pest control requirements are alike. Plant all perennials together at one end of the garden so that you won't have to plow around them every spring.

INTERPLANTING

Interplanting, also called *intercropping* or *companion cropping*, makes the best use of available space and reduces insect activity and numbers.

You can interplant in alternate rows such crops as radishes, tomatoes, onions, and broccoli. The radishes and onions will mature rapidly and be harvested before the tomatoes and broccoli need the space. So you can get four crops from the same area in which two would otherwise be planted. Similarly, you can plant winter squash next to a block of early corn. After the corn is harvested, the squash will use the space. It will also keep down weeds by shading the bare ground.

You can also interplant crops within the same row. Plant an early

Organic Snake Oil

Unlike succession planting, interplanting, or nurse cropping, there has been absolutely no scientific evidence that companion planting of repellent plants really contributes significantly to the welfare of the garden. It's like buying a bottle of snake oil: Many have fallen for the claims, but few have gotten results. There is some evidence that solid plantings of French marigolds grown over an entire season can reduce populations of root-knot nematodes, but French marigolds are the only ones that work, and they themselves are hosts for the northern root-knot nematode. When you tally the pluses and minuses, you haven't gained much. But it's chic to think so.

To be successful, companion plantings must reduce the damage caused by major pests. In one Illinois experiment, researchers planted wormwood, hyssop, thyme, catnip, rosemary, petunias, and marigolds in various arrangements among common vegetable plants over a three-year period. Not one controlled any major garden pest. Over those three years, Mexican bean beetles consistently destroyed the snap beans and then moved over to chomp down the petunias and marigolds. When the researchers dusted the beans with the insecticide rotenone, the beetles avoided them completely and went straight to the marigolds. In like manner, cucumber beetles destroyed the cucumbers, Colorado potato beetles ravaged the potatoes, cabbage worms ate the cabbage, and the flea beetles sucked the eggplants and potatoes dry.

Delighted that they were getting results, albeit negative ones, the researchers went on to plant leeks beside cabbage, snap beans with potatoes, radishes among the snap beans, onions with carrots, and tomatoes at the edge of the asparagus bed. Not one combination worked. So the conclusion after three years of experiments was that companion plantings simply don't control major garden insects pests. Now, if you want to plant flowers among your vegetables for beauty, that's fine. But if you insist on planting them to control insects, let me know. I've got a bottle of Dr. Bob's Bug-Off Elixir I'd like to sell you.

crop of leaf lettuce between tomato plants. The lettuce will be gone to salad before the tomatoes need the space. Combine this system with the one above, and you can plant leaf lettuce between cabbage plants, and radishes between the cabbage rows.

The idea behind interplanting is to make the most efficient use of space by planting a quick-maturing crop between plants or rows of a slower-maturing one. Because you're double cropping the space, you save cultivation time and space, better utilize the nutrients in the soil, and get higher yields per square foot of garden. You'll need to add more nutrients, however, and pay strict attention to watering and pest control.

SUCCESSION PLANTING

Succession planting requires you to supply more nutrients to the soil and to pay closer attention to watering but it will also give you greater yields per square foot of garden space. In this system, you harvest one crop and immediately plant another in the same place. This not only uses the soil well, but also makes the most of the growing season. The only requirements here are that there is enough growing season left for the second crop to mature, and that the crop will mature under the proper conditions. Rutabagas following onions will have enough time to mature in the cool fall, but peppers following onions might not work because they won't mature well in cool weather.

This term also refers to planting the same crop at ten-day intervals to spread out the harvest. It works very well with lettuce.

TRAP CROPPING

Trap cropping is the use of a crop to attract insects away from a more valuable crop. Of course, the trap crops will be destroyed. See Planting Trap Crops in the next chapter for examples.

VERTICAL CROPPING

Vertical cropping relies on the use of trellises or poles to allow certain plants to grow up instead of out, thus saving garden space. Pole beans climb poles and pole peas climb any fencing, poultry wire, net, or birch brush. Cucumbers, squash, melons, and gourds are often trained to climb trellises placed at a 45-degree angle, or even vertically. Some gardeners even train cucumbers and gourds to climb into trees. Support large fruits of climbing melon and pumpkin vines by enclosing them in wide-mesh onion bags and tying the bags to the trellis.

NURSE CROPPING

Nurse crops are those whose seeds are mixed with those of a crop that germinates more slowly in order to break the soil crust and to mark the rows so that you can begin to cultivate before the main crop emerges. Radish seeds mixed with those of carrots or parsnips will germinate rapidly and mark the rows nicely.

ROTATION CROPPING

Rotation cropping involves waiting two to four years before planting related crops in the same part of the garden. This makes better use of nutrients and helps control diseases and pests that may winter over. Cabbage planted in the same spot year after year draws the same nutrients from the soil in the same quantities. And when infected cabbage leaves fall from the plant, the spores remain in the soil beneath the plant, and infection will begin anew the following season if cabbage or one of its relatives is planted there again.

When planning your rotations, don't follow plants with members of the same family. Try to follow deep-rooted plants with shallow-rooted ones to make the best use of the soil profile, and follow heavy feeders with light feeders. Lettuce, green onions, radishes, and spinach do very well if they follow cabbage, peas, and beans, since the latter leave large quantities of organic matter in the soil.

RELAY CROPPING

Relay cropping is similar to intercropping and succession planting in that one crop will be harvested shortly after another is planted. For example, plant corn beneath the leaves of early cabbage. The cabbage will protect the young seedlings from late frost, and the heads will be harvested before the corn requires the space. You can also plant tomatoes between plants of early cabbage.

16

Beating the Bugs

If you have a garden, you will have pests. Of course, the pests are only doing what comes naturally. You are the one that has created an unnatural system of warm- and cool-season plants growing side by side in full sun, without drought to toughen them, without weeds to shade them, without nutrient deficiencies to stunt them. You have pushed them to perform to their maximum capacity, and you expect to harvest succulent, colorful, sweet vegetables. The bugs do too.

How you control pests, or even whether you do, is up to you. Some gardeners opt to do nothing, to let the pests have all they want. Others spend all their free time trying to kill every insect that violates the no-fly zone over the endive.

Consider pest control as a continuum of options in several lines of defense. If you choose to do nothing about pests, then plant plenty of extra cabbage to keep the loopers happy, and make up your mind not to lose your lunch if you find that the tomato you're eating contains only half a worm. But if you decide to maintain your artificial paradise until the end of the season, you'll have to fight for it. Start with a lot of common sense and the least intrusive methods. If these fail, then take stronger measures.

THE FIRST LINE OF DEFENSE
Sanitation

A clean garden is a healthy garden. Many pests hide and overwinter in crop residue and debris in the garden and at the garden's edge. Remove all crop remains right after harvest. Compost them if they are not diseased, bury or burn them if they are. If they carry a soil-borne disease, such as verticillium, get them off the property. Keep the area surrounding the garden clean and the grass mown. Weeds harbor many insects and diseases. Leaf miners often infest lamb's-quarters, and many pokeweed plants are infected with tobacco mosaic virus, which can easily spread to your tomatoes. Weeds also compete with your plants for water, nutrients, and light, which weakens your plants and makes them less resistant to pest attacks. Keep the garden cultivated or mulched.

Failure to turn under manure or compost will increase the grub, slug, and pill bug populations. And Japanese beetles are highly attracted to grapes, roses, and raspberries, so keep these plants away from your garden.

Part of garden sanitation also consists of controlling humans. Cigarettes or chewing tobacco may carry tobacco mosaic virus, which can infect tomatoes, peppers, eggplants, and some other crops, so tobacco users should wash their hands before entering the garden. Never walk through the garden when it's wet. If you brush against the wet foliage of a diseased plant, the spores can cling to your pant leg and brush off on a healthy plant you pass. This a great way to spread bean rust.

Rotation
Certain pests build up on certain plants. Moving the crops around each year will impede their spread. Crop rotation is most effective if practiced over a three- or four-year period. This means that you plant related crops in different places every year for three or four years. Then you can plant them where you initially did. Rotation is most effective in controlling diseases that live in the soil for up to two years. Clubroot of crucifers remains alive for up to three years, so you'll need a four-year rotation to control it. Root knot nematodes attack many plants but can be brought under control by planting resistant crops, such as corn and some cultivars of cowpea, for three years. Some diseases, however, such as potato scab and onion smut, remain alive in contaminated soil for a very long time and cannot be controlled by crop rotation.

Sodded areas are likely to be infested with grubs, so don't plant your garden in an area that a week ago was in lawn. Grubs, root maggots, and wireworms are especially troublesome with root crops and crucifers. If your soil is plagued by these pests, plant beans, spinach, peas, or Swiss

There are hundreds of insects that attack vegetable plants. Some are more common in some parts of the country than in others. (Shown at the right are a few of the most common pests.)

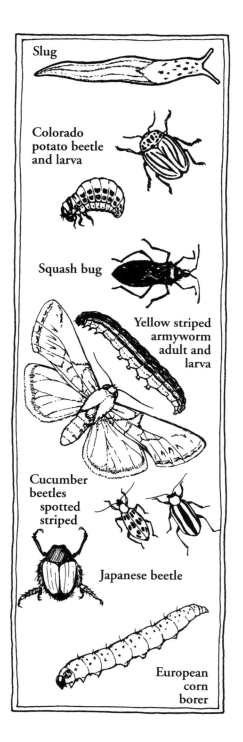

Slug

Colorado potato beetle and larva

Squash bug

Yellow striped armyworm adult and larva

Cucumber beetles
spotted
striped

Japanese beetle

European corn borer

chard, which tolerate them fairly well.

Rotation makes a lot of sense for controlling pests and for the best use of nutrients, too. No matter how small your garden, try to grow related plants in different spots every year.

Fall Plowing

Gardeners plowing in the fall not only turn under garden debris, but also may turn up burrowing insects to be killed by winter cold. But because fall plowing leaves the soil surface bare and subject to wind erosion—researchers estimate that U.S. soils lose about 80 tons of topsoil per acre per year—it's good to sow a winter cover crop to prevent erosion after plowing. That will also increase soil organic matter when plowed down in the spring.

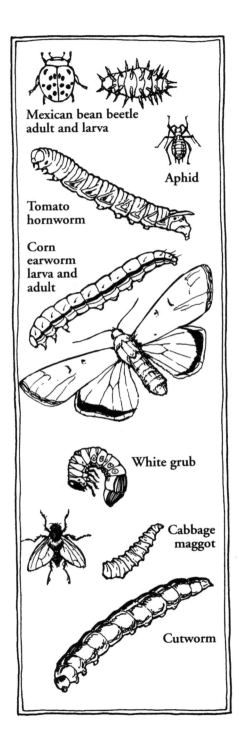

Mexican bean beetle adult and larva

Aphid

Tomato hornworm

Corn earworm larva and adult

White grub

Cabbage maggot

Cutworm

Seed and Plant Quality

When buying seeds, purchase cultivars that are adapted to your area and have resistance to some pests. New seeds generally are stronger and more viable and produce seedlings quicker. The faster they germinate and get out of the ground, the fewer rot and seed maggot problems you'll have.

Fungicide coatings protect the seeds from soil rot until they have germinated. This is particularly important in cool-weather crops, which are often planted before the soil has warmed sufficiently for rapid germination. The packages containing seeds treated with fungicide are clearly marked and the seeds are dyed a bright color. Some seeds, such as those of the crucifers, are treated with hot water to control seed-borne diseases like black leg. Purchase these whenever you can.

Use transplants, your own or the nursery's, whenever possible. You won't have seed maggot, rot, or damping-off problems in the garden, and your plants will get off to a faster start. Choose seedlings

Not all garden problems are caused by insect pests. Be sure you have a pest problem before you use a pesticide.

SYMPTOM	POSSIBLE CAUSE	POSSIBLE CONTROL
Wilt	Lack of water	Water
	Excessive water	Stop watering, drain
	Disease	Plant resistant cultivars
	Insect damage to stem or roots	Soil insecticide or protection
Leaves and stems spotted	Fertilizer burn	Follow directions next time
	Pesticide burn	Follow directions next time
	Disease	Plant resistant cultivars, fungicide sprays
Weak, spindly growth	Not enough light	Eliminate shade
	Excessive water	Improve drainage
	Crowding	Thin
	Excessive nitrogen	Reduce fertilizer
Leaves curl	Wilt	Plant resistant cultivars, remove diseased plants, rotate
	Virus	Control insects, remove diseased plants
Leaves roll	Virus	Plant resistant cultivars, remove diseased plants
	Drought	Water
Stunted or yellow growth	Excessive water	Stop watering
	Poor drainage	Drain
	Compact soil	Add organic matter or sand
	Improper pH	Adjust pH
	Insufficient fertility	Fertilize
	Disease	Plant resistant cultivars, fungicide sprays
	Virus	Remove diseased plants, control insects

Symptom	Possible Cause	Possible Control
Poor germination	Insufficient time	Wait
	Too cold	Pray
	Too wet	Pray
	Too hot	Pray
	Too dry	Water
	Bird depredation	Control birds
Young plants die	Damping-off	Fungicide
	Rot	Fungicide
	Fertilizer burn	Follow directions next time
Leaves have holes	Insects	Control
	Slugs	Control
	Hail	Swear
Abnormal, twisted growth	Herbicide	Follow directions next time; don't mulch with clipping from lawns treated with herbicides
	Virus	Remove diseased plants, control insects
Blossom ends rot	Improper soil pH	Adjust
	Insufficient calcium	Adjust
	Water imbalance	Adjust
	Compact soil	Add organic matter or sand
	Too-deep cultivation	Don't cultivate so deeply
Fruit does not set	Too cold	Pray
	Too hot	Pray
	Excessive nitrogen	Follow directions next time
	Poor pollination	Encourage bees, plant corn in blocks rather than long rows
	Immature plants	Wait

What pest is causing the damage? Most often you'll see the damage caused by a pest rather than the pest itself. Here's how to figure out what beast is in the beets.

Vegetable	Symptoms	Cause
Asparagus	Shoots are tunneled and the leaves have been eaten by beetle larvae.	ASPARAGUS BEETLES
Beans	Numerous small, green or black sucking insects, particularly on the undersides of leaves.	APHIDS
	Small plants cut off at soil level at night.	CUTWORM
	Wedge-shaped insects that hop when disturbed and suck sap from the leaves.	LEAFHOPPERS
	Lower surfaces of the leaves skeletonized (eaten between the veins).	MEXICAN BEAN BEETLES
Beets	Leaves eaten. Silvery trails of dried slime visible in the morning.	SLUGS AND SNAILS
	Larvae tunnels in leaves.	LEAF MINERS
Broccoli, Brussels sprouts, cabbage, cauliflower	Numerous small, green or black sucking insects, particularly on the undersides of cabbage leaves.	APHIDS
	Plants weak, maybe wilted. Maggots on underground parts.	CABBAGE MAGGOTS
	Holes in leaves eaten by large, green worms.	LOOPERS AND CABBAGE WORMS
	Small plants cut off at soil level at night.	CUTWORMS
	Many pinholes chewed into leaves.	FLEA BEETLES

Vegetable	Symptoms	Cause
Corn	Silks cut at ear. Large worm eats kernels.	CORN EARWORMS
	Larvae tunnel in ears and stalks.	CORN BORER
	Small plants pulled from ground.	BIRDS
	Small plants cut at ground level at night.	CUTWORMS
Cucumber	Numerous small, green or black sucking insects, particularly on undersides of leaves.	APHIDS
	All parts of the plant chewed.	CUCUMBER BEETLES
	All parts of the vine eaten. Larvae present.	PICKLEWORMS
Eggplant	Plants defoliated by black-striped beetles or reddish brown larvae.	COLORADO POTATO BEETLES
	Numerous small, green or black sucking insects, particularly on the undersides of leaves.	APHIDS
	Many pinholes chewed into leaves	FLEA BEETLES
Kale	Numerous small, green or black sucking insects, particularly on the undersides of leaves.	APHIDS
	Many pinholes chewed into leaves.	FLEA BEETLES
Lettuce	Numerous small, green or black sucking insects, particularly on the undersides of leaves.	APHIDS
	Wedge-shaped insects that hop when disturbed. Leaf tips brown.	LEAFHOPPERS

VEGETABLE	SYMPTOMS	CAUSE
Lettuce	Leaves eaten. Silvery trails of dried slime visible in the morning.	SLUGS AND SNAILS
Melons	Numerous small, green or black sucking insects, particularly on the undersides of leaves.	APHIDS
	All parts of the plant chewed.	CUCUMBER BEETLES
Mustard	See Broccoli.	
Okra	Holes chewed into pods.	CORN EARWORMS
Onions	Small, yellow insects feeding at base of leaves. Older leaves wither.	ONION THRIPS
	Plants weak. Underground parts attacked by maggots.	ONION MAGGOTS
Peas	Numerous small insects on undersides of leaves. Leaf tips often deformed.	PEA APHIDS
	Larvae burrow into pods and enter young peas. Blooms chewed by beetles.	PEA WEEVILS
Peppers	Numerous small, green or black sucking insects, particularly on the undersides of leaves.	APHIDS
	Leaves eaten by orange and yellow beetles.	BLISTER BEETLES
	Small plants cut off at soil level at night.	CUTWORMS
	Many pinholes chewed into leaves.	FLEA BEETLES
	Leaves and fruits chewed.	PEPPER WEEVILS

Vegetable	Symptoms	Cause
Radishes	Plants weak. Maggots chew underground parts.	ROOT MAGGOTS
Spinach	Numerous small, green or black sucking insects, particularly on the undersides of leaves.	APHIDS
	Larvae tunnels in leaves.	LEAF MINERS
Squash	Numerous small, green or black sucking insects, particularly on the undersides of leaves.	APHIDS
	All parts of the plant chewed.	CUCUMBER BEETLES
	Plants wilted. Flat, brown bugs present.	SQUASH BUG
	Vines suddenly wilt. Holes near base of stem.	SQUASH VINE BORERS
Swiss chard	Numerous small, green or black sucking insects, particularly on the undersides of leaves.	APHIDS
Tomatoes	Numerous small, green or black sucking insects particularly on the undersides of leaves.	APHIDS
	Many pinholes chewed into leaves.	FLEA BEETLES
	Small plants cut off at soil level at night.	CUTWORMS
	Leaves eaten by large, green worm with reddish horn.	HORNWORMS

with the same care that you choose your seeds. Be sure they are healthy and hardened properly for your area.

When planting onions, use sets to avoid the problem of onion smut, which attacks only seedling onions.

Location
Choose a sunny site with well-drained soil and good air circulation. Dead air pockets often have high humidity and increase the incidence of diseases. Poorly drained soil will lead to seed rot, damping-off, and sparse stands. Plants will have restricted or damaged root systems, which will put them under stress. And a stressed plant is more prone to pest attack.

Timing
Don't be overeager to get your crops in and plant in soil that's too wet and cold. Plant at the times recommended for your area. *Slightly* early planting is not all bad, though. Early spinach often matures before leaf miners become active, and early sweet corn can have less earworm damage than later cultivars. That's because the earworm must lay its eggs on fresh silk, and the silks on early cultivars have often dried before the worms arrive.

Keeping Plants Healthy
Healthy plants are better able to withstand pests. Adjust the soil pH, and fertilize your plants properly. Water only in the morning so that they will dry off before nightfall. Wet plants going into the cool of night are more subject to diseases, particularly the mildews.

Many diseases are transmitted by insects. Leafhoppers carry the carrot yellows virus and the curly top virus of watermelon, aphids spread mosaic to peas, and cucumber beetles can carry bacterial wilt to healthy plants. Good insect control will help control diseases as well.

Planting Trap Crops
Gardeners sometimes plant trap crops to draw insects away from a more valuable crop. For example, radishes planted among carrots attract wireworms. The radishes will be ruined, but the carrots will be nearly untouched. Kale and horseradish will draw harlequin cabbage bugs away from your cabbage, and a few plants of scallop squash among your cucumbers will attract pickleworms and leave your cukes virtually

unscathed. Beans interplanted with tomatoes will attract armyworms, which will devastate the beans but leave the tomatoes relatively sound. If you want both the beans and the tomatoes, forget about trap cropping.

Simple interplanting also traps the insects, because they often don't make it to another host plant when nonhost plants are in the way. Practice as much interplanting as possible, with the exception of corn, which should be planted in solid blocks.

THE SECOND LINE OF DEFENSE
Physical Barriers
Use paper collars to control cutworms. Make them yourself out of heavy paper or small milk cartons, and place them over or around the transplants, pushing them at least 1 inch into the soil and making sure they extend at least 2 inches above the soil line. Leave no more than 1 inch between the stem and the collar. An 8-penny, bright finish nail pushed into the soil and touching the stem also works well.

You can place hot caps or plastic milk jugs over young cucurbit plants to protect them from the cucumber beetle. Tarpaper collars that lie flat on the ground and fit snugly around the stems of crucifers will deter root maggots.

Wood ashes or sharp sand placed in a wide ring around your new transplants will discourage slugs and cutworms.

Traps
You can make beer traps to attract slugs. Though little research has been done on the kind of beer they prefer, my preliminary studies indicate that slugs prefer premium beer slightly over the cheap stuff. But when pushed into a corner, they'll drink any brand. If you want to treat your slugs well before you drown them, then buy the imported brew. Sink tunafish cans or other shallow cans into the ground so that their lips are at the soil line, then fill them with beer. The slugs will binge and then drown. Remove the bodies in the morning.

You can also trap slugs by placing boards on the ground. Slugs will crawl under them at night. Lift the boards in the morning and pick them off.

Although black-light traps do kill many insects, most of them are not harmful to the garden. So you're killing insects that really may not need killing.

Reflectors
Aphids hide and feed on the cool undersides of leaves, away from the sunlight. An aluminum foil mulch reflects sunlight back onto the undersides of the leaves, which disorients the aphids and reduces their feeding. It also reduces the number of Mexican bean beetles on your beans.

Hand Picking
Hand picking is a very old and very effective method of controlling some insects. And it leaves no harmful residue! Spend time every day picking the larger insects, such as tomato hornworm, Mexican bean beetles, and Colorado potato beetles, from your plants. Look for hornworms on the undersides of the foliage in the early morning. They won't bite you or stab you. Step on the hornworms, and drop the others into a can of kerosene or cooking oil. Of course, hand picking is not practical for controlling aphids, mites, or other tiny pests.

Hose and Soap Sprays
You can knock some insects off the foliage with a strong water stream from the hose. But there's nothing to prevent them from coming back. Spraying warm, soapy water onto plants has been used since 1787 for controlling some insects. There are commercial preparations made especially for this, or you can use a mild solution of Ivory soap in water. Because some soaps are toxic to some plants, follow the label directions carefully. Try your own preparation out on only a few plants at first to see if it causes any damage. Never use detergent solutions for this purpose.

Encouraging the Birds
Some birds eat huge quantities of insects. Provide them with cover and nesting areas, plant a couple of sunflowers or berry plants for feed, eliminate the cats, and these birds will work for you at no charge. Cherry, cotoneaster, crab apple, dogwood, elderberry, hawthorn, pyracantha, highbush cranberry, holly, mountain ash, red cedar, and Russian olive make wonderful cover for encouraging bird populations to alight near your garden.

While you're encouraging wild birds, buy some geese. These eat many insects and some weeds, and their eggs are wonderful for baking.

Box turtles and toads also feast on many insects and are great to have around. Bats eat some too, and bat houses aren't expensive. The garden snake is another wonderful predator that likes nothing better than to swallow insects and mice that hide under your plastic mulch.

THE THIRD LINE OF DEFENSE
Predators and Parasites
Predators are larger than the host insect, and parasites are smaller. Once you have established a good population of these, they should last a long time with almost no negative side effects. But many predators and parasites are not present at the time the harmful insects emerge, and many of our most voracious pests have no predators. Predators eat good insects as well as bad, and they are poor foragers. Some of them sit and wait for their prey to come to them or attack only what is in their immediate area. And as predators and parasites must have something to eat, there must be a certain population of harmful insects to begin with, so you'll have some damage before the harmfuls are destroyed. Still, some gardeners like to have them in the garden. It certainly won't hurt much, and it can reduce the number of harmfuls a little.

Lacewing larvae, also known as aphis lions, feed on aphids, mealybugs, scale insects, insect eggs, spider mites, and small insects by sucking out their juices.

Ladybugs feast on aphids, insect eggs, scale insects, mites, and mealybugs. In fact, one adult female of one kind of ladybug lays 1,700 eggs in her lifetime and eats 2,400 pea aphids. She must eat about 100 aphids before she begins to lay her eggs and must eat at least 2 aphids per day for each egg she produces. Unfortunately, if there are not enough aphids, the ladybugs eat each other or fly off to greener pastures.

Pirate bugs eat large quantities of small insects, aphids, and mites.

Damsel bugs eat aphids, caterpillars, leafhoppers, and mites.

Praying mantises are not effective garden predators. They sit and wait for their meals, and they prefer grasshoppers, crickets, bees, wasps, and flies, which are not really destructive to the garden. To make matters worse, they hatch in mid- to late summer after much of the damage has already been done, and the first mantises to hatch turn and eat subsequent mantises, so most are destroyed after the first week.

Syrphid flies look like wasps, and their maggots eat aphids as voraciously as do ladybugs and lacewings. Syrphid fly maggots can eat an aphid a minute.

Ichneumon wasps parasitize cutworms and caterpillars.

Tachinid flies glue their eggs to the skin of their hosts or lay their eggs on leaves where feeding hosts will ingest them. Once inside, the eggs hatch and maggots eat non-essential muscle and fat, eventually killing the host. Caterpillars, cutworms, and some beetles fall prey to this fly.

Chalcid wasps parasitize the imported cabbageworm.

Braconid wasps love to eat caterpillars and beetles. One species attacks the tomato hornworm. Eggs are injected into the worm by the adult. Larvae hatch and eat the worm from the inside, finally emerging from its body through a hole near its hind end.

Insect predators will eat huge quantities of harmful insects, but they may leave your garden if the food runs out. They're great to have around, but they're not miracle workers.

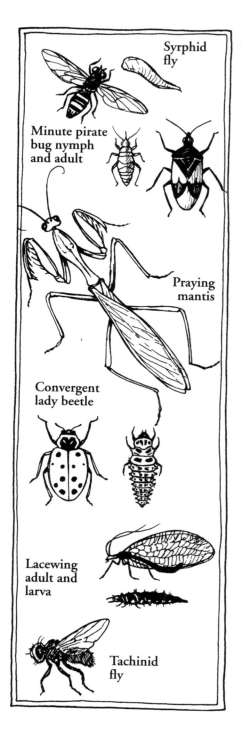

Syrphid fly

Minute pirate bug nymph and adult

Praying mantis

Convergent lady beetle

Lacewing adult and larva

Tachinid fly

All of these predators and parasites control some harmful garden insects, but probably none are worth buying. Instead, encourage the natural populations to remain in your garden by avoiding harsh pesticides.

Pathogens

A pathogen that is very effective is the bacterium *Bacillus thuringiensis*. Sold as Thuricide, Dipel, or BT, among other names, this bacterium attacks more than four hundred species of caterpillars, while leaving other insects and animals unharmed. It is one of the safest pesticides for the home garden and well worth the few dollars you'll spend.

THE FOURTH LINE OF DEFENSE

There comes a time in every gardener's life when it seems that the garden is being overrun by pests. Hand picking, hosing, and traps are not bothering the bugs a bit. Pests have broken through the first three lines of defense and are now threatening your very food supply. You can surrender . . . or you can fight.

The media have made *pesticide* a dirty word. But it's a fine word, derived from Latin, that means pest killer. Rodenticides are rodent killers, miticides are mite killers, fungicides are fungus killers, and herbicides are plant killers. A nontoxic pesticide is an oxymoron. It can't kill if it's nontoxic. All pesticides are toxic to the pests they are intended to kill, but some are relatively nontoxic to nontarget organisms, like birds and children. I say relatively, because everything is toxic if you ingest enough of it.

Scientists express relative toxicities of pesticides as acute oral LD_{50}, which stands for the number of milligrams of the pesticide that have to be ingested for every kilogram of body weight to cause half the test population to die. The smaller the number, the more poisonous the compound. For example, nicotine, a botanical insecticide, has an oral LD_{50} of 10. It is highly toxic to bugs and people. Gasoline is 150 and is about as toxic as rotenone, which varies between 80 and 400, depending on age and formulation. Concentrated caffeine has an LD_{50} of 200, making it close in toxicity to gasoline and rotenone. Carbaryl (Sevin) is about 700; malathion, 1,200; aspirin, about 1,300; and table salt, 3,300. These are classed as having low toxicity to nontarget organisms. The common fungicide captan is only slightly toxic, with an LD_{50} of about 12,000,

Pesticides are the fourth line of defense against garden pests. Use only the less toxic ones, and then only as a last resort. Follow label directions carefully. Given for comparison are relative toxicities of some common household products.

A chemical's toxicity is expressed by a number called the LD50. This means the lethal dose for 50 percent of the test population, usually rats. The dose is given in milligrams of the pure compound per kilogram of body weight. The smaller the number, the more toxic the compound. "Acute oral" means the entire dose of the compound must be swallowed at one time. A compound's relative toxicity is given by a signal word on the label.

Toxicity	Approximate Acute Oral LD50	Probable Lethal Dose for a 150-Pound Person	Signal Word
High*	1–99 Gasoline, nicotine, caffeine	Few drops to 1 teaspoon	Danger Skull & Cross- bones Poison
Moderate	100–499 Diazinon, rotenone, Tylenol	Over 1 teaspoon to 1 ounce	Warning
Slight	500–4999 Acephate, aspirin, ibuprofen, carbaryl, pyrethrins, sabadilla, malathion, ryania, table salt	Over 1 ounce to 1 pint or 1 pound	Caution
Relatively none	greater than 5000 Glyphosate, pyrethrum (natural), captan, bordeaux mixture, sulfur	Over 1 pint or 1 pound	None

*Not recommended for the home garden

and BT is essentially nontoxic to things other than the target organisms. Now, some of these compounds may have debilitating effects on the gardener with long exposure, but then so do nicotine and caffeine.

The point of all this is that pesticides are tools, no more and no less. They can help you control pests in the garden, but they must be handled carefully. Don't be afraid of them, but educate yourself about every one you use, and respect it for what it can do. Whatever you use, follow the label directions closely.

A pesticide with a low LD_{50} has no place in the garden. Of the synthetics, carbaryl, malathion, Diazinon, and captan are considered relatively safe at the moment. BT is a good choice for foliage-feeding insects, and sulfur and mineral oil are relatively safe inorganic compounds. Many botanicals also are relatively safe, but some may not be too effective.

Pesticides can be divided into several categories: the biologicals, the botanicals, the synthetic organic compounds, and the inorganic compounds.

If you choose to fight your pests with pesticides, start with those that have the least toxicity to nontarget organisms: the biologicals. If you do not get the level of control you need with these, then go to the botanicals.

Biologicals

These controls are the microbial insecticides, such as *Bacillus thuringiensis,* that cause insect diseases. They are very effective and relatively nontoxic to predators and beneficial insects.

Botanicals

The botanicals are derived from plants and generally are relatively nontoxic to humans and pets when used as directed. Nicotine, however, is highly toxic.

Rotenone is made from either the derris root of East Asia or the cube root from South America. It is broad-spectrum—effective against a wide variety of pests—but slow acting and may not adequately control insects that feed rapidly, such as cabbageworms and caterpillars. It degrades in about a week and has a low toxicity to mammals and birds but is extremely toxic to fish.

Ryania is derived from a plant native to the Amazon and Trinidad. It controls only a few insects in the home garden.

Pyrethrum is made from the dried and ground flowers of a chrysan-

Controlling insects and diseases in the vegetable garden. Use chemical controls only if the nonchemical controls fail. Follow label directions carefully, and be sure all chemicals are still legal to use in your area.

| | | CONTROL | |
PLANT	PEST OR DISEASE	NONCHEMICAL	CHEMICAL
Asparagas	Asparagas beetles	Hand pick Sanitation	Carbaryl Malathion Rotenone
	Rust	Resistant cultivars	Maneb
Beans	Aphids	Water stream Soap Spray	Malathion
	Bean beetles	Hand pick	Carbaryl Malathion
	Flea beetles		Carbaryl Malathion
	Mites	Soap spray	Sulfur
	Leafhoppers		Carbaryl Malathion
	Seed-corn maggot	Avoid high organic matter soil	Treated seed
	Bacterial blight	Rotation	
	Anthracnose	Sanitation	
	Mosaic	Resistant cultivars	
	Sclerotinia white mold	Rotation	Benomyl
	Downy mildew	Avoid wetting foliage	Maneb
	Powdery mildew		Sulfur
	Rust	Resistant cultivars	
Beets	Flea beetles		Carbaryl
	Leaf miner		Malathion
	Aphids	Water stream	Malathion
	Cercospora leaf spot	Resistant cultivars	Fixed copper

		CONTROL	
PLANT	PEST OR DISEASE	NONCHEMICAL	CHEMICAL
Cabbage, cauliflower, collards, broccoli, Brussels sprouts	Aphids	Water stream	Malathion
	Cabbage worms	BT	Carbaryl
	Flea beetles		Carbaryl Malathion
	Cabbage maggot		Diazinon
	Clubroot	Rotation	Terraclor
	Downy mildew	Avoid wetting foliage	Maneb
	Blackleg	Treated seeds	
	Black rot		
Carrots	Six-spotted leafhopper		Carbaryl Rotenone Malathion
	Cercospora Alternaria	Rotation	Maneb
	Yellows	Aluminum foil mulch	
Corn	Earworm	Half medicine dropper	Carbaryl
	Borers	mineral oil onto silks as they begin to dry	Ryania
	Seed-corn maggot	Avaoid high organic matter soils	
	Flea beetles		Carbaryl
	Sap beetles	Remove all ripe fruits from garden at once	Carbaryl Rotenone
Cucumbers	Aphids	Water stream Soap sprays	Malathion

		CONTROL	
PLANT	PEST OR DISEASE	NONCHEMICAL	CHEMICAL
	Cucumber beetles	Hand pick	Carbaryl
			Rotenone
	Mites	Soap sprays	
	Vine borer	Pinch vine tips to force branching. Cover main stems with mulch or soil. If borer present, slit through hole and part of stem with razor blade lengthwise to cut insect.	Carbaryl Rotenone
	Powdery mildew		Benomyl
	Angular leaf spot	Resistant cultivars	Fixed copper
	Wilt	Resistant cultivars	
	Scab	Resistant cultivars	
	Mosaic	Resistant cultivars	
Eggplant	Aphids	Water stream Soap spray	Malathion
	Flea beetles		Carbaryl
	Potato beetles	Hand pick	Carbaryl Rotenone
	Mites	Soap spray	Sulfur
	Anthracnose	Rotation	Maneb
	Phomopsis	Treated seed	Maneb
	Wilt	Rotation Resistant cultivars	
Lettuce	Leafhoppers		Carbaryl Rotenone
	Cabbage loopers	BT	Malathion

| PLANT | PEST OR DISEASE | CONTROL | |
		NONCHEMICAL	CHEMICAL
	Aphids	Water stream Soap spray	Malathion Rotenone
	Downy mildew	Space head lettuce 12 inches apart	Fixed copper
Muskmelons	Aphids	Water stream Soap spray	Rotenone Malathion
	Cucumber beetles	Hand pick	Carbaryl Rotenone
	See diseases and controls under Cucumbers		
Mustard	Downy mildew	Avoid wetting foliage	Maneb
	See diseases and controls under Cabbage		
Okra	Aphids	Soap spray	Malathion
Onions	Onion maggot	Avoid high organic matter soils and excessive moisture	Diazinon
	Thrips	Soap sprays	Rotenone Malathion
	Downy mildew	Avoid wetting foliage	Maneb
	Smut	Plant sets	Thiram
Peas	Aphids	Water stream Soap spray	Malathion
	Powdery mildew	Sanitation	Sulfur
Peppers	Aphids	Water stream Soap spray	Malathion
	Flea beetles		Carbaryl

		CONTROL	
PLANT	PEST OR DISEASE	NONCHEMICAL	CHEMICAL
	Hornworms	Hand pick	Carbaryl
			Rotenone
	Pepper weevil		Carbaryl
			Rotenone
	Corn borer	Resistant cultivars	Carbaryl
			Ryania
	Bacterial spot		Fixed copper
	Fruit rot		Maneb
Potatoes	Aphids	Water stream	Malathion
		Soap spray	
	Flea beetles		Carbaryl
			Rotenone
	Leafhoppers		Carbaryl
	Potato beetles	Hand pick	Carbaryl
			Rotenone
	Scab	Resistant cultivars	Sulfur
	Blights		Maneb
	Rhizoctonia	Use whole seed pieces	Captan
Pumpkins, squash	Aphids	Water stream	Malathion
		Soap spray	Rotenone
	Cucumber beetles	Hand pick	Carbaryl
			Rotenone
	Squash bugs	Hand pick	Carbaryl
		Trap under boards placed beneath plants	Sabadilla
	Vine borer	Butternut squash is resistant	Malathion
			Rotenone
	Mites		Pyrethrins
	Powdery mildew		Benomyl
	Mosaic	Remove pokeweed	
		Aluminum foil mulch	

		CONTROL	
PLANT	PEST OR DISEASE	NONCHEMICAL	CHEMICAL
Radishes	Aphids	Water stream Soap spray	Malathion Rotenone
	Flea beetles		Carbaryl
	Radish maggot		Diazinon
Spinach	Leaf miner		Malathion
	Downy mildew	Resistant cultivars	Maneb
Tomatoes	Aphids		Malathion Rotenone
	Cutworms	Paper collars	Carbaryl Rotenone
	Flea beetles		Carbaryl
	Blister beetles		Carbaryl Rotenone
	Hornworms, Fruitworms	Hand pick	Carbaryl
	Sap beetles	Remove ripe fruits	Carbaryl Rotenone
	Blights		Maneb
	Wilts	Rotation Resistant cultivar	
	Bacterial spot		Fixed copper
Turnips	Aphids	Water stream	Rotenone Malathion
	Flea beetles		Carbaryl
	Turnip maggot		Diazinon
Watermelons	Aphids	Water stream	Malathion
	Cucumber beetles	See Cucumber	

themum that grows in Ecuador and Kenya. It knocks down the insects very rapidly but kills them slowly. For this reason, it's usually combined with another insecticide, like rotenone, or with an activator, such as piperonyl butoxide, that increases its potency. It breaks down rapidly and is nonhazardous to birds and wildlife, though slightly toxic to fish.

Quassia bark can control many soft-bodied insects, especially aphids.

Sabadilla, also called Red Devil, is made from the seeds of a tropical bush and kills many bugs, beetles, and caterpillars. It gets stronger with age if kept in a dark place but breaks down rapidly in sunlight.

Synthetic Organic Compounds

These contain organic phosphates like malathion and Diazinon, carbamates like carbaryl, and pyrethroids. All of these pesticides have relatively low mammalian toxicity and are broad-spectrum, killing a wide variety of pests.

Captan is a broad-spectrum carbamate fungicide that is usually an ingredient in all-purpose sprays. It is not highly toxic to mammals and birds and breaks down relatively quickly.

Carbaryl (Sevin) is a broad-spectrum insecticide that has low toxicity to birds and mammals, is slightly toxic to fish, and is extremely toxic to bees. Never apply this compound to plants in bloom. About half of the compound degrades in three days, and it is nearly all gone within two weeks.

Malathion is an organic phosphate that degrades quickly and has broad-spectrum action. It has low toxicity to birds and mammals but is highly toxic to fish and bees. Malathion is one of the safest synthetic home pesticides.

Diazinon is another organic phosphate that is moderately toxic to humans and animals. Use this to control soil insects.

Inorganic Compounds

The once-common arsenic, lead, and mercury compounds have been laid aside. Mineral oil is still useful for controlling corn earworm, copper compounds control some diseases, and sulfur is used for disease, mite, and insect control.

More Organic Snake Oil

Frustrated gardeners have thought up some odd remedies. Being the scientist and curious gardener that I am, I've tried several of these "surefire" remedies myself.

Hot sauce. I mixed 2 tablespoons per gallon of water and sprayed it on my rose bushes to control Japanese beetles. The beetles loved it. I doubled the concentration. They devoured it. I finally poured hot sauce right out of the bottle onto the little critters. Nothing happened. They continued chomping my roses. Obviously, this doesn't work on Japanese beetles. Maybe it will work on aphids.

Garlic juice. I tried this a few times on my tomatoes. My hornworms got fatter, and the aphids went right on feeding. I did, however, get bushels of garlicky tasting tomatoes. Other strong-smelling condiments, like onions and horseradish, are also thought to control insects. The idea probably comes from the medieval notion that spices and herbs repel the evil spirits that cause disease. Some of these, like oil of citronella, might work to control mosquitoes, but they are all questionable for controlling insects in the vegetable garden.

Bug blending. Perhaps the idea here is to terrify the enemy. You collect many specimens of the insect that is troubling you, process them in a blender into a thick frappé, let the puree stand overnight, then mix it in equal parts with water and spray the concoction back onto the plants. This will get a little cumbersome if you're bothered by aphids. And the simple act of picking the insects will control their populations more than their frothy return. Spraying certain unidentifiable deliquescent remains onto your maturing peppers is a sure way to ruin your appetite, and who wants to eat yellow summer squash covered with green slime? More important, who will drink the next vanilla milkshake?

Sulfur, one of the oldest fungicides, will wipe out mites, thrips, newly hatched scale insects, and some caterpillars. It can, however, damage the foliage of some crops, and its long-term use will acidify the soil. Ask for garden sulfur, sulfur dust, or wettable sulfur. Lime-sulfur, a combination of hydrated lime and sulfur, controls insects on fruit trees but is not usually used in the vegetable garden.

Cryolite is mined and ground for use in controlling chewing insects. It is not highly toxic to humans and pets, nor does it harm most predators.

Copper is another old fungicide that can be used alone as a dust or in combination with other minerals. Bordeaux powder, a combination of copper sulfate and hydrated lime, is an effective fungicide and has insecticidal properties as well. Some other copper compounds are used to prevent seed rot. Copper compounds can damage plant tissue, particularly of cucurbits, if used incorrectly, especially when relative humidity and air temperature are high.

CAUTIONS

There are hundreds of pesticides on the market. Some are highly toxic, some are relatively nontoxic. Some work, some don't. There is absolutely no need for the home gardener to use highly toxic compounds or to waste time on idiotic schemes to control insects. If the pesticides listed above don't work in your garden, then pave it over for a parking lot. Be sure to follow the label directions religiously whenever you use a pesticide, and be sure the compound is still legal to use in your area. Laws change fast.

17

Picking and Putting By

Now that you've grown the finest vegetables in the world, you've got to get them out of the garden and into the pot or storage at the right time. You need only a little basic knowledge and some common sense for this step.

WHEN TO HARVEST

You must cut, pick, pull, or dig your crops when they are horticulturally mature. This means when they have achieved their peak flavor and tenderness, which is not necessarily when they are botanically mature. Botanically mature green bell peppers are red, mature sweet corn is pasty and full

Maturity indexes for some vegetables. Use the criteria in the left-hand column to judge whether the vegetables on the right are ready to pick.

Abscission layer forms	Muskmelons
Dry foliage	Potatoes, onions, garlic, horseradish, Jerusalem artichokes
Size	Most vegetables
External color	Most vegetables
Compactness	Cauliflower, broccoli
Solidity	Cabbage, head lettuce, Brussels sprouts
Tenderness	Peas, sweet corn, asparagus

of starch, and mature cucumbers are yellow and seedy. On the other hand, horticultural and botanical maturity are about the same in tomatoes, watermelons, and winter squash. Delaying harvest just a day or two in hot weather might allow your crop to mature from palatability to inedibility. You've put a lot of work into the garden—don't waste it all now.

Harvest in the cool of the day—early morning after the dew has dried or evening. Spinach is an exception. The leaves are full of water and brittle in the morning and apt to crack or break if you cut them at that time. Cut them during the day.

After you've harvested your crops, get them out of the sun and cooled down as soon as possible. The higher the temperatures, the faster the vegetables will lose their quality. Sweet corn can lose up to a quarter of its sugar in just a few hours at 80 degrees F. If you want to eat starchy corn, you can always buy it at the supermarket.

STORAGE

Between harvest and eating, you need to store your crop. Knowing the conditions involved in storage and the limitations of the crop will help you choose the best method. You also need to know how much room you're going to need.

Temperature is the most important consideration for storage. Low temperatures slow respiration, the chemical reactions taking place in the vegetable, and the growth of disease organisms. The rate of respiration increases two to three times for every 18-degree F. rise in temperature. A pod of peas gets stringy and loses sugar two to three times faster at room temperature than it does at 50 degrees F. It shrivels faster and rots faster too. By lowering the temperature as soon as possible, you'll preserve the freshness of the crop as long as possible.

Most crops store best at temperatures between 32 and 35 degrees F. Lower temperatures will freeze the tissue and cause it to break down, and higher temperatures will increase respiration and development of rot and lower the quality of the vegetables. Exceptions are the warm-season crops, most of which store best at around 50 degrees F. Storing them at lower temperatures for any length of time causes chilling injury. Cucumbers and eggplants stored in the refrigerator for two weeks will develop pitted areas on their surface. That's chilling injury, and it allows water to leave the fruit and rot to develop. Potatoes convert their starch into sugar

Knowing how much you can expect to harvest per 100 feet of garden row will give you some idea of your storage needs.

VEGETABLE	YIELD	VEGETABLE	YIELD
Asparagus	40 lbs.	Lettuce, leaf	50 lbs.
Beans, lima, shelled	35 lbs.	Muskmelons	100 fruits
Beans, snap	130 lbs.	Mustard	100 lbs.
Beets	150 lbs.	Okra	1000 pods
Broccoli	100 lbs.	Onions	100 lbs.
Brussels sprouts	75 lbs.	Parsley	25 lbs.
Cabbage	50 heads	Parsnips	100 lbs.
Cabbage, Chinese	80 heads	Peas, pods	30 lbs.
Carrots	80 lbs.	Peas, black-eyed	40 lbs.
Cauliflower	50 heads	Peppers	60 lbs.
Celeriac	60 lbs.	Potatoes	85 lbs.
Celery	200 stalks	Pumpkins (small)	75 fruits
Chard	70 lbs.	Radishes	100 bunches
Collards	100 lbs.	Rhubarb	100 lbs.
Corn, sweet	100 ears	Salsify	600 roots
Cucumbers	110 lbs.	Scallions	140 bunches
Eggplant	120 fruits	Spinach	50 lbs.
Endive	65 plants	Squash, summer	160 lbs.
Garlic	40 lbs.	Squash, winter	250 lbs.
Kale	100 lbs.	Sweet potatoes	100 lbs.
Kohlrabi	75 lbs.	Tomatoes	150 lbs.
Leeks	300 plants	Turnips	75 lbs.
Lettuce, head	85 heads	Watermelons	35 fruits

when stored below 38 degrees F. The high sugar content will cause the potatoes to turn brown or black when fried as the sugar caramelizes. It won't hurt you, but it doesn't look very nice. Pay attention to proper storage temperatures.

Relative humidity is another important consideration. Most vegetables are 90 to 95 percent water. If they are stored in air with less than 95 percent relative humidity, water will leave the tissue and the vegetables

Store your vegetables at the right temperature and humidity. Storage life also depends on the cultivar, the condition of the vegetable at harvest, and how it was handled after harvest. Store only mature, sound vegetables of a good-keeping cultivar.

VEGETABLE	TEMPERATURE	RELATIVE HUMIDITY	LIFE
Asparagus	34°F	95%	2–3 weeks
Beans, snap	45	95	7–10 days
Beans, lima	40	95	5–7 days
Beets	32	95	1–3 months
Broccoli	32	95	10–14 days
Brussels sprouts	32	95	3–5 weeks
Cabbage	32	95	1–6 months
Cabbage, Chinese	32	98	2–3 months
Carrots	32	95	1–3 months
Cauliflower	32	95	3–4 weeks
Celery	32	98	1–2 months
Corn, sweet	32	95	5–8 days
Cucumbers	53	95	10–14 days
Eggplant	53	95	1 week
Garlic	32	65	6–7 months
Honeydew melons	45	95	2–3 weeks
Horseradish	32	95	10–12 months
Kohlrabi	32	95	2–4 weeks
Leeks	32	90	1–3 months
Lettuce	32	98	2–3 weeks
Muskmelons	48	95	7–14 days
Okra	50	90	2 weeks
Onions, dry	32	65	1–7 months
Onions, green	32	95	3–4 weeks
Peas	32	95	1–2 weeks
Peppers	50	95	2–3 weeks
Potatoes	39	95	4–8 months
Spinach	32	95	10–14 days
Squash, summer	50	95	1–2 weeks
Squash, winter	50	60	1–3 months

Tomatoes, mature green	55	95	1–3 weeks
Tomatoes, ripe	48	95	4–7 days
Turnips	32	95	4–5 months
Watermelons	50	90	2–3 weeks

will shrivel. Higher relative humidities, on the other hand, can cause rot. Some crops, such as winter squash and dry bulb onions, must be stored in a fairly dry environment of about 65 percent relative humidity or they will rot.

Ventilation is also important, but it is often overlooked. All vegetables give off heat as they respire. This is called the *heat of respiration,* and it can be a substantial amount, as in the case of celery. Without proper ventilation, heat will build up around the produce, increasing the temperature and destroying quality. This is worsened as water given off by the produce increases the humidity. As relative humidity builds to 100 percent and the temperature rises, the likelihood of rot increases. If you're storing in the cellar, open a window and run a fan near the vegetables to circulate fresh air.

Ripening vegetables and fruits release a colorless, odorless gas called ethylene. The higher the temperature, the faster it is released. Ethylene causes fruits and vegetables to ripen faster, and the faster they ripen, the more ethylene they release. The less ethylene in the air, the longer the produce will keep. Lowering the temperature and increasing the ventilation reduce the amounts of this gas. Rotting fruits and vegetables give off large quantities of ethylene. Look them over frequently and get rid of any that are rotting. Apples, pears, plums, avocados, peaches, muskmelons, and papayas are high ethylene producers; store them away from your vegetables. Cigarette smoke, engines, and fluorescent lighting also emit substantial quantities of ethylene.

Keep your storage area dark, since light can raise the temperature and cause greening in some vegetables, such as onions, potatoes, endive, and garlic. The greening is serious in potatoes because it signals the buildup of the toxic alkaloid solanine.

A pepper will not keep as long as a potato, and some vegetable cultivars will store better than others. For example, late cabbage stores better than the early type, and pungent onions are better keepers than mild.

Select appropriate cultivars if you plan to store your crop for any length of time.

All vegetables to be stored should be free from bruises and injury. Rot will quickly attack an open wound, and the damaged tissue will release ethylene gas.

Vegetables for storage also must be in the proper stage of ripening. Broccoli should be slightly immature, winter squash must have hardened rinds, and beets and turnips must be picked before they become woody, since woodiness will increase in storage. Onions, sweet potatoes, and pumpkins need to be properly cured before storage.

Most of us don't have elaborate storage facilities—the household refrigerator, kept at 35 to 40 degrees F., serves as common storage for everything. We wrap greens in plastic to increase the humidity and prevent wilting. There are other areas around the house, however, that are great for storing some things. An unheated, dry, well-ventilated basement is fine for several crops. Hang onions and garlic in mesh bags or slatted baskets from the ceiling, and place sweet potatoes, winter squash, and pumpkins on shelves along the walls so that they do not touch each other. Hang tomato plants with mature green tomatoes upside down from the shelves to ripen the fruits. On the floor near the outside entrance, build a box or bin filled with moist sand in which you can bury your beets, carrots, parsnips, turnips, rutabagas, and cabbage.

If you have the room, build a pit storage right in your garden. Dig a shallow hole and lay 6 inches of straw on the bottom. Pile cabbage, kohlrabi, and root crops on the straw, and cover them with about 12 more inches of straw. Place over this several inches of soil. Leave some straw sticking out of the top of the pile to provide ventilation. As the weather gets colder, pile on more soil until you have about 8 inches above the straw. Continue to cover that with alternating layers of fluffy snow and straw. If there is no snow, use only straw. The beauty of this method is that it is inexpensive to construct and easily removable the fol-

Many vegetables can be stored on shelves in a cool basement. Hang onions and garlic from the shelves in mesh bags, place squash so that they don't touch each other, and hang tomato plants upside down to ripen the green tomatoes. Beneath the shelves, fill a wooden bin with damp sand, and sink your turnips, cabbage, carrots, and parsnips into it for fresh keeping.

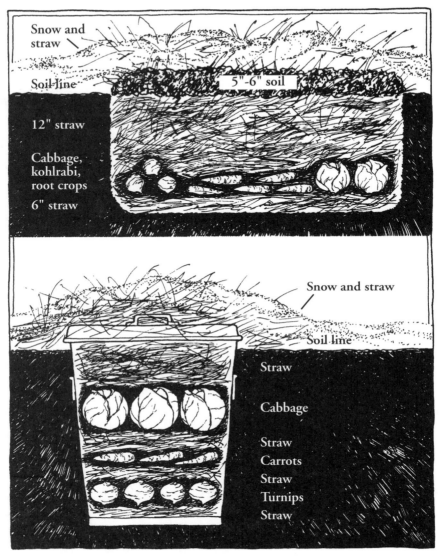

Snow and straw

Soil line

5"-6" soil

12" straw

Cabbage, kohlrabi, root crops

6" straw

Snow and straw

Soil line

Straw

Cabbage

Straw
Carrots
Straw
Turnips
Straw

Pit storages. Top. *Pit in the garden filled with alternating layers of straw, produce, straw, and soil, then covered with a snow-straw mixture. Leave straw sticking out above the soil to allow ventilation of the pile.* Bottom. *Modified pit storage using a garbage can with lid. It's handy and allows periodic removal of vegetables throughout the winter.*

lowing season, when the straw can be turned into the soil. What's hard is when you want a head of cabbage in January. With everything frozen, it's difficult to get at, and it's even more difficult to cover the pile again. An alternative is to construct several small piles that can be opened and their contents removed all at once. Modify this process by sinking a garbage can into the ground to within 6 inches of the rim. Place straw in the bottom, then a layer of produce, a layer of straw, repeating until the can is full. Top off with straw, and place the lid on the can. Cover this with straw, leaves, and snow, and use the vegetables when you need them.

Pit storages like those described above are crude but reasonably effective, although they have no good means of temperature and humidity control and relatively poor ventilation.

18

Cool-Season Crops

Cool-season crops all tolerate some degree of cold, and they make their best growth in the cool temperatures of spring, fall, and in southern gardens, winter. Some, like the perennial crops, go dormant during the coldest months. None of these crops grow well in the summer heat.

PERENNIALS

Perennial crops occupy the land year-round. Plant them to one side of the garden so that you will not have to till around them each year.

Few of these crops are related, and aside from their vegetative propagation, their cultures differ widely. All should, however, be planted in fertile, well-drained soil high in organic matter. Because you will not prepare the ground fresh each year, apply phosphorus and potassium to the deeper soil layers when initially preparing the area, since these nutrients do not move down to the roots readily when applied as a top dressing.

Asparagus

This plant originated along the seashores and riverbanks of Europe. The ancient Romans were familiar with the plant. In 200 B.C., Cato gave directions for its cultivation. Later writers Pliny and Columella spoke highly of it, and Suetonius claimed that the Emperor Augustus relished the young shoots. Although it was introduced into the United States very early, it was not planted extensively until after 1850.

Asparagus is a hardy herbaceous perennial grown for its tender spears. It is dioecious, meaning that some plants have male reproductive organs and some female. It tolerates severe cold during its dormancy and grows best when daytime temperatures average about 80 degrees F. and nighttime temperatures about 60 degrees F. Very high temperatures result in poor plant development. In addition, the crowns require a dormant season of three to five months of temperatures below 50 degrees F. This is really a plant for northern gardens.

Crown development: Rhizomes and fleshy roots form the crown of the plant. The rhizomes are underground stems that grow up to 2 inches per year and point slightly upward. (This is why old beds have crowns near the surface.) The fleshy roots grow about 6 feet outward from the plant and 5 feet downward. Fibrous roots, necessary for absorbing water and nutrients from the soil, develop from the fleshy roots but die back each fall. The fleshy roots and the rhizomes are perennial.

Spear development: Edible stems, or spears, arise from buds on the rhizomes. They have scalelike leaves at their tips and become increasingly woody as they elongate. The rhizome buds show some apical dominance, like the eyes of a potato, and unless the early shoots are harvested, will produce only a few shoots. With continuous harvest, more shoots develop. The growth of spears depends on the temperature. It takes about five days to produce a 6-inch spear at 53 degrees F. but only two days at 78 degrees F. Warm temperatures cause such rapid growth that the scales at the tips may loosen and quality will suffer. Too-cool temperatures will cause the spears to become woody and bitter.

Fern development: The spears continue to elongate into shoots 4 to 6 feet tall with frondlike leaves. Shoots will bear flowers and, on the female plant, berries. The ferns produce carbohydrates that are transported to the crown to replenish the supply used in overwintering and early spear development.

Prepare the soil by turning under manure and compost as well as a green manure crop if possible. Because the plant is long-lived and the roots deep, it is important to till under some phosphorus and potassium before planting to get it deep into the root zone.

Deep, loose, well-drained, sandy loams are best. Soil that is too sandy will dry too much for good production. Since asparagus is susceptible to fusarium, try to plant on ground that was not previously planted with asparagus.

Select plump, one-year-old, certified disease-free crowns containing two or more well-formed clusters of buds. Be sure the roots are not dried or moldy.

Dig a trench about 8 inches deep, and place the crowns at the bottom, spreading the roots and ensuring that the buds are pointing upward. Cover them with 1 or 2 inches of soil. As the shoots grow, continue to fill in the trench, always keeping the top inch or two of the shoots above the soil, until you have brought it up to soil level. If your soil is a little on the heavy side, plant the crowns only 4 to 6 inches deep.

Space the rows about 4 feet apart, with 1 foot between crowns in the row.

The amount of fertilizer you need depends on the soil and growing conditions. Fertilize in the early spring to encourage spear growth and again after harvest to promote the best frond growth. If your soil is a bit sandy, or your plants don't look too healthy, fertilize a bit more heavily. Many gardeners also apply manure over the crowns after harvest. Always keep the plants as vigorous as possible.

Watering is critical for the first two years of the bed, while plants are becoming established. During this time, apply at least 1 inch of water per week during the growing season. By the third season, the plants will have established an extensive root system, and you won't need to water as frequently. When you do water, try to wet the soil down to a 2-foot depth.

Keep all weeds out of the bed. This can become a problem as the crowns begin to spread and the rows fill in. You may have some volunteer asparagus seedlings appear after a few years. Keep them out of the bed as much as possible by regular hoeing, as they will not be as vigorous or productive as the mother plants and will compete for water and nutrients.

Many older cultivars are based on the 'Martha Washington' strain. 'Waltham Washington' and 'Mary Washington' are good ones. Breeders have recently developed a number of all-male or predominantly male cultivars. 'Viking' and 'Jersey Centennial' are fine selections for the home garden. Male plants can produce three to five times as many spears as a mixed population and don't waste their energy on berry production.

Don't harvest any spears for the first two seasons. During this time, let the plants become established. In the third season, harvest spears for only about three weeks. Extend the harvest period by two weeks each year to a maximum of six to eight weeks. Allow spears developing after

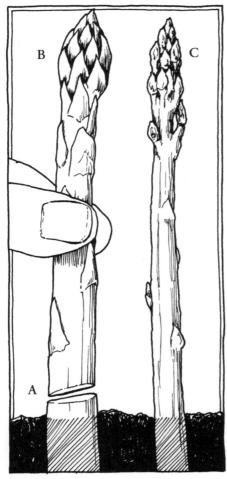

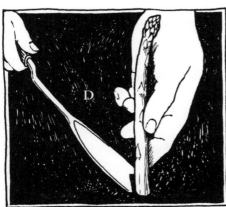

Break off the asparagus spear just above the soil surface and leave the tough lower stem behind (A). Tight tips on these spears (B) mean that they are at their best quality. Spears that grew when the temperature was too warm or are old and overmature are spindly and have loose tips (C). Harvesting with an asparagus knife (D).

this time to produce leaves and fruit. They will manufacture carbohydrates, which will be stored in the roots for winter. If spears begin coming up spindly and pencil thin, stop harvest immediately—the crowns are running out of energy.

The best spears for eating are about 6 to 10 inches long and have tight tip scales. Because the scales may open sooner during warm weather, you may have to harvest every day.

To harvest the spears, cut or snap them from the crowns. Use a special knife with a V-shaped blade to cut the spears about 1 inch below the soil line but at least 2 inches above the crowns. The portion of the spear that was below ground will be blanched and a little tough, so you'll have to trim it off. If you snap the spears at the soil line, you'll eliminate the tough white base and have less trimming to do. Whichever method you use, be careful not to injure the crown or its buds.

Let all later shoots develop fully and overwinter. Remove them before growth begins in the spring.

Asparagus doesn't store well, so cool it to below 40 degrees F. fast and use it rapidly.

What's Wrong?

Why is my asparagus stringy and woody?
Both of these conditions indicate slow growth. Most likely, your bed has become too crowded or you did not supply enough water when the spears were developing.

Why do my plants have rusty-looking areas?
They probably have asparagus rust, the most common cause of failure in asparagus beds. Destroy the existing plants and plant rust-resistant cultivars in a new bed.

Why is my asparagus bitter?
It's probably too warm in the garden. Quit harvesting.

Globe Artichokes

This herbaceous perennial, which resembles a giant Canada thistle plant, originated in north Africa and in areas surrounding the Mediterranean Sea. The globe artichoke was first cultivated in Naples for its large flower bud, and, by the sixteenth century, it had become popular in European gardens. It reached England in 1548 and was introduced to the United States before 1800 by French settlers in Louisiana and by Spanish and Italian farmers in California.

The globe artichoke, an herbaceous perennial, grows best during the winter where the climate is cool and mild. It's very sensitive to frost, and the buds are killed when the temperature falls below 30 degrees F. Too-high temperatures will cause the edible bud scales to become fibrous and tough and to partially spread.

The terminal bud on the globe artichoke is usually the largest bud. Axillary buds are smaller.

A rich, well-drained, moderately fertile loam will produce the best artichokes. Seedlings are highly variable, so you're better off planting crown divisions or rooted offshoots in the early fall, 6 inches deep and 6 feet apart in rows 8 feet apart. Moisture is critical, and the plants should receive 1 to 2 inches a week, particularly when the buds begin to form. Harvest the buds in the late spring or early summer by cutting the stem 2 inches below the base of the bud. The terminal buds will be the largest, sometimes growing to 3 to 5 inches in diameter. Axillary, or side, buds are slightly smaller.

Remove the tops of the plants after harvest, and do not fertilize or water until late summer. This allows the plants a short rest period. When temperatures begin to cool in the fall, apply plenty of water and fertilizer to stimulate new growth.

A planting of globe artichokes will usually last six to nine years.

Jerusalem Artichokes

This is one of the few vegetables that originated in North America. Many Native American tribes cultivated it, and some ate it mixed with spring greens. Early colonists observed the natives growing the plant along the Massachusetts coast and soon sent specimens back to Europe. The plant bears no relation to either Jerusalem or globe artichokes, but gets its name from the Italian *girasoli articocco*, which means "sunflower artichoke." The Italian name was then corrupted and anglicized to "Jerusalem artichoke." By 1806, the plant had become a common garden perennial in the United States, and cultivars bearing white, yellow, and purple skin were described by the time of the American Civil War.

The plant is grown for its small, knobby tubers, which are planted in the early spring 2 to 3 inches deep, 2 to 3 feet apart in rows 3 to 4 feet

The Jerusalem artichoke is neither from Jerusalem nor an artichoke. It's grown for its starchy tubers rich in the carbohydrate inulin. Don't confuse this with the protein insulin.

apart. Light soils make harvest easier but produce smaller yields than slightly heavier soils. Harvest is difficult in very heavy soils.

The tubers produce plants that may grow several feet high and resemble sunflowers. Tubers begin to form during the shortening days of late summer and early fall. They are usually ready for harvest about five months after planting. Dig the tubers after the tops have been killed by a heavy frost. In areas with mild winters, you can harvest the tubers throughout the winter months, but where winters are cold, dig them before the soil temperature drops below freezing. Stored at about 32 degrees F., they will keep for three to five months.

What's Wrong?

How can I keep my Jerusalem artichoke plants from spreading and becoming weedy?

Dig up all the tubers each year. If you're afraid you'll miss some, dig a trench 18 inches deep completely around your planting, line the sides with double-thick polyethylene sheeting, then refill the trench. This will keep the patch from spreading.

Horseradish

As Jerusalem artichoke has nothing to do with either the Holy City or artichokes, so the horseradish has nothing to do with either horses or radishes. The name is supposedly an anglicized rendering of the German *meerrettich*, which means "mare radish."

A native of southeastern Europe, the plant was apparently not recognized by the ancient Greeks or Romans. It has long been used as one of the bitter herbs in celebration of Passover as described in Exodus 12:8. It was first used in Europe for medicinal purposes during the Middle Ages, when both its leaves and roots were eaten in Germany. The Germans cultivated the plant as early as 1542, the Italians by 1563, and the English by 1586, where it was used as a condiment in sauces served with meat. Colonists brought it to the United States by 1800.

The horseradish plant is a perennial grown as an annual. It grows best where the summers are warm and the falls cool. Southern gardeners will have a tough time growing it unless they live in a mountainous area.

Plant root cuttings, or sets, in the early spring in rich, fertile, loamy soil well prepared by turning under manure, compost, and a green manure crop. Do not apply a lot of fertilizer at this time, since excessive nitrogen will cause too much top growth and highly branched, irregularly shaped roots.

Select fairly straight sets about 10 inches long and dime or nickel thick. Plant them 4 to 5 inches deep, 18 inches apart in rows 30 inches apart, laying them at a 45-degree angle with the tops of the roots pointed upward.

The plants will produce much foliage at first, but by midsummer the taproot will begin to enlarge and make rapid growth until fall. Keep all weeds away from the planting until the tops are large enough to shade the area between rows.

Dig the roots after the tops have been killed by a heavy frost. Remove the dead tops, and trim off the largest side roots for planting the next year. When you remove the side roots, cut their tops square but make a slanting cut on the bottom to help you orient them properly when you plant. Store the roots at 32 degrees F., or leave them in the ground over winter and dig them in the spring before growth resumes. It' best to leave roots from which sets will be cut for propagating right in the ground until time to plant.

Rhubarb

This hardy herbaceous perennial is grown for its tender, tart, leaf stalks, or petioles. A native of Siberia, it was introduced to Europe around

1608, appearing first in Italy. The first documentation of it being grown in America was in 1778, but it was common in American gardens by 1806.

The plant is highly resistant to both drought and severe cold. Where summers are hot and dry and the winters mild, rhubarb will go dormant during the summer and grow during the fall and winter. Where winters are severe, it will go dormant during that time and grow best in the spring and fall. The plant does best in northern gardens where summer temperatures average 75 degrees F. and winter temperatures average 40 degrees F. It begins growth when the temperature reaches 45 degrees F. and grows rapidly during the cool spring, when the leaf stalks become red. In summer, vegetative growth is severely reduced, the leaf stalks turn green, and the plant produces a long flower stalk. Vegetative growth picks up again in the cool fall, and the stalks become red again. The plant finally dies back when the temperature drops to 26 degrees F.

Rhubarb is a voracious feeder and requires well-drained soil rich in organic matter. Prepare the soil deeply, turning under rotted manure, compost, and a green manure crop, as well as some fertilizer.

Using the vigorous outer portion of the old crown, cut crown divisions into as many pieces as there are strong buds. Where winters are severe, plant these in the spring; in areas with mild winters, plant in late fall after the leaves have died down. Set the divisions 2 feet by 4 feet apart and 2 inches deep, and firm the soil around their sides, leaving the soil directly over the buds loose and fluffy.

Once the planting has been established, side-dress the plants in the spring with a complete fertilizer, and cover them in the fall with rotted manure.

'Ruby', 'Valentine', and 'Canada Red' produce bright red leaf stalks, their color made more intense by cool temperatures. Another old Canadian cultivar, 'McDonald', produces pink stalks, and the very old cultivar 'Victoria' produces large green stalks.

Plants of cultivars producing red stalks are generally smaller than those producing green stalks. 'Valentine' and 'Canada Red' are somewhat better adapted to warmer climates, since they are not as apt to produce seed stalks as other cultivars.

The plants need to become established before you harvest them. You usually can harvest for a week or two from vigorous plants during their second season. By their third season, they should be established enough to support a longer harvest of eight to ten weeks. Don't harvest for longer than that, though, and never harvest in both spring and fall.

Harvest the stalks by pulling them from the plant. Don't cut them, since the knife could injure the bud and ruin the next crop. Remove the leaf blades, which are poisonous, before storage.

The plants become crowded after eight to ten years, and the stalks will be small and spindly. When that happens, divide the plants, transplant the divisions to new areas, give the old plants a good dressing of manure, and you're back in business.

What's Wrong?

What is the tall, central stalk that has formed on my rhubarb plants? Should I remove it?

Yes. It's a seedstalk. The energy needed to ripen the seeds could be put to better use in resupplying the crown with nutrients to produce a larger plant with more stalks.

Why can't I start rhubarb from seeds?

You can, but viability of the seeds is terrible. Stick with crown divisions.

Why discard rhubarb leaves? Can't I use them like spinach?

Absolutely not. The leaf blades are poisonous. Do not eat them. Eat only the leaf stalks.

Sea Kale

Sea Kale is a hardy perennial native to western Europe and popular in England, where it's grown for its tender shoots and greens. It's nearly unknown in this country.

You can start sea kale from seeds or root cuttings. Sow seeds in rich, well-prepared soil in a corner of your garden in early spring. Thin the seedlings to stand 5 to 6 inches apart. Transplant them to their permanent locations the following spring. If you prefer to use 4- to 5-inch-long root cuttings, plant them in their permanent locations 3 feet by 3 feet apart.

Care for the plants as you would rhubarb. Remove the dead leaves in

Sea kale is grown for its greens and tender shoots. It's very popular in Europe but is little known in America.

the fall, and cover the plants with manure or compost for the winter.

Harvest the most vigorous shoots for a week or two the second year, cutting them when they are 4 to 5 inches long.

By the third year, the plants should be established enough to support a harvest of three to six weeks.

ALLIUMS

This group of plants all belong to the genus *Allium* and resemble onions in their culture, flavor, and use. The group includes garlic, leeks, chives, shallots, and onions. All are hardy, cool-season vegetables. Most are grown for their bulbs, with the exception of leeks and chives.

Chives

The cold-hardy chives grow in a clump, form only small bulbs, and are harvested for their leaves, which have a mild onion flavor. The plant was cultivated at least as long ago as A.D. 812, when its name appeared in a list of plants compiled for Charlemagne. It was grown in England prior to 1600 and was introduced in the United States before 1800.

Chives are propagated from seed or from clump divisions. The latter is the easier method. Divide and reset the clumps every two to three years in the fall, being sure that the new clumps contain at least ten to twenty bulblets each. Give the plants the same care as you would onions, and harvest them by cutting the leaves every four to six weeks throughout the season, beginning when the plants have made several inches of top growth.

Harvest chives by snipping off their tops.

Garlic

This native of southern Europe has been grown for over five thousand years. As early as 3200 B.C., the ancient Egyptians considered it an important crop. The Greek historian Herodotus wrote that the laborers who built the Cheops pyramid around 2900 B.C. lived on mostly garlic and onions. According to the Bible, the Israelites complained to Moses that they had neither garlic nor leeks in the wilderness. Roman and Greek nobles didn't care too much for garlic, but they belived that it provided strength and courage, so they fed it to their laborers and soldiers. The Chinese and Indians were using garlic by 500 B.C., and from those countries it spread throughout Asia. Cortez brought it to Mexico and so introduced it to North America in the early 1500s.

Garlic differs from the onion in that its bulb is compounded of several small bulblets, or cloves, each of which has two mature leaves and a vegetative bud.

Plant garlic in the early spring in northern gardens and as a winter crop in the South. It will survive heavy frosts, but it will not take the heat of summer, forming no bulbs if the temperature rises above 77 degrees F. and the days are long. Garlic needs rich, friable soil. Sandy loams are better than heavier soils, which cause irregularly shaped bulbs.

Before planting, store bulbs at 40 to 50 degrees F. for several months to break their dormancy so that they will sprout more readily. Separate the cloves just before planting, and set them into the soil 2 to 6 inches apart in rows 12 inches apart. Care for them as you would onions. Water them well—dry soil will cause small bulbs.

'New York White', 'Extra Select', and 'German Extra-Hardy' are good cultivars that keep well. 'Elephant' is a very large-bulbed, mild cultivar that must be used soon after harvest.

Pull the plants when the tops have died down, and cure and store them as you would onions.

What's Wrong?

Why do my garlic plants grow very weakly and produce poor bulbs?

You may not have fertilized enough, or you may have planted too late, as garlic doesn't do well in the heat of summer.

Why are my garlic bulbs lopsided and not shaped nicely?

Your soil may be too heavy. Lighten it with sand.

Leeks have flattened stems and leaves and taste like mild onions. The soil mound has been pulled away from the base of the plant on the right, revealing its blanched stem.

Leeks

Leeks are nonbulbing biennials grown for their blanched basal leaves. They are seeded directly in the garden in the South and grown over the winter. In the North, plants can be started in hotbeds or cold frames and transplanted in the garden in early spring, where they are given the same care as onions. When the plants are several inches tall, hill the soil around their bases to blanch the lower portions. Continue this practice as the plants grow. Don't begin this process too early, because the young seedlings rot easily, and don't pack the soil over the leeks; leave it loose.

'American Flag' is the most popular cultivar grown in the United States.

To harvest, you can pull the plants about 120 days from planting. At that time, they should be at least 1/2 inch in diameter at the base and have several inches of blanched stem. Well-grown leeks can have an edible portion 6 to 8 inches long and 2 inches in diameter.

What's Wrong?

Why did all my leeks rot when I hilled them?
You may have hilled them too soon, packed the soil too firmly, or covered the entire plant.

Onions

The Greek Hippocrates, the Father of Medicine, wrote that onions were very popular among the people of his time (430 B.C.) and that several cultivars were grown. And although they were used in Europe during the Middle Ages, they were not as popular as either leek or garlic, a reversal of today's preferences.

Columbus brought onions to Isabela Island in 1494. They spread fast through the Americas and were popular among the tribes of Native Americans. Massachusetts colonists grew them in 1629, and Virginia had its first crop in 1648.

The common onion is a biennial grown as an annual. Its bulb is a mass of concentric leaf bases, the outer ones of which swell when exposed to the proper day length. The inner leaves usually do not swell, but if they do, the bulb will have a thick neck and will not keep well.

The onion grows best at temperatures between 55 and 75 degrees F. and does poorly when the temperature reaches 85 degrees F. or drops below 45 degrees F. For most onions, the weather must be cool during the early phase of development and warm during bulbing.

Onions form bulbs in response to day length and can be divided into three categories. Short-day types form bulbs when exposed to twelve- to thirteen-hour days; intermediate types, thirteen- to fourteen-hour days; and long-day types, fourteen- to sixteen-hour days. When bulbing begins, leaf growth stops, and the bulb must draw upon existing leaves for its nourishment. That's why it's important to plant onions early in the season to get as much top growth as possible before the onset of bulbing.

Though onions grow in nearly all types of well-drained soil, they grow best in rich soil high in organic matter and nutrients. Work in as much rotted manure and compost as you can and broadcast some fertilizer before you plant.

The planting method depends on why and where you are growing onions. If you want them for dry bulbs and you live in the North, you can plant either seeds or sets in the very early spring after danger of hard freezes has passed. Most gardeners prefer sets, since they produce a crop three to four weeks earlier and yield more than seeded onions do. Southern gardeners plant sets, seeds, or seedlings in the fall or winter.

Dime-size onion sets produce the best dry bulb plants. They must be planted right side up, as they appear here.

Whether you start with seeds, seedlings, or sets, space your onion rows 16 inches apart. If you choose to seed, plant thinly in the row and don't bother to thin. The bulbs will push through the soil as they grow and separate themselves from one another. Bulbs occasionally become misshapen if the soil is very heavy or compact.

Plant sets 2 to 3 inches apart in the row, and cover them lightly with soil. Plant them right side up—the dried roots at the bottom and the point at the top. They don't grow well upside down. The best sets are dormant and about the size of a dime. Smaller sets won't yield as well, and plants from larger sets are likely to bolt.

Seedling onions should be pencil thick, about 6 inches tall, and eight to ten weeks old. Plant them 3 to 4 inches apart in the row.

Side-dress the young plants about a month after planting to keep them growing actively, but don't add any nutrients after that, as they would keep the plants growing and delay maturity.

The onion plant has a very small, shallow root system that is a terrible competitor and forager and must be well watered throughout the season. Give them 1 to 2 inches each week, but no more than that. Too much water, like too much fertilizer, can delay maturity and will cause the plants to produce soft bulbs that will not store well. Stop watering when the tops begin to fall over to encourage the plants to harden up.

Premature seed stalks are the result of the sets' being stored at improper temperatures. Large sets stored at 40 to 50 degrees F. are most likely to produce plants that bolt. Most of us buy our sets and do not have control over how they were stored. If they went directly from storage in the unheated back room to your garden, they will likely produce a lot of seeders. If they were taken from the unheated room and displayed in a warm showroom for a couple of weeks, they will have lost their tendency to bolt and should produce suitable plants.

There are many different types of dry bulb onions: round, flat, or globe-shaped bulbs in red, white, or yellow. They can be pungent or mild and come in short-day, intermediate, or long-day types.

Pungent, or American-type, onions are small, dense, and strong-flavored. The most popular cultivars produce yellow bulbs, although they also are available in red or white. Pungent onions store better than mild.

Mild, or foreign-type, onions are typified by the Bermuda onion, a short-day type grown widely in the South.

Long-day types grow best above 35 degrees north latitude and are therefore best for northern gardens, where they are planted in early spring for late-summer harvest. Short-day types grow best below 28 degrees north latitude, where they are grown for a winter and early-spring crop. Intermediate types do best at northern latitudes between 32 and 40 degrees and are usually planted in the fall for a late-spring harvest.

Some good long-day cultivars include 'Cuprum', 'Norstar', 'Sweet

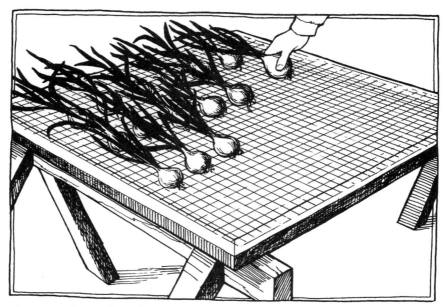

To cure onions, place them on a wooden frame covered with hardware cloth or 1-inch mesh poultry wire and supported on sawhorses. Lay the onions flat, and let the tops of the each row sparsely cover the bulbs of the previous row to prevent sunburning. Place the frame in a well-ventilated place. Keep them out of direct sunlight if the temperature is very warm.

Sandwich', 'Early Yellow Globe', 'Sweet Spanish', and 'Stuttgart'. Short-day cultivars include 'Grano' and its improved strains. Choose a cultivar adapted to your area.

Any densely planted onions can be pulled and used as green onions starting when they are about pencil thick.

Pull onions for dry bulbs when the tops on most of the plants have fallen over but before the foliage has dried completely. If you wait too long, the bulbs may sprout new roots and will not keep well.

After harvest, you must cure them for good keeping. Put them into rows in the garden with the tops of one row covering the bulbs of another, and leave them until the tops are completely dry. This will usually take between three and fourteen days, depending on the weather. If the weather is wet or damp, put them in a shed or garage on a piece of hardware cloth supported by two-by-fours between two sawhorses so that air can circulate around the bulbs. Leave the door open for ventilation.

Remove the tops when they have dried completely, cutting them about 1 inch above the bulb, and place the sound, firm bulbs into a large-mesh bag or wire basket for storage. The bulbs must have good ventilation to prevent rotting. They'll keep best in a cold, dry place, so long as they don't freeze. Garages and unheated attics are fine, but basements might get too damp. Hang the bag or basket from a rafter so that air can circulate through the bulbs.

Bruised or damaged bulbs and those with thick necks will not store well, so use them right away.

What's Wrong?

Why didn't my dry bulb onions get big?

You may not have supplied enough water or fertilizer, or there may have been too many weeds, especially during bulb formation.

Should I break over the tops of my onions before I pull them?

No. As onions mature, their tops will fall over naturally. It's time to pull the onions when most of them are bent. Breaking them on purpose doesn't hasten harvest.

Shallots

Shallots are perennial plants grown as annuals for their clusters of cloves. They are closely related to onions and have a delicate onion flavor without their pungency.

Shallots are usually started from bulblets, or cloves, planted 2 inches deep and 4 inches apart in rows 18 inches apart. In northern gardens, they are planted in the early spring and grown as a summer crop, and their dry bulbs are harvested near the end of the season. In southern gardens, the plants are grown as a winter crop for green onions. They are very hardy and can be left in the ground all winter.

If you want the dry bulbs, grow, harvest and cure them as you would onions. If you want the green onions, bank the soil 2 inches deep around the plants five weeks before harvest. Wait another two weeks, and bank the soil another 2 inches high. This will blanch the stems and create a more mild-flavored product. Pull the plants when the tops are 6 to 8 inches long and at least pencil thick.

Celeriac is a celery grown for its enlarged root. It deserves to be more widely grown.

There are few cultivars of shallots, but 'French Shallot' is a fine one.

CELERIAC

Celeriac is also known as turnip-rooted celery, or celery root. It is simply a type of celery grown for its enlarged, celery-flavored tuberous root that can grow to about the size of a fist. Grow these plants just as you would celery, and harvest them when the roots are 3 to 5 inches in diameter.

There are few cultivars, but 'Brilliant' and 'Large Smooth Prague' are two good ones.

CELERY

The ancient Greeks used celery leaves in funeral wreaths and as rewards for athletes. Romans seasoned their food with celery seeds. Chinese doctors used celery widely in the fifth century A.D. It was not cultivated then, but gathered wild in marshes from Sweden to Algeria and east to India. The plant was used almost exclusively for medicine through the seventeenth century, though its use as a vegetable for flavoring broths began during the Middle Ages. By the end of the sixteenth century it was being cultivated in Italy and, by 1623, transplanted to gardens in France. Slowly, it came once again to be used in soups and broths and to be eaten raw, though it was still used in early eighteenth-century England to "purify the blood."

Celery is a biennial grown as an annual. It forms a very short stem surrounded by leaves with stalks, or petioles, up to 2 feet high. It has a small, very shallow root system, with most of the roots in the top 6 to 12 inches of soil and within 6 to 12 inches of the plant.

Celery grows best at temperatures of 60 to 65 degrees F. and will bolt if young plants with more than five leaves are exposed to temperatures of 40 to 50 degrees F. for more than ten days. Temperatures in the 70s or higher while the plants are maturing will cause them to become stringy and strong flavored.

Celery is not easy to grow. It is very exacting in its requirements and needs a well-drained loam high in organic matter and moisture retention. Soil pH must be between 5.5 and 6.7, and the plant should make rapid, unchecked growth to avoid stringiness.

Celery is planted in the spring in northern gardens and grown as a fall crop in the South. In areas with a long growing season, celery can be direct seeded in the garden. Presoak the seeds for twenty-four hours for more rapid germination. As the seeds are very small, it is difficult to space them properly; you'll have to thin and waste many of the seeds. Also, the stand will be poor if the seeds are planted too deeply or the soil crusts. You'll be better off using transplants.

Move plants to the garden when they are 4 to 6 inches tall and space them 6 to 8 inches apart in rows about 24 inches apart. Unfortunately, celery plants grown from transplants have even smaller root systems than those direct seeded.

Celery soil should be very high in organic matter. Turn under rotted manure, a green manure crop, and all the compost you can spare. Because they're heavy feeders but lousy foragers, broadcast fertilizer before you plant, and side-dress the plants a few times during the season. Always push them in order to develop the most tender stalks.

Celery doesn't compete well with weeds. Keep it cultivated or mulched with straw, and don't let weeds gain a foothold.

Because of its marshy origin and highly restricted root system, celery requires large quantities of water continually throughout the season—from 1 to 2 inches a week. Any water stress will result in poor growth and stringiness.

Several nutrient disorders affect celery. These can be caused by an actual mineral deficiency or by insufficient watering.

Black heart is the result of a calcium deficiency, exacerbated by high

Blanch celery by mounding soil over the stalks several weeks before harvest.

temperatures, rapid growth, and water stress. The inner leaves and the growing point blacken and die. To prevet this, plant at the right time and provide sufficient water.

Cracked stems are the result of boron deficiency. The stalks become brittle, crosswise cracks develop, and surrounding tissue turns brown. Have your soil tested for boron.

Pithiness is the result of too-rapid growth and excessive nitrogen. The cells of the stalks break down, causing corky tissue and hollow cavities to form.

There are two types of celery grown: golden and green. Golden types are self-blanching and were quite popular in this country years ago. Cultivars of this type mature earlier but are less vigorous, more stringy, and have thinner stalks than the green types. 'Golden Plume', 'Golden Self-Blanching', and 'Lathom Blanching' are some good golden cultivars.

The green types are most common today. 'Utah 52-70' and its strains, and 'Ventura' are great green cultivars.

There is no absolute time to harvest celery. Cut the stalks at the soil line when they are large enough, about 100 to 150 days after transplanting. If you wait too long before harvesting, the outer stalks will become stringy and tough.

Blanching results in a golden-colored, mild-flavored stalk. You can plant one of the self-blanching cultivars, or blanch a green one by mounding soil over the stalks or covering them with boards or heavy paper several weeks before harvest. You can at least partially blanch your celery by crowding the plants in the row.

What's Wrong?

My celery seems stunted and the leaves are yellow. Why?
Because of the plant's fussy nature, this could be due to almost anything. The weather might be too hot, the soil too dry, the nutrients too low, or the cultivation too deep. Water and side-dress the plants, take care not to hoe too deeply, and keep your fingers crossed.

COLE CROPS

The cole crops are all hardy, cool-season crops. All belong to the mustard family, Cruciferae. With the exception of broccoli raab and Chinese cabbage (*Brassica rapa*), all are members of the species *Brassica oleracea*.

Kale and collards also are cole crops but are discussed under Greens.

Broccoli

There are two kinds of broccoli: heading broccoli, actually a late over-wintering kind of cauliflower, and sprouting broccoli. The latter is the more commonly known and the kind planted in most gardens.

Scientists believe that sprouting broccoli developed from wild cabbage on the coasts of Europe. Both purple and green types of broccoli were known in England in 1724, and the plant was commonly called "sprout colli-flower" or "Italian asparagus," because of its supposed Italian origin. The plant was introduced to the eastern United States around 1800 by Italian immigrants, but it remained obscure until after World War I, when doughboys returning from Europe, having become accustomed to eating the vegetable there, began to demand it from our producers. The popularity of broccoli skyrocketed when a group of Italian farmers in Northern California shipped the first trainload of the vegetable to eastern markets in 1920.

Like all cole crops, broccoli will tolerate light frost, which some say

Harvest the central head of broccoli before the florets open. Then side-dress to help the lower side shoots develop.

improves its flavor, but it won't take midsummer heat. It does best at temperatures between 57 and 68 degrees F. Above 68 degrees F., the heads become leafy and go to flower quickly, and above 77 degrees F., the plants form no heads at all.

Because of its heat intolerance, broccoli must be transplanted in the very early spring or seeded later in the garden as a fall crop. Try to use younger transplants of both broccoli and cauliflower; older plants, if exposed to temperatures of 50 degrees F. or less, will button, forming only tiny, miserable heads.

Space your plants 18 to 24 inches apart in rows 30 inches apart. Like its cousins, broccoli requires a rich, loamy soil to produce the best crops. Work in compost, manure, and fertilizer before planting, and side-dress after you cut the central head.

When you have your soil tested, have the lab test for boron and molybdenum as well. Broccoli is very sensitive to deficiencies of these nutrients. If the lab suggests that you add these minerals, follow their recommendations to the letter, since too much of these, particularly boron, can be worse than not enough.

Be sure that your broccoli gets at least 1 inch of water a week. Dry spells during heading can cause poor-quality heads.

Prevent competition from weeds by cultivating shallowly or, better still, applying an organic mulch to keep the soil moist and cool.

'Goliath' and 'Packman' are good early-season cultivars; 'Everest' and 'Green Valiant' are popular main-season ones. If you want a spring crop but are afraid the cool weather won't last long enough, try a heat-tolerant cultivar like 'Saga'.

Broccoli raab, or de rapa, is a nonheading type grown for its greens, which are eaten like kale. It goes to flower very quickly in warm weather and often does better as a fall crop.

Broccoli may suffer from a couple of nutrient deficiency disorders. Molybdenum deficiency causes whiptail, the development of straplike leaves that are sometimes reddened. A deficiency of boron causes browning, a disorder in which the stems develop water-soaked areas that later discolor. This discoloration moves up the stem to the flower head, where the individual florets become brown.

Plan your crop so that it does not mature in hot weather, which will cause the heads to become leafy and the plants to go to flower too fast.

To harvest, cut 8 to 10 inches of stem, along with the tight central head, when the head is 3 to 6 inches in diameter. Pick before the florets open and the head becomes loose. After your first harvest, side-dress the plants to promote good development of the lateral shoots. Harvest these when their heads are 1 to 3 inches in diameter.

You can store broccoli in the refrigerator for several weeks, but keep it away from ethylene-producing fruits and vegetables, such as apples. The quality of all cole crops degenerates rapidly when exposed to this gas.

What's Wrong?

Why does my broccoli form leaves in the flower head?

Temperatures are too high. Next season, time the planting so that the heads will mature in the cool of late spring or early fall.

My broccoli seems to go to flower overnight. I can't pick it fast enough. Why?

Again, it's maturing when it is too warm. Try a fall crop.

A few weeks after transplanting, my broccoli plants began to wilt, and the leaves become stunted and yellow. Why?

Pull one up and check for root maggots. If that's the problem, the plant will have no side roots, and you'll find tiny, white maggots tunneling into the stem. Use the proper soil insecticide, and rotate your crop next year. If there are no root maggots, check to see whether the main root is malformed. If so, suspect clubroot. Raise your soil pH to slightly above 7, and rotate your crop next year.

Brussels Sprouts

Like its sister broccoli, this plant too developed from wild cabbage and became popular in northern Europe long before the rest of the world had heard of it. Though it was probably grown in Brussels as early as the 1600s, it was not until 1821 that it had become widely known in Belgium. Gardeners grew it in the United States around 1800 and in England by 1854. It was not until the end of World War I that it became popular throughout Europe and the United States.

This crop is a nonheading cabbage grown for its axillary buds. Brussels sprouts tolerate cold better than some other cole crops and can survive temperatures as low as 14 degrees F. with little damage. In fact, low

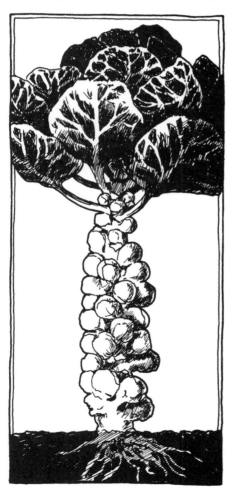

temperatures improve the flavor and, together with the sunny days of fall, help the plant produce a tight, compact, mild-flavored bud. Heat will make the sprouts soft, open, and strong flavored.

Like the other cole crops, Brussels sprouts need a rich, fertile soil. Prepare the soil as you would for cabbage.

You can transplant young plants in late spring for a fall crop or direct seed in spring for a late-fall crop. In either case, space the plants 30 inch-es apart in rows 3 feet apart. Since this is a long-season crop, side-dress it after a month or so in the field.

'Oliver', 'Widgeon', 'Jade Cross', and 'Prince Marvel' are all fine cultivars.

Remove the lower leaves on Brussels sprouts to make harvesting easier.

Begin harvesting your sprouts about 12 to 14 weeks after planting, when the lower leaves first begin to yellow and the lower sprouts are firm and about 1 or 2 inches in diameter. Don't wait too long after you see their color fade, or the sprouts will turn tough and strong. Remove the lowest leaf, and cut the bud from the stem. Then do the same to the one above it, and so on up the stem. The plant will continue to produce up to one hundred sprouts right up until winter. Don't remove the lower leaves too long before harvest; this will substantially reduce total yields.

English gardeners remove the plant's terminal bud after the lower sprouts have begun to form. This is useful in shorter seasons and will increase the size of each sprout and the total yield, but it will reduce the total number of sprouts.

Do not store sprouts with ethylene-producing fruits or vegetables.

What's Wrong?

Why have my plants stopped growing and the sprouts stopped forming?

There could be any number of reasons. If you removed the uppermost leaves during harvest, this would have suddenly arrested plant growth.

The bottom sprouts on my plants are large and firm, but the upper sprouts are not so good. Why?

This will happen if you remove all the leaves at once. Snap them off gradually, just before the sprout next to the leaf is ready to harvest. Taking a leaf off too soon will cause the nearest sprout to be of poor quality.

Cabbage

Cabbage has been grown for food for more than three thousand years. Before that, it was used as medicine by the ancient Egyptians. These ancient cabbages did not form solid heads. Our modern heading cultivars probably originated from the wild, nonheading forms growing along the chalky cliffs of England and northwestern France. These are the remnants of plants introduced from the coastal Mediterranean area by the Romans and Celts two thousand years ago. By A.D. 900, cabbage was common in European fields and, by 1536, essentially modern types were grown in England. Most of these were developed in northern Europe, though the soft-headed Savoy type was developed in Italy. They were introduced into the Western Hemisphere (Haiti) in 1556 and finally into Virginia by 1669.

Although cabbage is technically an herbaceous biennial, it is grown as an annual for its enlarged vegetative bud. The first leaves produced remain the outer leaves, and the head grows from the inside out, with leaves curving inward and overlapping to form a tight head. Under conditions of excessive moisture and high nitrogen fertilizers, the first head will split open and several smaller heads will form.

The best temperature range for cabbage growth is 60 to 65 degrees F. Although well-hardened cabbage plants will tolerate temperatures as low as 20 degrees F., they won't grow below 40 degrees F., and they again stop growing above 75 degrees F. Don't plant it to mature during the warm summer months.

If exposed to temperatures of 40 to 50 degrees F. for more than thirty days, or to a lower temperature for a shorter time, the cabbage head will split and send up a seed stalk, which ruins the head. Not all cabbage will do this, however. Plants will not bolt unless they have at least three to four leaves, or stems thicker than a pencil, at the time of exposure.

Cabbage needs adequate moisture and fairly high fertility. A soil with a pH of 6.0 to 6.8 is about right, but if there's a clubroot problem and fungicides fail, you'll have to raise the pH to 7.5 or slightly above. You'll also have to put cabbages into a four-year rotation if your plants develop this disease.

Spring cabbage is usually transplanted in the garden a couple of weeks before the last frost is expected. Use stocky, medium-size plants. If you are eager to get your cabbage in and want to try planting earlier, use hardy smaller plants with no more than three leaves to avoid bolting during the cool early spring. Space your plants 16 inches apart in rows 30 inches apart. If you're transplanting for a fall crop, give the plants a bit more room, spacing them 18 to 24 inches apart in the row. The closer you space your cabbages, the smaller the heads.

Fall crops are often sown where they will mature. Thin the young plants to their final spacing—18 to 24 inches apart—when they are 2 to 4 inches high and before they become crowded. Direct-seeded cabbage often matures two to three weeks earlier than transplants.

Cabbage is a heavy feeder that requires a fertile soil and responds well to the addition of nutrients. Turn under green manure crops and manure, and add compost to the soil at every opportunity. Broadcast fertilizer before you plant, and side-dress the plants when they are 4 to 6 inches tall. Don't add too much fertilizer or fertilize when they begin to mature; both can cause the heads to loosen and split. Excessive fertilizer, particularly nitrogen, can also cause tip burn.

Although they have extensive, dense, fibrous root systems, cabbages are poor competitors for water and nutrients. You must cultivate to kill weeds, but they won't tolerate deep cultivation. Because their systems are shallow and fill the area between the rows when the plants are half grown, discontinue hoeing them at this time to prevent damaging the roots.

Cabbage is relatively tolerant of drought, probably because of the heavy waxy coating on the leaves that prevents water loss. Nevertheless, they need at least 1 inch of water a week. Apply it with a soaker hose or watering can; wetting the foliage can spread black rot and *Alternaria* diseases. Try to keep the moisture supply constant, as dry spells followed by rains or heavy watering during head formation can cause the heads to split.

Cabbage comes in a number of different head types. The following classification system was instituted in 1915.

Wakefield. Small, pointed heads; early maturity; cold tolerant; bolt resistant.

Copenhagen Market. Medium-large, round heads; early maturity; will bolt in cold weather; grown for fall crops.

Flat Dutch (Drumhead). Large, flat, solid heads; various maturities; bolt resistant.

Danish Ballhead. Medium-size, round-oval heads; late maturity; intolerant of cold; good keeper.

Savoy. Medium-large, flat-globe heads; crinkly leaves; excellent quality.

Red. Medium, round; red to purple.

Alpha. Very small, round heads; early maturity.

Volga. Medium, flat-globe heads; late maturity.

There are many cultivars within each type. Some garden favorites include 'Emerald Acre', 'Tucana', and 'Early Jersey Wakefield', popular early green cabbages; 'Stonehead' and 'Prime Choice', midseason cultivars; 'Apex' and 'Perfect Ball', late green cabbages; 'Regal Red' and 'Red

Head', red cabbages; and 'Julius' and 'Savoy Queen', excellent savoy types.

Nutrient deficiencies that affect cabbage include internal tip burn, characterized by a breakdown of tissue near the center of the head. The tissue becomes dry and papery and turns black or brown. Athough its exact cause is unknown, it is related to an imbalance in calcium in the plant, made worse by uneven watering. It is most prevalent in fast-maturing cultivars when the water supply cannot keep up with rapid growth. Keep the water supply plentiful and constant.

Cut the heads from the plants when they are firm and mature and weigh from 3 to 5 pounds. Leave a few of the older wrapper leaves on the head unless they show worm damage. Do not let the heads remain on the plants too long after they mature, or they will split. Late cabbages store the best, holding up for several months. Early cabbages keep only a month or two. Don't store cabbage with apples or other fruits or vegetables that give off ethylene gas. This will cause the heads to lose their green color and drop their leaves.

What's Wrong?

How do I prevent my cabbage heads from splitting open?

Maintain a steady water supply, and harvest the heads as soon as they mature. If they begin to crack, stop watering, and twist the plant, in order to break some of the roots. This will decrease the water supply to the head and stop the splitting. The heads of early cultivars sometimes split a week or so after they mature in warm weather, so harvest them quickly.

Why are my cabbage heads and leaves full of holes?

This is probably the work of the cabbageworm. If you see small, white butterflies around the plants, apply BT immediately.

Why are my heads small?

You may have planted too closely or may not have thinned enough. Crowding will cause the heads to be smaller than normal. Or you may have planted a small-headed cultivar.

Cauliflower

Cauliflower is grown for its tight flower head, called a *curd*.

This crop does best in a cool, moist climate. It will not tolerate as much cold or as much heat as cabbage and grows best at temperatures between 57 and 68 degrees F. Above 68 degrees F., heads will be of poor quality, with many leaves developing in the heads; above 77 degrees F., heads will not form at all. Temperatures below 32 degrees F. can injure the plants and prevent heads from forming as the plants mature.

Though cauliflower can be grown in northern gardens as both a spring and a fall crop, it is grown mostly as a fall crop because of the summer heat. You can transplant young plants to the garden or direct seed in rows 30 inches apart. If you direct seed, thin the plants to stand 18 to 30 inches apart in the rows.

These plants have the same soil requirements as cabbage and must have good drainage to produce a good crop. They are fussy about soil acidity and do best in the pH range of 5.5 to 6.5. Yields are reduced in soils with pH ranges above or below this.

Like cabbage, cauliflower requires high fertility. Turn under organic matter, broadcast fertilizer before you plant, and side-dress the plants when they are several inches tall. They also have a high magnesium requirement, so use dolomitic limestone for adjusting the pH of the garden.

A number of disorders can affect cauliflower. Crowding in the flat, nitrogen deficiency, or any other condition that restricts growth can cause buttoning, resulting in small, exposed, inedible heads. The plants remain small and develop small leaves that don't cover the curds.

Whiptail is caused by a molybdenum deficiency and usually shows up when the soil pH is below 5.5. The leaves become straplike and extremely savoyed, and the plant is stunted.

Browning (also brown rot or red rot) is the result of boron deficiency and shows up as water-soaked areas in the stem and the center of the branches of the head. These turn rusty brown, the heads become bitter, and the foliage also becomes thick and brittle and curls downward. Have your soil tested for boron, and follow the recommendations of the testing agency.

Blindness, a condition in which no terminal bud forms, can be caused by insect or mechanical damage to the apex and is irreparable.

Gather a few leaves over the cauliflower curd when it is the size of a silver dollar, and fasten them with a rubber band. The blanched curd will continue to increase in size for the next several days.

Cauliflower curds may be white, green, or purple, depending on the cultivar. The purple-curded cultivars are becoming more popular among gardeners. These plants are a cross of broccoli and cauliflower that develop the curd shape of cauliflower and the sweet tenderness of broccoli. These "broccoflower" types require no blanching, and the color disappears when the curd is cooked. Another such cross produces plants with green curds.

Popular white-curded cultivars are 'Early Snowball', 'Snow Crown', and self-blanching 'Siria'. 'Violet Queen' and 'Burgundy Queen' are purple-curded cultivars that require no blanching. They develop a deep purple color when grown as a fall crop. 'Romanesco' produces an attractive conic lime green curd and is popular at gourmet shops.

The leaves of self-blanching cultivars naturally curl over the curd, shutting out the sunlight and whitening it. But you'll have to blanch the heads of the other white-curded cultivars to get a nice white curd. For the spring crop, when the weather is warm and the plants are growing rapidly, tie the outer leaves over the curd when it is a couple of inches in diameter. Leave them tied for two to three days before harvest. For the fall crop, when the weather is cooler, you may have to leave them for eight to ten days or longer. Check their development every day. Leaving them tied too long in hot weather can cause the leaves to rot over the curd, and in cool weather can cause the curd to flower. If the curd flowers, the production of stamens and anthers turns it fuzzy and brown-gray. This is called *riciness* and is undesirable. Instead of tying, some gardeners break several outer leaves and arrange them over the curd. Another alternative is to gather several outer leaves over the curd and hold them in place with a toothpick.

When the curd is blanched and about 6 inches in diameter, cut it from the stem as you would cabbage. Trim the leaves square across the top to protect it, and cool immediately.

What's Wrong?

Why does my cauliflower produce small heads?
Small heads can be caused by uneven or insufficient watering. If the heads are very small—the size of a quarter—the plant has probably buttoned.

Why are my cauliflower curds off-color?
You waited too long to cut them. Old curds will begin to flower, and the flower parts will cause a brown, gray, or pink hue to develop on the curds' surface.

Why are leaves growing in my curd?
The weather is too hot. Plant earlier or later next year.

Chinese Cabbage

This native of China developed from the wild turnip and rape of the Middle East about three thousand years ago and was introduced to Europe around 1837. There are two types of Chinese cabbage. The bok choy type forms a leafy plant resembling chard or mustard and is also known as Chinese mustard or mustard cabbage. Pe-tsai types form a head and resemble cos lettuce but have much thinner leaves.

Both types are cool-season crops. They are sensitive to cold temperatures below 40 degrees F. and do best at 60 to 70 degrees F. Both bolt under the long days of summer.

Chinese cabbage requires a fertile soil; prepare it as you would for cauliflower. It has the same pests as cauliflower and cabbage. It's grown as a winter crop in southern gardens and as a fall crop in the North. You can transplant young plants, less than four weeks old, in the garden for a spring crop, but it's chancy, since you may run out of cool weather before they mature. The fall crop can be sown in place and thinned to stand 12 to 15 inches apart in rows 2 feet apart.

'Crispy Chou', 'Pac Choy', and 'Lei Choy' are popular cultivars of the leafy bok choy type. 'Michihli', 'Wong Bok', and 'Jade Pagoda' are common pe-tsai cultivars.

Cut the heads from the stem at the soil line when they are firm and fully developed, about sixty-five to one hundred days after planting. You can harvest the entire leafy plant this way too, about thirty-five to sixty days after planting, or you can simply harvest the outer leaves and allow the plant to grow continuously until frost.

Kohlrabi

Kohlrabi is a strange plant grown for its aboveground, swollen, turniplike stem.

It's a cool-season crop that is sensitive to cold. It bolts when exposed to temperatures below 45 degrees F. and makes its best growth at 60 to 70 degrees F.

Most gardeners grow kohlrabi as a fall crop, sowing it directly in the garden and thinning the plants to stand about 6 to 8 inches apart in rows 18 inches apart. If you want to try it as a spring crop, start the plants in a hotbed and transplant them in the garden.

Prepare the soil as you would for cabbage, and give this crop the care you would cauliflower. It has the same pests as cabbage.

'Early White Vienna', 'Early Purple Vienna', and 'Triumph' are some good garden cultivars.

This kohlrabi is ready for harvest. Pull the plants, and remove the stems and taproots.

Pull your plants when the swollen stems reach 2 to 3 inches in diameter. Larger stems are woody. Trim the leaves and the woody taproot, and store the stems as you would turnips.

GREENS

These vegetables, also called *potherbs*, are grown for their green leaves and tender stems. They are usually served cooked, whereas the salad crops are usually eaten raw. Some plants may fall into both categories. Endive, for example, which is usually eaten raw and is classed as a salad crop, can also be cooked; the dandelion, included here with the greens, makes a dandy salad vegetable. Turnip greens and beet tops also are used as greens, but as those plants are grown primarily for their roots, they are discussed under Root Crops.

All the greens are high in minerals and vitamins, and all are cool-season crops, with the exception of New Zealand spinach, which is discussed under warm-season crops. The only green produced on a large commercial scale in the United States is spinach.

Swiss Chard

Swiss chard is actually a beet grown for its tops. This is a cool-season crop that will tolerate warm weather better than other greens and so can be grown through the summer. Its culture is similar to that of the beet, but the plant is larger and it does not develop the swollen root of its cousin.

You can transplant chard as soon as the danger of hard frost has passed or, like most gardeners, direct seed it in your garden. Space your rows 18 inches apart, and set your transplants 10 inches apart in the row. If you direct seeded, thin the young plants to stand 3 inches apart at first, then 10 inches apart as they begin to crowd. Use the thinnings for tender greens.

A spring planting of chard will last through the summer and into the first hard freeze if you treat it properly. If you garden where winter temperatures rarely fall below 25 degrees F., try growing chard all winter long.

Chard isn't fussy about soil, although it must be fertile and well drained. The crop responds well to high organic matter content, so spread manure in the fall or turn under a green manure crop or compost in the spring before planting. Broadcast fertilizer before planting, and side-dress at least once if you want to grow the plants through the summer.

Regular Swiss chard cultivars have thick, crumpled, dark green leaves and green-white leaf stalks. 'Fordhook Giant', 'Silverado', and the old standby 'Lucullus' are popular. Rhubarb chard is a type of Swiss chard that develops bright red leaf stalks.

The plants are ready to harvest about sixty days after planting. Cut the entire plant at the soil line, as you would spinach, or remove only the outer leaves 1 or 2 inches above the soil line. If you take care not to injure the small bud at the center of the plant, it'll continue to produce new leaves throughout the summer.

Collards

Think of collards as nonheading cabbage. They are biennials grown as annuals and, although a cool-season crop, are most popular in the South, where they are grown for boiled or fried winter greens.

This plant is hardier than cabbage to both heat and cold—it'll even tolerate temperatures of 15 degrees F. if acclimated—but it is best grown as a spring or fall crop.

You can direct seed or set out transplants. In either case, space the plants 18 inches apart in rows 3 feet apart. Spring crops are usually transplanted, and fall crops sown in place. Prepare the soil as you would for cabbage.

There are only a few cultivars of collards. 'Champion' and 'Vates' are popular for home gardens.

The greens are ready to harvest about seventy-five to ninety days after seeding, just before they become fibrous and woody. Harvest the older, larger leaves, and let the bud continue to produce younger leaves as the stem elongates. After several weeks, the plant will look like a tuft of new leaves stuck on a long stalk, and you may have to stake it for support. Alternatively, you can cut the entire plant at the soil line when it is 6 to 12 inches tall.

Dandelions

All of us are familiar with that pesky weed that invades our lawns with bright yellow flowers. Why in the world have breeders improved it? Because it tastes good.

The dandelion is popular for salads and greens in Europe. Unfortunately, it is best known in this country as a favorite target for weed killers. But the plant has been so improved that some cultivars actually resemble expensive endive.

Sow this hardy perennial in the early spring in rows 16 inches apart. Thin the plants to stand 10 inches apart in the row.

To harvest, cut the entire plant at the soil line, as you would spinach, before it begins to flower—about sixty to ninety days after planting. If you wish, blanch the plants before harvest as you would endive, by tying the outer leaves over the center or by covering the plant with boards or tarpaper. This will encourage tenderness and mild flavor.

Some gardeners let the plants overwinter and harvest them for spring greens before growth begins. For extra-early crops, you can force these plants by covering them with a portable cold frame, or you can you can start plants in cold frames.

Kale

Kale is a winter-hardy, non-heading cabbage grown as a spring and fall crop in the North and as a spring, fall, and winter crop in the South. It will not tolerate warm summer weather.

You can transplant kale in the garden in the very early spring for spring use, or direct seed it in late summer for fall use. Light freezes in late fall

Kale comes in dwarf (top) and tall (bottom) types. Harvest the entire plant or remove the lower leaves as they mature.

improve the quality of the leaves. Don't plant kale so that it will mature during the heat of summer; you won't be pleased with the result.

Kale is a heavy feeder, and you must broadcast some fertilizer before you plant, then side-dress when the plants are about four weeks old. Kale does well with high organic matter soils, so turn in manure and compost. Push the plants, and the leaves will be tender and succulent. Otherwise, grow it as you would spinach.

There are two types of kale commonly grown in the United States. 'Scotch' kale has curly, crumpled, gray-green foliage; 'Siberian' kale has blue-green leaves that are less crinkled. There are dwarf and tall forms within each type, though the dwarf is more popular. Common cultivars are 'Vates Blue Curled', 'Green Curled Scotch', and 'Squire'.

Harvest the plants before they become large and their leaves tough and fibrous. This will be about forty to fifty days after seeding. Cut the entire plant for use, or simply harvest the older, outer leaves, leaving the inner leaves to grow. Cool the greens rapidly to about 32 degrees F., and they'll keep for a couple of weeks.

What's Wrong?

Why is my kale pale and making very slow growth?

Temperatures are probably too high. If you can't get the seeds or the plants into the ground in the very early spring, plant them for a fall crop only. A lack of nutrients, particularly nitrogen, can also cause poor performance. You have to push kale to get the best-quality plants.

Why is my kale bitter and strong flavored?

Temperatures are too high or you're waiting too long to pick it. Kale that has been exposed to a few light frosts has a wonderful mild flavor.

Mustard

White mustard, leaf mustard, and spinach mustard are grown for their tasty leaves. Commercially prepared mustard is made from the seed of the black mustard, which belongs to a different genus. Once popular in home gardens, mustard has been replaced for the most part by the milder-flavored spinach and kale, though it still remains popular in the South.

Mustard is a hardy annual grown for its compact foliage. Like the other greens, it is a cool-season crop that will bolt quickly in summer heat.

Sow the seeds in the very early spring for spring greens or in late summer for fall use. Gardeners in the Deep South grow the plant through the winter.

Like other crucifers, mustard does best on fertile, well-drained soil high in organic matter. So don't spare the manure and compost.

Sow the seeds thickly in rows 1 foot apart. Thin the plants to stand 4 to 5 inches apart as they begin to crowd the row. Make successive plantings every ten days for plenty of greens. Plan additional plantings for a fall crop, since you'll soon run out of time for plantings to mature before the summer heat.

The leaves of mustard cultivars range from very curled to nearly smooth. 'Southern Giant Curled' is a popular bolt- resistant, curly-leaved cultivar. 'Slobolt' has smooth leaves and resists bolting well. 'Green Wave' and 'Florida Broadleaf' are other popular cultivars.

Begin harvesting your greens about forty to fifty days after sowing by cutting the entire plant at the soil line or by snapping off the outer leaves as you would those of kale. Cool them immediately, and store them as you would spinach.

What's Wrong?

Why do all my mustard plants go to seed very early and quickly? I hardly get any greens.

If this is happening in your spring planting, you're probably running out of cool weather too soon. Try fall plantings for a better crop.

Why is my mustard so strongly flavored?

The weather may be too hot.

Spinach

This green, native to central Asia, was first cultivated by the Arabs, who introduced it into north Africa. From its homeland, the plant also spread into China, where it was being cultivated by the seventh and eighth century. The Moors carried the plant from north Africa into Spain around 1000 A.D. and from there it spread into the rest of Europe by the fourteenth century, though it was not widely grown in northern Europe until the eighteenth century. Its use as an edible plant suitable for fast days was first recorded by monks in 1351. It was a common garden plant in the United States by 1800.

Spinach is another cool-season crop that withstands light freezes to 20 degrees F., though it makes its best growth at between 60 and 65 degrees F. and is intolerant of temperatures above 77 degrees F. It is grown as a spring and fall crop in the North and through the winter in the South.

Spinach is one of the few vegetable crops that are very susceptible to air-pollution injury. Both ozone and sulfur dioxide will cause leaf speckling and the death of tissue along the leaf margins.

The plant forms a rosette of leaves when grown under cool conditions but will bolt quickly under the long days and high temperatures of summer. It is shallow rooted; most of its roots are within 2 inches of the soil surface.

This crop does well in almost any soil. The pH must be between 5.5 and 6.5, however. Too high, and the plants will be severely stunted; too low, and the leaves will become yellow.

Sow the seed directly in the garden in the early spring,

Flower

Spinach will bolt, or go to flower, quickly under hot, long-day conditions of summer, and its leaves will become tough and bitter.

Some spinach cultivars bolt more easily than others. Select one that has a low tendency to bolt if you live where springs are short.

CULTIVAR	TENDENCY TO BOLT
America	Low
Bloomsdale (Dark Green)	Medium
Bloomsdale (Long Standing)	Low
Bloomsdale (Winter)	Low
Bounty	Low
Chesapeake Hybrid	High
Dixie Market	Medium
Hybrid #7	High
Hybrid #424	Medium
Hybrid #612	High
Hybrid #621	High
Melody	Low
Olympia	Low
Packer	Low
Seven R Hybrid	High
Tyee Hybrid	Low
Vienna	Medium
Viking	Low
Virginia Savoy	High

spacing the rows 12 inches apart. If you want large, uniform plants, thin them to stand 4 to 5 inches apart in the row. If you care only for the greens and not the shape or size of the plants, don't bother. Instead, harvest the largest plants and let the smaller ones grow, harvesting them in turn until those that remain have enough space. Sow seeds for fall crops about six weeks before the first frost.

This crop loves high fertility, so spread manure in the fall prior to spring planting and turn under a green manure crop to boot. Broadcast some fertilizer before planting, and side-dress when the plants are a few inches high.

Keep the soil uniformly moist throughout the growing season, being sure the plants receive at least 1 inch of water a week. Use a soaker hose to avoid wetting the foliage, which would promote the growth of mildew.

Spinach comes in two types: the savoy, which has very crinkly leaves, and the smooth leaf. The savoy is the more common garden variety, grows larger, and looks nicer, but unfortunately holds the grit and is not as easily washed. 'Melody', 'Hybrid 7', 'Long Standing Bloomsdale', and 'Winter Bloomsdale' are popular cultivars. The long-standing types are slow to bolt in warm weather and so are best adapted for spring crops. The small, smooth-leaved cultivars are used mostly for commercial canning purposes because they can be washed more easily.

Begin to harvest your crop when it has developed five to six leaves, and continue until just before it bolts, cutting the entire plant at the soil line. Try not to harvest spinach early in the morning or after a rainfall or heavy dew, because the leaves will be turgid and brittle and are apt to tear and crack.

What's Wrong?

Why does my spinach flower before I can pick most of it?
Temperatures are likely getting too high. Plant your crop earlier in the spring or try a fall crop.

What causes the little tunnels in my spinach leaves?
Leaf miner maggots burrow between the upper and lower epidermises. The leaves become maggot-infested and inedible. Plant early in the spring so the leaves can be harvested before the maggots develop, or consider fall planting.

PEAS

This is an ancient crop thought to have originated in the eastern Mediterranean area and the Near East. From there it spread very early throughout Europe. The Chinese were enjoying peas by 2000 B.C., and the Egyptians, Greeks, and Romans all used them long before the birth of Christ. Europeans used both the fodder-type peas for livestock feed and the edible, shelled peas for their table. Because of their versatility and plain good taste, peas became an important crop by the eleventh century. But only dried peas were used, green peas being thought unfit to eat. Early American colonists brought the garden pea, by then called the English pea, to the New World.

The garden pea is first cousin to the bean. Unlike the bean, however, this is a hardy, cool-season crop that will not tolerate warm summers. The black-eyed pea, or cowpea, is not really a pea, but a bean.

Although young pea plants can withstand some frost, they will not grow in temperatures below 45 degrees F. and make their best growth between 55 and 65 degrees F. Plant peas as spring crops in northern gardens and in the late fall or early winter in southern gardens. Pea seeds won't germinate in temperatures less than 40 degrees F., and the flowers and pods cannot withstand frost.

There are several types of peas. All are viny annuals, but they differ in height and growth habit. The determinate types, which are the dwarf, or bush, peas, are the most popular for the garden. They generally reach heights of 18 to 30 inches and seldom require staking. The indeterminate types—climbing, telephone, or pole peas—can reach heights up to 6 feet and require support.

Within each type, there are edible-poded peas. These were developed by breeders and belong to separate botanical varieties of the pea species (*Pisum sativum* var. *macrocarpon* and *P. s.* var. *saccharatum*). They are much more fussy about their environment than shell peas, need more attention to watering, and are more susceptible to mildew.

Early cultivars begin to bloom after producing about ten leaves, and late cultivars, fifteen. Peas can be single-podded or double-podded. All of the peas our ancestors raised were single-podded—they produced one, two, or three flowers at each node, but only one of the flowers produced a pod. Some newer cultivars are double-podded; two flowers set pods, and the plants produce twice as many peas.

Peas need well-drained soil high in organic matter. Turn under manure six months before planting and a green manure crop a few weeks before planting. Broadcast fertilizer before you plant. You may want to side-dress lightly once the crop is up and going, but don't overdo it; peas are sensitive to salts.

Plant the seeds 1 or 2 inches apart in rows 16 inches apart. Some gardeners plant in double rows 3 to 4 inches apart, with 2 to 3 feet between the double rows. The idea is that the vines will give each other mutual support. That never happened in my garden, however—both sets fell down.

Pea plants have many feeder roots near the soil's surface, as well as taproots that may extend to depths of 3 to 4 feet. The roots contain small nodules that hold *Rhizobium* bacteria, which fix atmospheric nitrogen into a form useful to the plant. So before planting, some gardeners treat their seeds with a *Rhizobium* inoculant (vetch group IV). They claim that this is important, especially if the ground was not planted to peas within the last five years. Some scientists don't believe it's that important, and it's difficult to show a real increase in yields from inoculated seeds. But the inoculant is inexpensive, and if it makes you feel good to inoculate, then by all means do it. It can't hurt anything. Sprinkle a bit of water onto the seeds to dampen them, then put them and the inoculant into a paper bag and shake until the seeds are covered with the dust.

Lodging, or falling over, reduces yields and can increase the amount of bird damage to the peas. Pole peas must be staked or trellised, and it's a good idea to get the stakes into the ground at planting. Seven-foot poles set firmly into the ground several feet apart along the row will serve as a good trellis framework. Run heavy twine between the stakes 2 feet above the ground and again 3 feet above that, then run twine between the horizontal strands in a zigzag fashion. The peas will grow up the trellis. You can also use chicken wire supported by the posts. An old, effective method is to stick birch branches into the ground along the row. Peas love to climb them. When the harvest is over, simply throw away the branches with the vines.

Most gardeners don't plant pole peas anymore. But if you want to try them, 'Alderman' is a fine cultivar. Good bush pea cultivars include 'Little Marvel', 'Sparkle', and 'Freezonian', which all do well in cool springs. 'Wando' tolerates some heat and usually is a good bet where spring runs into summer overnight. 'Olympia' is a fine new double-podded pea. 'Dwarf Gray Sugar', 'Dwarf White Sugar', 'Oregon Giant', and 'Sugar Snap' are wonderful edible-podded peas.

Peas mature their crop about fifty-seven to seventy-five days after planting. By that time, the pods should be well filled, with no hard, starchy seeds. Pods that feel hard and look crinkly are overmature. Most pea cultivars produce eight to ten seeds per pod, though the newer ones may have up to fourteen. If the weather remains cool, you can stretch the harvest over several days. In warm weather, however, the sugar in the peas turns into starch very rapidly, and the peas keep their good quality for only a day or two. Edible-podded peas lose their fine quality quickly and must be harvested within twelve to twenty-four hours of peak maturity. Seeds should be no larger than BB shot, the pods stringless, brittle, and succulent. If they get ahead of you, let them develop as you would regular pod peas, and shell them for use. Harvest peas by grasping the pods in your hand and snapping them from the stem with your thumb. Cool them to 32 degrees F. rapidly to prevent the sugar from converting to starch.

What's Wrong?

My pea vines look beautiful—strong and lush—so why do I get only a few peas?

Wait. They'll produce. If you're impatient, pinch back the tips of the stems to push them into setting pods.

The tips of the leaves of my pea plants are browning and dying, and the plants look awful. Why?

If the days are warm and dry, your peas may be drying out. Give them plenty of water. If you're into summer, pea season is over. Plant them earlier next year.

Why are my pea pods hard and a little shriveled when I pick them?

You waited too long. They are overmature.

POTATOES

Potatoes probably originated in southern Chile, then spread into northern Chile and Peru, where the Incas cultivated them. By the time Columbus sailed to America, potatoes were widely cultivated throughout South America.

In the early 1500s, potatoes were brought to Europe by Spanish explorers, who learned that eating them during long trans-Atlantic crossings prevented scurvy. Sir Walter Raleigh introduced the Irish to the potato in 1585, but it was not until the mid-1700s that it came into general cultivation in Europe; the early potatoes were watery and bland-tasting.

Slowly, gardeners and farmers in Europe improved upon the old strains and people began to appreciate the potato more. The impoverished Irish became so dependent upon them that an estimated three quarters of a million of them starved to death when their crops were destroyed by an infestation of late blight two years in a row (1845 and 1846). That blight also sparked a huge wave of Irish emigration to the United States.

The Irish, or white, potato is grown for its fleshy underground tubers. It is a cool-season crop that is moderately tolerant of frost. Growing temperature is critical and is one of the most important factors in good yields. The plant stops growing when temperatures fall below 45 degrees F. or rise above 75 degrees F. It produces the best yields at 60 to 65 degrees F. Organic mulches will cool the soil and help produce a better crop.

Stolons, or runners, arise from buds on seed pieces before the plant emerges from the ground. At first, one stolon arises from each bud. Later, more can arise. The stolons continue to grow under the long days of summer, then stop and begin to swell, forming tubers at their tips when the days shorten. This time of tuber forming, or tuberization, roughly coincides with bloom.

Potato cultivars can form tubers of many flesh colors. Though only the white-fleshed tubers are acceptable to U.S. consumers, yellow-, pink-, red-, and blue-fleshed tubers are common in other countries.

The top of the plant is upright at first, then begins to sprawl like a multibranched vine. The fruit, which is poisonous, resembles a small tomato and can contain as many as three hundred seeds. But don't bother to save the seeds, since they are genetically unstable and will produce many off types of potato plants. In other words, if you plant the seeds of 'Katahdin', you will get many plants, but none will be 'Katahdin', and most, if not all, will be inferior to the parent.

Potatoes are very sensitive to poor soil aeration and drainage. Roots will not grow in compacted soil. Therefore, don't plant so early that the soil is too wet. Be sure your soil is in good condition, with plenty of compost and green manure crops turned under. The tubers will develop a lighter skin color and better shape in light soils.

Potato tubers are susceptible to scab, caused by a fungus. Fortunately, the fungus doesn't grow well in acid soil, and keeping your potato soil down to a pH of about 4.8 to 5.4 will reduce the chances of raising a scabby crop.

Before planting, cut seed potatoes into 2-ounce pieces about the size of a silver dollar, each having at least one eye.

Purchase your seed potatoes from a reputable company. Potato tubers can carry many diseases, so be sure they are certified seed. If the seed tubers are large, cut them into several blocky, 2-ounce pieces, each about the size of a silver dollar. Be sure each piece has at least one eye. Larger pieces might produce slightly more vigorous plants, but there isn't much difference among them, so long as none have sprouted before planting. The plant will live for its first month on food it gets from the seed piece, so it's important to start with large, healthy pieces. If you have bought small seed potatoes, you can plant the entire tuber.

Some gardeners hold the cut seed pieces at 60 degrees F. for about a week before planting to allow them to cure, or heal, making them less apt to rot when planted. Removing them from cold storage and planting them immediately can cause them to sweat and rot in the soil.

Plant the pieces after the danger of hard frost has passed—several weeks before the last frost is expected—and the soil temperature has warmed to about 45 degrees F. Where summer temperatures are high, plant them so that they will mature in the cool of the fall. Space the pieces 5 inches deep and 8 to 12 inches apart in rows 3 to 4 feet apart.

An old-fashioned way of growing spuds is to set the seed pieces in a wide, 3-inch-deep trench. As the stems grow, build up a mound of pine needles or straw gradually. Never bury the tips of the shoots. Tubers will form in the mulch at ground level. To harvest, simply pull back the mulch and gather the potatoes.

These plants have small root systems and require high fertility. Turn under rotted manure and a cover crop, and apply all the fertilizer before planting. Never apply fresh manure to potatoes, since it may increase the incidence of scab. Side-dressing does little good with potatoes, unless you have very sandy soil. If that's the case, side-dress about a month after planting.

Keep the weeds out of potatoes, but do not cultivate more than 2 inches deep. In the middle of the season, when weeds are well under control, hill the plants by mounding soil over their bases. Don't wait too long to do this, since the potato roots will have spread between the rows, and hoeing the soil from that area for hilling will injure them. By hilling, you'll be sure that the tubers are covered with soil and not exposed to sunlight, which will cause them to turn green and bitter.

Always provide at least 1½ to 2 inches of water a week. This cools the soil and supplies water to the growing tubers. A dry spell for a couple of weeks will substantially reduce yields, though excessive water after the tubers have formed can cause them to rot. There are many physiological disorders that affect this crop, and most of them are caused by uneven or inadequate moisture supplies.

For northern gardens, early cultivars include 'Irish Cobbler', 'Norland', and 'Superior's, and late cultivars are 'Katahdin', 'Kennebec, and 'Russet Burbank'. Midwestern gardeners prefer 'Pontiac' and 'Red LaSoda' for an early crop, and 'Katahdin' and 'Russet Burbank' for a late crop. 'Russet Burbank' and 'Kennebec' are popular in the Pacific Northwest. 'Irish Cobbler', 'Red Pontiac', and 'Red LaSoda' are prized in southern gardens.

Several disorders can affect your potato crop. Internal black spot is the result of a bruised seed piece in combination with excessive water and nitrogen. The tissue just beneath the skin of the tuber turns black, and the potato loses a lot of eye appeal.

Hollow heart is the formation of a cavity near the center of the tuber. It's caused by uneven growth as a result of uneven moisture supply.

Tuber greening occurs when the tuber is exposed to light. Because the tuber is a stem, not a root, it can manufacture chlorophyll when it is exposed to light. Though the chlorophyll won't hurt you, another compound, the alkaloid solanine, builds up along with the chlorophyll, and it *can* hurt you. Solanine is bitter tasting and can give you a bad stomachache if eaten in large quantities. Most of the chlorophyll and solanine are located near the surface of the tuber and can be removed by peeling. But if you just take the time to hill the crop, you can avoid this problem.

Dig your potatoes before a hard freeze, but about two weeks after the vines have been killed by the first frosts, as tubers dug from living vines will skin and bruise easily. Put the dug tubers into storage immediately without exposing them to much sunlight, or tuber greening will occur. To store them properly, hold them at 50 to 60 degrees F. for about a week to allow them to cure and for digging wounds to heal. Then lower the temperature to about 40 degrees F., where they will keep for up to six months. Though they will not sprout if held at 40 degrees F., lower temperatures will cause their starch to turn into sugar and they will taste sweet. That's good, as long as you are baking and not frying them; frying will cause some of the sugar to caramelize, and the chips or fries will turn dark brown.

What's Wrong?

My potatoes stick out of the ground and the upper sides turn green. What can I do?

Next year, hill them to protect the tubers from sunlight. Green potatoes contain a toxic compound.

Why should I cut my seed potato pieces?

The tuber is a stem. As on all stems, the topmost bud will suppress the growth of all the other ones; this is known as apical dominance. Cutting the tuber into pieces will remove the apical bud and its dominance, and all the buds will sprout.

My potatoes turned sweet in storage. What happened?

The storage temperature was too low and the starch turned to sugar. Keep them for about ten days at temperatures above 55 degrees F. and the sweetness will disappear.

Why are my leaves brown and rotten?

This could mean blight, which begins as a purplish spot on the leaves. If the plants lose their leaves, your crop will suffer badly. Use the proper fungicide for protection next time.

ROOT CROPS

All root crops do best in deep, friable soil and cool seasons. Most are grown as spring and fall crops in northern gardens and through the winter in southern gardens. All are sown directly in the garden, although beets can be transplanted for an extra-early crop. They are all hardy and can be planted very early in the spring or left in the ground until early winter.

Beets

Garden beets are related to Swiss chard and spinach. Europeans call them *beetroot.*

Pliny recommended that garlic-lovers eat a roasted beet to sweeten their breath and Greeks began to revere the red root, offering them in silver bowls to the god Apollo. Galen tells us that beets were used as medicine in the second century A.D., and we know they were eaten as food by the third century. Roman gardeners of this time developed both red- and white-rooted types for the table, while others developed beets for their edible tops. Barbarian invaders carried large-rooted beets into northern Europe, where they were first grown for cattle feed. By 1558, beets were widely grown throughout Europe, where they had become segregated by color; those with red roots were used for the table and those with white roots for stock feed. Beets were being grown in the United States by 1800.

Beets are a fairly hardy crop and do best in the cool climate of spring and fall in the North and in spring, fall, and winter in the South. Though they will tolerate warm weather better than other cool-season crops, plants that mature in the heat of summer will develop poor-quality roots. They make their best growth at 50 to 65 degrees F.

The beet is a biennial, forming a tuft of leaves, or rosette, and an enlarged taproot the first year and a flower stalk the second. Sudden drastic changes in the weather or low temperatures (40 to 50 degrees F.) for more than a couple of weeks while seedlings are small will cause the plants to bolt. Prolonged high temperatures result in zoning and low sugar content in the roots. Zoning is the undesirable development of alternating light and colored bands in the flesh of the root. Beet roots also develop poor color if heavy rains follow a dry period during which you did not water.

Deep, friable loams produce the best beets; heavy soils will produce asymmetrical roots. Germination is best when soil temperatures are between 65 and 75 degrees F., though beet seeds will germinate in temperatures as low as 40 and as high as 80 degrees F.

Though you sow directly in the garden, you are not actually planting beet seeds directly. The knobby, shriveled things in the seed packet are really the dried fruits, each containing several tiny seeds. Because the seeds are planted this way, seedlings emerge over a long period of time in clumps. Since the seeds are so small, the seedlings are weak and cannot tolerate soil crusting. A bit of radish seed mixed with your beet seeds will mark the rows and help break soil crusts.

Plant the seeds in rows 18 inches apart, and thin the plants when the roots are large enough to eat. The tops make tasty greens. Beets remaining in the row after thinning should stand 3 to 4 inches apart.

To keep your supply of beets coming, make successive sowings about three weeks apart through the spring and again in late summer for a fall crop.

Beets must make rapid growth to develop the best quality. They respond well to organic matter, so apply well-rotted manure in addition to preplant fertilizer, and side-dress about four to six weeks after planting. Take care not to apply too much nitrogen, however; that will force excessive top growth, and the roots will develop poor color.

Beets are sensitive to strongly acid soils, which will cause their leaves to look ragged. Old gardeners used them as indicator plants to see if their soil pH was right. Have your soil tested for boron too, since beets are sensitive to low levels of this nutrient. Beets are attacked by few pests, but boron deficiency will show up as internal black spot. Corky black spots appear in the flesh of the root, and the young leaves resemble straps and sometimes turn deep red. Boron deficiency is more likely to occur under droughty conditions and on soils that are neutral or alkaline, so don't add too much wood ash.

The most popular beets have globe-shaped roots. These include 'Early Wonder', 'Ruby Queen', 'Red Ace', and 'Detroit Dark Red'. Cultivars with long, cylindrical roots are popular in Europe. Try 'Long Dark Blood' or 'Formanova' for something different.

Lately, odd-colored beets have become popular in the home garden. Grow them as you would regular beets, but be prepared for a splash of color. 'Chioggia' is a pretty beet, with scarlet skin and white and pink zoning. 'Burpee's Golden Beet' is a bright golden-yellow. 'Albino White' has white roots. 'Winter Keeper' is a large-rooted, long-season cultivar (eighty days) that remains tender and keeps its sugar over a long period of time.

Beets in prime condition have a high sugar content, dark color, and little zoning. Pull them when they've reached about 1¼ to 1½ inches in diameter, and store them just above freezing. They'll keep longer if you remove the tops, but leave about 1 inch of the stem attached to the root to prevent them from shriveling and bleeding.

What's Wrong?

Why are my beets tough and woody?

Any slowdown in growth will cause this. Often, planting too thickly and not thinning properly are the reasons, since the increased competition among plants for water and nutrients checks their growth. Very hot weather will also cause the roots to become woody.

The leaves on my beets are ragged and don't look healthy. Is this caused by an insect?

No. It's probably caused by a soil pH that is too low. Old-time gardeners used beets to see if the soil needed lime. If the tops looked ragged, the soil pH was probably too low.

Why have my beets bolted?

Early sowings, where plants have been exposed to temperatures below 40 degrees F. for several weeks, sometimes do this. Beets are biennials, and they can get fooled into thinking they just went through a winter. Use the leaves in salads and resow.

Why are my leaves small and pale?

Check your soil pH. You might need lime. If the pH is okay, side-dress with superphosphate. Pay attention to soil phosphorus next year.

Why do my beet roots have black, pitted areas?

Beets need plenty of boron. When they don't get enough, they develop corky black spots. Have the soil tested for boron next year. In the meantime, mix ¼ teaspoon of regular borax with 12 gallons of water and sprinkle the soil where you're going to plant your second crop of beets. Don't use too much boron, or you'll sterilize the soil.

Carrots

Carrots as we know them, the yellow gold of the garden, are native to Europe, Asia, and northern Africa, where they have been grown for thousands of years. The earliest carrot roots ranged in color from purple to almost black. The yellow-orange color arose as a mutant of these dark strains.

The ancient Greeks knew the wild carrot as a medicinal herb but did not cultivate it. Galen, a second-century A.D. Greek physician, was the first to mention that carrots were cultivated in gardens at that time. These were both the purple and yellow-rooted strains. By the third century A.D., cultivation of this plant had spread from France and Italy to other parts of Europe, where it became a staple food by the thirteenth century. It was brought to China around A.D. 1300 and was widely grown there. It crossed the Atlantic into the New World by 1565 and was grown in Virginia by 1609 and in Massachusetts by 1629. By this time, the purple-rooted cultivars were being discarded in favor of the yellow-rooted ones.

Carrots are herbaceous biennials grown as annuals for their enlarged taproots, which can reach diameters of 1 to 2½ inches and lengths of 2½ to 36 inches, depending on cultivar and conditions.

The carrot grows best at temperatures between 60 and 65 degrees F. Above 82 degrees F., top growth is stunted and the roots develop a very strong flavor. Below 60 degrees F., the roots become long and tapered and develop poor color, and they grow very little below 50 degrees F.

Carrots can be white, yellow, orange, red, purple, or purplish black, but orange is the most popular. Red-rooted carrots will bolt when exposed to the long days of summer, as will carrots of any color that are at least ¼ inch in diameter and have been exposed to temperatures below 50 degrees F. for several weeks. This situation is unlikely to occur in the home garden, however.

The shape and color of carrot roots depend on temperature, age, and genetics. Young carrots are usually lighter in color than more mature carrots. Carrots develop their best color at temperatures between 60 and 70 degrees F. and the longest roots between 50 and 60 degrees F. The higher the temperature, the shorter the roots. Droughty conditions will also produce longer roots.

Light soils produce the earliest crops, and soil that is free of clods and stones will produce the best roots. In compacted soils, the roots will be

Carrots come in different sizes and shapes. Select cultivars of the best type for your garden. (A) Hutchinson, (B) Danvers, (C) Nantes, (D) Imperator, (E) Chantenay

short and conical instead of long and tapered. Heavy soils may crust, and this will decrease your stand, since carrot seeds require a long time to germinate and seedlings are weak. Because of this trait, mix radish seeds with those of your carrots when you plant. These will germinate rapidly, marking the rows and breaking the soil crust. Cultivate to destroy weeds before they become established and to break any soil crust that might form.

Plant the seeds thinly in 3- to 4-inch-wide rows, spaced 18 inches apart. You really don't have to thin the plants. Though thinning might give you bigger, better-shaped roots, it will also give you fewer useful roots. If you are entering carrots into the fair, then by all means thin. If not, don't bother.

Carrot growth must be rapid and uninterrupted for the highest quality. Apply preplant fertilizer, and side-dress when the plants are four to five weeks old. Rotted maure is fine, but never apply fresh manure, which would cause the carrots to have forked roots.

Carrots need plenty of water: 1 to 1¹/₂ inches a week. If the weather is hot and dry and you don't water, the roots will become strong and pungent in flavor. But don't overwater, as that can result in poor color development.

There are a few different types of carrots, classified by shape. Nantes-type cultivars produce roots that are cylindrical and medium long; Imperator-type, long and slightly tapering; and Chantenay-type, short and shaped nearly like a toy top. The Chantenay are useful for growing on heavy or shallow soils. 'Long Nantes', 'Napoli', and 'Pioneer' are some popular cultivars.

Pull carrots when the roots are 1 to $1\frac{1}{2}$ inches in diameter at the top, about sixty to eighty-five days after planting.

The upper part of the carrot root is made up of stem tissue, so it will green up if exposed to sunlight. Though this won't hurt you, it does detract a bit from the vegetable's visual appeal. To prevent this, mound the soil up over the root crowns a couple of weeks before harvest to block out the sunlight.

Remove the carrot tops before storing; they will pull water and nutrients out of the roots and lead to rapid deterioration.

What's Wrong?

My carrots have poor germination and stands. Why?

Carrot seeds are small, and the soil may have crusted or the seeds may have dried out before germinating. Place a board or sheet of plastic over the row right after sowing, and remove it when the seedlings appear. Or plant a nurse crop along with the carrot seeds to break the soil crust.

Why are my carrots twisted and forked?

The twisting is probably from overcrowding. Thinning them will reduce this. Forked roots could be caused by a number of things, but most commonly by stony soil. Remove as many stones as possible before planting. If your carrot roots are stubby or grew vertically for a while and then ran horizontally, you have a hardpan. Before you plant your next crop, spade deeply.

Why are the tops of my carrot roots green?

The top of the carrot root is actually made of stem tissue. Like all stems, it can turn green when exposed to sunlight. This is not harmful, but you can prevent it by mounding the soil just enough to cover the tops of the roots.

Parsnips

Another native of Europe and Asia, these plants were relished by the ancient Greeks and Romans. Pliny wrote of their medicinal virtues and the Roman emperor Tiberius is said to have liked them so much that he had them imported fresh from Germany. But these ancient parsnips did not have the characteristic large, white, fleshy root, which began to develop during the Middle Ages, when the roots were eaten by the English during Lent.

The plant was cultivated in Virginia in 1609 and in Massachusetts by 1629.

Parsnips require a long season, up to 130 days, to mature their roots. They are not as heat-tolerant as carrots and grow best where summers are cool, making the most growth when temperatures are between 60 and 65 degrees F.

This crop requires a deep, rich soil that is free from hardpan and stones. Shallow soils will cause the roots to crook, and heavy soils, where the surface crusts before germination, will produce you a poor stand and roughened roots.

Prepare a fine seedbed as you would for beets, and plant in the early spring as soon as you can work the ground. Make the rows 18 inches apart, and thin the plants to stand 2 to 4 inches apart in the row after they become well established (five to six weeks). Do not overthin. If the plants are too far apart, they'll grow too large and will quickly become woody and fibrous; if left close together, the roots will be small but tender.

Parsnip seeds take a very long time to germinate, and you'll usually have to cultivate the weeds out before the parsnips even begin to show. Parsnip seedlings are very delicate and cannot compete with weeds or soil crusting. Plant radish seeds with your parsnip seeds to mark the rows and break the soil crust, or cover the seeds with peat moss, vermiculite, sand, or a board to keep the soil from crusting over them. Begin cultivation as soon as weeds emerge or the soil crusts, and continue until the plants become large enough to shade the area between the rows. Fertilize parsnips as you would beets and carrots.

The standard cultivars are 'Hollow Crown', 'Model', and 'All American'.

Starch in the parsnip root is converted into sugar when temperatures fall below about 37 degrees F. This is when they're at their best. Dig the roots after several hard frosts, and store them in a root cellar. (Because the roots are very long, you can't pull them.) Alternatively, you can leave them in the garden, mulched with leaves, and dig them through the winter into early spring. Dig them before the tops resume growth in the spring, since growing tops will use the stored sugar, and the roots will shrivel and lose their flavor.

There is absolutely no truth to the old belief that parsnip roots, in any form, are poisonous.

Radishes

The Greeks loved radishes and made small golden replicas of the roots. When they made oblations to Apollo, they placed the beloved roots in golden bowls. Radishes were brought to China around 500 B.C., where new elongated and mild forms were developed. The roots reached England in 1548, and, by 1597, were widely enjoyed, raw on bread or stewed into a tangy sauce for meat.

Radishes are a cool-weather crop that will not tolerate summer heat. They are grown as a spring or fall crop in the North or a spring, fall, or winter crop in the South.

Any check in growth, as might be caused by hot weather, will cause the roots to become pithy and pungent. Warm weather may also cause the plants to bolt.

The familiar spring, or salad, radish matures in three to six weeks; the winter radish, in forty-five to seventy days.

Light soils favor early planting and maturity of the spring crop; heavier soils are best for summer radishes. Stony soils will cause the roots to become misshapen, and overcrowding will cause poor root development. In fact, if the radishes are crowded, you may wind up with all tops and no swollen roots.

Plant your radishes in rows 16 inches apart. Thin salad radishes to stand twelve to eighteen plants per foot of row, and winter radishes two to four plants per foot of row. Because they germinate quickly, you can mix radish seeds with those of parsnips or carrots to mark the rows so that you can begin cultivation even before those crops come up. Radishes also make a good intercrop for beans, cabbage, or squash, because they will be harvested before the other crops need the space.

Radishes mature so rapidly that you'll have no time to side-dress.

Broadcast fertilizer before you plant, and hope that it doesn't all wash away in a spring downpour before your radishes are mature.

Spring radishes are the most popular. The little, globe-shaped, red roots are attractive in salads and garnishes. Try 'Cherry Bell', 'Sparkler', and 'Early Scarlet Globe'. 'French Breakfast' is olive shaped and 'White Icicle' long rooted.

Late-summer radishes are not widely grown in the United States, but you can try some in your garden. They take slightly longer to mature than the spring cultivars. 'White Vienna' and 'Stuttgart' are good long-rooted cultivars, and 'Golden Globe' is a fine round one.

Winter radishes generally take about twice as long to mature as spring cultivars and are grown for a fall crop. Some are mild, some are pungent; some have black roots, some white. Try 'White Chinese' (also called 'Celestial'), 'China White', and 'Sakurajima'. The last one can grow to weigh 50 pounds or more.

Pull your radishes as soon as they reach 1 to 1 1/2 inches in diameter. If you leave them in the ground too long, they'll get strong and pithy, particularly if the weather is hot. Summer cultivars remain edible longer than spring cultivars, and winter cultivars even longer. You can store spring and summer radishes in the refrigerator for a few weeks, but treat your winter radishes as you would turnips: Put them in a root cellar, where they'll keep for several months.

What's Wrong?

Why do my radishes produce all tops and few good roots?

You may have planted the seeds too late in the spring or too thickly. Plant earlier next season, and thin the plants to stand at least 1 inch apart in the row.

Why are my radishes very pungent?

If you do not water and your soil dries, growth is checked and the roots get very strong. Water thoroughly and consistently.

Why are my radish roots wormy?

You probably have an infestation of cabbage root maggot. Turn the plants under, and treat the soil with an insecticide before planting next time.

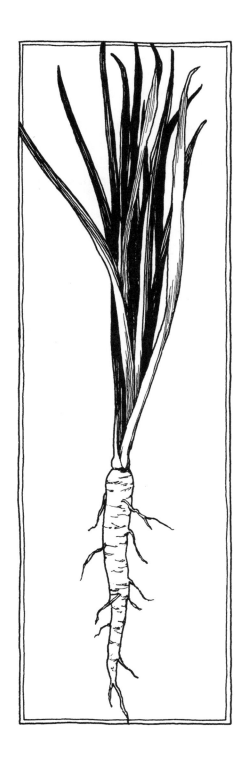

Salsify

Salsify, also called *oyster root*, is a worthy but relatively unknown member of the sunflower family. This plant deserves to be better known. The sweet roots have an unusual, delicate, pleasant flavor reminiscent of oysters and are a prime ingredient of mock oyster stew. Although the wild plant was eaten by Albertus Magnus in the thirteenth century, salsify was not cultivated as a garden plant until about 1600. It was grown in France in 1612 and was brought to America in the late 1700s; Thomas Jefferson grew it in his garden. It remains obscure today.

The crop requires a long growing season of about 110 to 150 days; grow it as you would parsnips.

Sow the seeds very early in the spring in rows 12 inches apart. Thin the plants to stand 2 inches apart in the rows. Broadcast fertilizer before you plant, and side-dress when you thin the crop.

Supply at least 1 inch of

Salsify is a long, slender root vegetable with a flavor reminiscent of oysters.

water a week, and try to keep the plants growing vigorously. Any check in growth can cause the roots to become woody.

Only one cultivar, 'Mammoth Sandwich Island', is commonly available to American gardeners.

As you would with parsnips, dig the roots late in the fall or mulch them and dig them right into the winter. They become sweeter after exposure to cold, so delay digging until several hard frosts have occurred. The roots will be about 12 inches long and 1 to 2 inches in diameter. Store them in a root cellar.

Scorzonera

Also called *black salsify*, scorzonera is native to central and southern Europe. It came into cultivation relatively late, being considered a new plant in the kitchen garden in 1600, though it was used as a remedy for snakebite in Spain around 1550. Its culture had spread into French, Belgian, and English gardens by the end of the sixteenth century, but it was not introduced into American gardens until around 1800. Despite its popularity in Europe, it never caught on in America.

Scorzonera is grown for its long, black roots, which must be soaked in water to remove their bitterness, then boiled before being eaten. Grow, har-

Scorzonera is a black-rooted relative of salsify that is nearly unknown in this country.

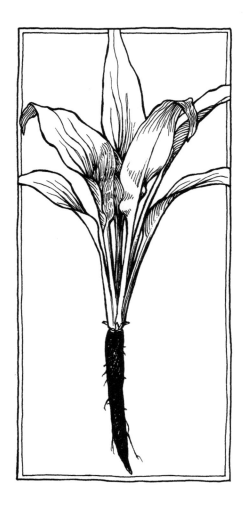

vest, and store it as you would salsify, but allow a bit more room for this larger plant.

Turnips and Rutabagas

The turnip and the rutabaga are closely related plants native to northern Asia, the Near East, and Afghanistan. The turnip grows wild in Siberia and has been used as food since prehistoric times. It was first cultivated around 2000 B.C. in the Near East. The Romans grew it for the enlarged root and for the leaves, which they cooked as greens. It was widely grown in France in the Middle Ages, and by 1540, the French explorer Jacques Cartier had planted the first turnips in Canada.

The rutabaga was developed in Europe by an accidental crossing of kale and turnip during the Middle Ages. Also called the winter turnip or the Swede turnip, it found its way into American gardens around 1800.

Turnips and rutabagas have similar cultural requirements and are both grown for their enlarged fleshy root. Both have cultivars with white and yellow flesh, although typically you find the rutabaga with yellow flesh and the turnip with white. The similarities stop here. The turnip is a smaller plant, with a smaller root that may be round, elongated, or conical, and slightly flattened. The root has no neck and is usually white to tan, with purple near the top. The leaves are hairy, rough, thin, and green. The rutabaga has a larger, round root with a thick, leafy neck and smooth, fleshy, blue-green leaves. The root is usually tan to yellow.

Both turnips and rutabagas tolerate low temperatures and do poorly when temperatures get too warm. Turnips get bitter and pithy in hot weather. On the other hand, prolonged exposure of young rutabaga plants to temperatures of 50 to 55 degrees F. will cause them to bolt before harvest.

Since both are cool-season crops, you must time the planting so that the roots will mature during cool weather. Turnips, which need about sixty days to mature, are grown as a spring or fall crop in the North. The fall crop usually has better flavor. Rutabagas, which require from eighty-five to ninety-five days to mature, are better grown as a fall crop in the North. Southern gardeners can grow either plant as a fall, winter, or early-spring crop.

Both are sown directly in the garden. Plant turnips in rows 18 inches apart, and thin them to stand 2 to 6 inches apart in the row. Rutabagas need a little more space; plant them in rows 30 inches apart, and thin them to stand 4 to 8 inches apart in the row.

Fairly high fertility is necessary to push the spring planting to maturity before warm weather. Broadcast fertilizer before planting, and side-dress the plants when you thin them. High fertility is not so important for the fall crop; there is no rush to mature the plants, since the weather is getting cooler.

Both crops are sensitive to boron deficiency, and you may have to add some to get a good crop. Have your soil boron levels tested, and watch for brown heart (water core or raan), characterized by the browning and breakdown of flesh at the center of the root. It usually shows up in August when the plants are growing rapidly. It is caused by a boron deficiency and can be corrected by adding borax to the soil. Excessive levels of boron will sterilize your soil, however; always follow the recommendations of the testing agency before applying boron.

Turnip cultivars grown primarily for their roots include 'Early Purple Top Strap Leaf' and 'Purple Top White Globe'. Those grown for their leaves are 'Shogoin', 'Seven Top', and 'Just Right'. Some fine rutabaga cultivars include 'American Purple Top', 'Laurentian', and 'Purple Top Yellow'.

Both crops taste best when the roots are medium-size and mature in cool weather. Pull your turnips when they are 2 to 3 inches in diameter, and harvest the entire crop before the weather gets too hot. If you're growing turnips for the greens, harvest them about four to six weeks after planting. Pull rutabagas when their roots reach 3 to 5 inches in diameter. In moderate climates, you can mulch your fall crop heavily and pull them through the winter.

SALAD CROPS
Salad crops supply fiber, bulk, vitamins, and minerals, and are an important part of our diet. They thrive in spring and fall in northern gardens and through the winter in the South. They must make rapid and continuous growth to attain highest quality.

Lettuce
Lettuce is a native of the Mediterranean area and Asia Minor, and was cultivated for food by the Egyptians at least seven thousand years ago.

The Greek historian Herodotus mentions this vegetable being served to Persian kings in the sixth century B.C.. Common lettuce found its way into Roman gardens, where a dozen cultivars were grown. These spread slowly throughout the empire. Romaine was a popular type. Augustus Caesar had a monument erected to lettuce because he thought its use had helped him recover from illness. By the fifth century, lettuce had spread to China, and it was brought to the New World by Columbus on his second voyage. Both head and leaf types have been popular among American gardeners since the eighteenth century.

Common garden lettuce is well known to every gardener and comes in head and leaf varieties. A less common type, stem lettuce, is grown not for its leaves but for its stems. Because it reminds some gardeners of asparagus or celery, it is also called *asparagus lettuce* or *celtuce*. It's very popular in the Far East but is relatively rare in American gardens.

All lettuce requires warm days (66 to 73 degrees F.) and cool nights (45 to 52 degrees F.) to make the best growth. Above 75 degrees F., head lettuce will become soft, and above 85 degrees F., all lettuce will become bitter and bolt. The crop will withstand light freezes, below 45 degrees F., but all growth will be extremely slow. Well-hardened seedlings can tolerate temperatures as low as 22 degrees F. with little damage, but the ability of lettuce to withstand cold temperatures decreases with age. The higher the temperatures, up to about 75 degrees F., the faster heads develop. Above that, however, quality will suffer.

Lettuce is a cool-season biennial grown as an annual. Growth begins slowly but then speeds rapidly. The plant makes 75 percent of its growth in the three weeks preceding maturity. The heads form from the inside out.

Lettuce often bolts before you can pick it all. This is because exposure to warm temperatures or long days—typical summer conditions—makes this biennial think it is in its second season, and it produces a seed stalk. Lettuce is a spring or fall crop. Don't try to grow it during the summer.

Lettuce seeds will germinate when soil temperatures are between 35 and 86 degrees F., but it's best to wait until the soil has warmed to 50 or 60 degrees F. Direct seed in rows 18 inches apart. Thin plants of head lettuce to stand 10 inches apart and those of other types to stand 4 inches apart in the row. Spacing affects the size of the lettuce heads, so give them adequate space. As you thin, transplant the seedlings to other areas of the garden, and you'll get more than enough lettuce from a packet of seeds.

Lettuce transplants easily, and you can reduce the time it takes to mature by two to three weeks by doing so. This is particularly important with head lettuce, because it requires a longer season than the other types.

Lettuce needs to make rapid growth to have the best quality. Because of this, and because of its small root system, lettuce has a fairly high fertilizer requirement, although it removes only a small amount of nutrients from the soil. Apply preplant fertilizer, and side-dress when you thin the plants. Since you want succulent leaves, give your lettuce plenty of nitrogen.

Because of its need for rapid growth, lettuce also requires a constant supply of water, although excessive amounts during high temperatures late in the season will cause head lettuce to become loose and puffy. Provide 1 inch of water a week before heading begins, and increase this a bit afterward.

There are four types of lettuce commonly grown in American gardens: looseleaf (bunching), crisphead (iceberg), butterhead (Boston, bibb), and cos (romaine).

Looseleaf is a short-season lettuce that is the easiest to grow, and it's the one most often found in American gardens. 'Black-seeded Simpson', 'Oakleaf', and 'Salad Bowl' are popular cultivars.

Crisphead, or iceberg, lettuce is the most popular in markets, but it's the most difficult to grow because of its longer season and extreme sensitivity to heat. 'Ithaca', 'Bounty', and 'Empire' are good cultivars.

Butterhead is a semiheading type of lettuce that forms loose heads with a delicate flavor. Try 'Bibb', 'Buttercrunch', or 'Summer Bibb'.

Cos lettuce forms a long, narrow, upright plant that is more tolerant of bad weather than either crisphead or butterhead. 'Parris Island' and 'Dark Green Cos' have very fine flavor.

Lettuce suffers from a couple of disorders caused by poor environmental conditions. These are not pathogenic, so don't try to control them with pesticides.

Tip burn is characterized by brown spots along the outer margins of the leaves and is more common in hot weather. The calcium content of affected tissue is low. Anything that slows the growth of the plant will reduce the problem, so it appears that tip burn occurs when the plant grows so rapidly that it cannot supply itself with enough calcium. Crisphead cultivars seem to be more tolerant to tip burn than others.

Bolting is usually the result of exposure to long days and temperatures above 85 degrees F. Extreme environmental stress, such as drought, can also cause lettuce to bolt.

Looseleaf lettuce is ready for harvest about 40 to 50 days after seeding; butterhead and cos, 55 to 70; crisphead, 70 to 120. Cut the plants at the soil line, and cool them to 32 degrees F. as rapidly as possible. Leaf varieties can also be harvested by simply removing the outer leaves and allowing the rest of the plant to continue growing.

Brown spots sometimes develop on the lower midrib of the leaves while the lettuce is in the refrigerator. This is called *russet spotting*, and it's caused by the plant's reaction to ethylene, a ripening gas given off by many fruits and vegetables. Apples are big emitters, so keep lettuce away from other fruits and vegetables as much as possible.

What's Wrong?

My lettuce gets too bitter to eat. Is this from planting it next to cucumbers?

No. It's probably from temperatures too high for the plant. Plant your lettuce earlier next year.

My lettuce begins to flower before we can harvest it all. What can I do?

Again, this is due to high temperatures, and there is nothing you can do but plant earlier next year.

Sometimes my head lettuce does not form heads. Why?

You probably didn't thin your plants enough. Give them more room, and they'll produce heads.

Why is my lettuce stand so spotty?

You may have planted the small seeds too deep. Cover them very lightly.

Why do the heads on my head lettuce rot?

It's probably too warm and humid in your area. Lettuce needs to mature in cool temperatures.

Endive is a loose-headed let-tucelike plant with decorative, frilly leaves.

Endive and Escarole

Endive is a loose-headed, let-tucelike plant with curled, frilly leaves; escarole is a broad-leaved type of endive with slightly bitter outer leaves. Both can be used in salads or as cooked greens.

These are cool-season plants that are grown as annuals. They with-stand moderate freezes and cool weather better than lettuce, and many gardeners in temperate regions leave them in the garden until Christmas.

Endive and escarole must make rapid, unchecked growth for best quality. They grow best between 60 and 75 degrees F. and, like lettuce, will bolt under long days and higher temperatures.

Sow endive and escarole seeds in the garden in rows 18 inches apart. Thin the plants to stand 10 inches apart in the row. You can also use transplants to get a jump on the season. Both plants are often grown as fall crops because they have a fairly long maturity season and can tolerate cold but not heat.

The plants will take on yellow-white color and a milder flavor if blanched just before harvest. Do this by crowding them in the row, by tying the outer leaves over the head as you would cauliflower, or by plac-ing tarpaper or boards over the plants for a week or two.

There are not many cultivars of endive on the market. 'Green Curled' and 'Salad King' are two that do well. 'Florida Deep Heart', 'Broad Leaved Batavian', and 'Full Heart Batavian' are excellent cultivars of escarole. Some red cultivars are beginning to appear in seed catalogs.

You can begin harvesting these plants about eighty to one hundred days after planting, when the heads are well developed. Cut the entire plant at the soil line. Remove damaged leaves and the outer leaves, which are often tough and bitter. Store as you would lettuce.

Chicory

Chicory is related to endive and is sometimes called *French endive, Belgium endive, witloof,* or *succory.* It's native to the Mediterranean area and popular in Europe, where it's grown for both tops and roots. The earliest mention of its being grown is in Germany in 1616. From there its culture spread throughout Europe and into the New World, where the leaves were used in salads and as cooked greens, and the roots roasted, ground, and used for a coffee substitute or coffee additive. In the mid-eighteenth century, Flemish gardeners discovered that the roots could be forced in the off-season to produce a top called a chicon that is very popular in European house-

holds—hence the name Belgian endive. Its distinctive flavor is similar to that of endive, and like endive, chicory will bolt

Chicory adds a continental flavor to your garden. After you harvest the leaves, dig and store the roots near freezing for several weeks, then force them in the dark at warmer temperatures. Use the creamy white heads as you would lettuce.

under high temperatures and should be grown only as a spring or fall crop.

Both annual and biennial forms of the plant are known. Most form an open rosette of leaves, but some form a head when they mature. Their development is similar to that of lettuce.

Sow seeds directly in the garden in rows 18 inches apart. Thin them when they have two leaves to stand 6 to 8 inches apart in the row. You can also use transplants.

'Flash' is an excellent cultivar.

To harvest, cut the tops about sixty to seventy days from seeding, when the leaves are 6 to 8 inches long. Blanch the plants as you would endive, by tying the outer leaves over the plants. When you cut the tops, leave the growing points attached to the roots. After harvest, dig the roots and store them at 32 to 45 degrees F. for five to six weeks. Then pack them together tightly in a box full of sand, and place them in a cellar or room at about 60 degrees F. Exclude all light; cover them with a tarp if necessary. After about a month, your roots will have sprouted creamy yellow, tight heads 3 to 5 inches long. Cut these from the roots, and use them as you would lettuce. Then relegate the roots to the compost pile.

19

Warm-Season Crops

Warm-season crops are tropical or semitropical in origin. None will tolerate a frost, nor will any grow well at temperatures below 60 degrees F. All are planted when the soil has warmed, and most benefit from black plastic mulches. They are relatively large plants, most of which are grown for their fruits.

BEANS
Snap Beans and Lima Beans
Beans were cultivated in Central America at least seven thousand years ago. Columbus carried their seeds back to Europe, where they were disseminated throughout the world by Portuguese and Spanish explorers. Colonial settlers in New England found the local natives growing beans and adopted their way of growing and preparing them. Our famous succotash and Boston baked beans are derived directly from native dishes.

The snap bean is also known as the *string bean*, though today most cultivars have no strings attached. It got its name from the fibrous, stringy material that ran along one side of the pod. Snap bean pods are cylindrical or flat, 3 to 8 inches long, and may be green, yellow, or purple. Yellow-podded snap beans are also called *wax beans*. Purple pods turn green when cooked. Seed color can be yellow, white, green, purple, red, brown, or black. Snap beans are also classified by pod shape—cylindrical or flat—and by whether or not they will be shelled. Beans grown for their immature green seeds are called *horticultural*, or *shelley*, *beans*; those grown for their mature seeds are called *dry beans*.

Lima beans come in two types: small-seeded and large-seeded. Lima bean pods are flat and bear either large or small seeds. The small-seeded varieties are the baby lima, sieva, and butter beans. The large-seeded types are more vigorous growers.

All beans are warm-season crops that grow best between 60 and 85 degrees F. Seeds will not germinate at 50 degrees F., and germination is severely retarded at temperatures above 95 degrees F. Seedlings will not emerge from the soil if days are shorter than sixteen hours.

The plants are chill sensitive, and seedlings will be injured if temperatures fall below 50 degrees F. High humidity and rainfall usually result in disease infestation, and high temperatures during flowering will cause the flowers to abort. Hot, dry winds will also injure the flowers and reduce fruit set.

Lima beans are more sensitive to their environment than snap beans and require 60 to 110 days to mature their fruit, compared with the 50 to 70 days necessary for snap beans.

Beans are annual vines that grow in one of three habits. Indeterminate cultivars, the pole, or runner, beans, produce climbing vines that reach heights of 10 feet or more. These plants must be supported by a trellis or stakes. Bush beans have determinate vines that reach heights of 8 to 24 inches and end with flower clusters at the tips of the stems. The half-runner, an intermediate type, is semideterminate and can reach heights of several feet. Bush beans are the gardener's favorite, but pole beans produce more fruits per plant.

The bean root system is highly branched and grows to about 4 feet deep. The roots contain small nodules that hold *Rhizobium* bacteria, which convert atmospheric nitrogen into a form the plant can use. Some gardeners treat their bean seeds with *Rhizobium* inoculant (see discussion under Peas).

Wait until the soil has warmed to at least 60 degrees F., then plant bush beans in rows 30 inches apart. Thin the seedlings to stand about eight to a foot of row. You can plant pole beans 6 to 12 inches apart in rows 3 to 4 feet apart, or plant a half dozen seeds in hills 3 to 4 feet apart each way. Thin these plants to three or four healthy seedlings per hill. Trellis or cage your pole beans when you plant the seeds; you'll damage the root systems if you try to erect a trellis after the plants are up. Many gardeners center over each hill a tripod made of 10-foot poles 2 inches in diameter and tied at their tops. The vines climb the poles and form a sort of tepee.

Beans are moderate feeders and are among those vegetables least responsive to fertilizers. Your preplant fertilizing should be enough to satisfy their needs. They are very sensitive to salt, so keep all fertilizers away from the roots and plant stems. Excessive nitrogen will cause overly vigorous vine growth, reduce pod formation, and delay maturity.

Beans are very sensitive to moisture stress and should receive about $1^1/_2$ inches of water a week. Lack of water during flowering will sharply decrease yields.

Green bush snap bean cultivars include 'Bush Blue Lake', 'Greencrop', and 'Provider'. Yellow bush snap bean, or wax bean, cultivars are 'Goldrush', 'Sungold', and 'Goldcrop'. Green pole snap bean cultivars include the old standards 'Kentucky Wonder' and 'Romano'.

Large-seeded bush lima bean cultivars include 'Fordhook 242' and 'Fordhook 169'. Small-seeded bush lima cultivars are 'Henderson Bush' and 'Dixie Butterpea'. 'Challenger' and 'King of the Garden' are large-seeded pole limas. 'Sieva' is a small-seeded pole lima.

Harvest snap beans about forty-five to eighty days after planting, depending on cultivar. Bush types mature faster than pole types. Pick the pods when they are about half to three-fourths their maximum size, while the seeds are still small, tender, and juicy. You should see no large bumps along the pods where seeds are swollen.

Lima beans need an extra thirty to forty days to mature. Harvest green shell limas when their seeds are nearly full-size and the pods are still green.

Dry shell beans of both types should remain on the plants until the pods mature and dry.

What's Wrong?

The ground beneath my beans is covered with flowers and pods. What happened?

Hot, dry weather with moisture stress during flowering can cause both the flowers and the young pods to abort.

My bush beans are running like small pole beans. Was the seed mixed up?

You probably applied too much nitrogen, which causes overly vigorous growth.

> **My beans have white, cottony patches on the undersides of the leaves. Is this normal?**
>
> No. This probably is mildew. Avoid brushing against infected plants, which would spread the pathogen through your beans. Apply the right fungicide to prevent the spread of the disease.
>
> **My lima bean pods have no seeds in them. What happened?**
>
> Lima bean pod borers sometimes eat the seeds inside the pod. This is a problem particularly in southern gardens. Practice good garden sanitation, and plant your beans as early as possible next year.

Other Beans

There are several less well known types of beans grown in some home gardens. Most of these require long, warm seasons and the proper photoperiod to produce fruit.

The scarlet runner, a pole bean, is grown for both its ornamental flowers and its immature pods. A white cultivar, 'Dutch Caseknife', is prized in Europe for its white flowers and pods.

Black-eyed peas (cowpeas or southern beans) are beans, not peas. They are grown in the South or Southwest and are more sensitive to cold than snap beans. One type, the 'Crowder', is so named because its seeds are crowded into the pod.

Asparagus beans (yardlong beans or tau kok) produce pods up to 3 feet long.

Catjang beans (Bombay cowpeas) do best in semiarid tropical regions and are limited in this country to Florida gardens.

Garden soybeans are close relatives of the black-eyed pea and produce shell beans or edible pods in 75 to 110 days. They are highly sensitive to photoperiod and are subdivided into nine U.S. maturity groups. Be sure to select the right group for your area.

Fava beans (Windsor beans, horsebeans, or broad beans) need a long, cool to moderately warm-season and have other narrow growing requirements.

Garbanzo beans (Indian gram or chickpeas) require at least one hundred days of warm temperatures to produce their crop.

Mung beans (green gram or golden gram) are very susceptible to cold, and their culture is limited to southern gardens. You can eat them in their green stage or remove the dried seeds for sprouts.

Adzuki beans are a drought-resistant short-day crop suitable for southernmost gardens.

Hyacinth beans (lablab beans or Egyptian beans) will tolerate poor soils. Eat only the white seeds; those with colored coats contain a cyanide compound. The starchy root is also edible.

NEW ZEALAND SPINACH

In 1770, on Captain James Cook's expedition of the South Seas, Sir Joseph Banks noticed this plant growing wild along the shores of Queen Charlotte Sound, New Zealand. The sailors on the expedition boiled the leaves and found them an adequate substitute for spinach. Specimen plants were brought to Kew Gardens in 1772, and by 1820 English gardeners were growing it as spinach. Seeds were sent to New York in 1827 and the plant found its way into American seed catalogs the following year. Curiously, the plant was not used in New Zealand.

New Zealand spinach is not related to true spinach. This is the only warm-season green, or potherb, crop commonly found in American gardens. It is drought and heat resistant but is chilled by the first cool nights of autumn. It will provide tasty greens after early summer, when all your spinach has bolted.

This large, spreading plant reaches 1 to 2 feet tall and 3 to 4 feet wide and bears inconspicuous white or yellow flowers.

Plant this warm-season crop, after all danger of frost

New Zealand spinach is a warm-season potherb and is not related to regular spinach. Harvest 3 to 4 inches of the tender branch tips as you need them.

has passed and the soil has warmed. As with beets and chard, you do not plant individual seeds, but the dried fruit containing several seeds. Germination takes two weeks to three months. Soaking in water for twenty-four hours before planting will hasten germination a bit. Space the dried fruits 1 to 2 feet apart in rows 3 to 5 feet apart, and keep the soil from crusting until seedlings emerge.

Broadcast fertilizer before planting; this should be adequate in most cases. If the lower leaves begin to yellow, side-dress each plant with a handful of fertilizer.

Begin to harvest this plant about forty to fifty days after seedlings emerge. Clip 3 to 4 inches of the tender branch tips with their leaves as you need them. This will stimulate the plant to produce new branches and foliage, and the harvest can continue until fall frost. Boil or steam the greens as you would spinach, or use them fresh in salads.

What's Wrong?

Why hasn't my New Zealand spinach seed germinated?
You probably planted when the soil was too cold. This is a warm-season crop that requires warm soil for the best growth.

SOLANACEOUS PLANTS

The soleanaceous plants are all warm-season members of the nightshade family and have similar cultural requirements and pests. All are grown for their fruits, occupy the soil for the entire season, and require much heat to produce a good crop.

Eggplant

The common, large-fruited eggplant is believed to have originated in the area around India and Burma. Smaller-fruited varieties, such as the snake eggplant (*S.m.* var. *serpentium*), the dwarf eggplant (*S.m.* var. *depressum*), and the Chinese, scarlet-fruited, or tomato, eggplant (*S. integrifolium*) probably originated in China at about the same time. It was cultivated in China as early as the fifth century B.C., where fashionable women used a black dye extracted from the fruit to stain their teeth.

Use of the eggplant, also called the Jew's apple and the mad apple, spread westward from its place of origin. Invading Moors introduced it into Spain in the seventh century A.D. The Arabs and Persians brought it to Africa before the Middle Ages, and it made the journey from there into Italy in the fourteenth century. Spanish explorers carried the purple- and white-fruited cultivars with them to the Americas, where they were grown in Brazil as early as 1658. Like their cousin the tomato, eggplants were also considered poisonous in early New England and, prior to the twentieth century, U.S. gardeners grew the plants mostly as ornamentals.

The eggplant is a very tender plant that requires a long, warm growing season of 100 to 140 days to mature its fruit. It is killed by even light frosts and can be injured by long periods of chilly weather. Both vegetative growth and fruit set suffer at temperatures below 65 degrees F., and growth ceases below 63 degrees F. Temperatures below 61 degrees F. result in a great deal of pollen deformity, which in turn will produce misshapen fruits. Any check in growth, no matter how slight, will decrease fruit quality. The plant achieves its best growth and fruit quality when daytime temperatures remain between 80 and 85 degrees F. and nighttime temperatures at about 70 degrees F.

The eggplant is insensitive to photoperiod. Flowering begins after the sixth leaf has opened on early cultivars and after the fourteenth leaf has opened on late cultivars, as long as conditions are favorable. Spiny, star-shaped, purple flowers give rise to large, berrylike fruits at temperatures above 65 degrees F.

Eggplant fruits are pendant, fleshy berries that are oval, oblong, or round and between 2 and 8 inches in diameter. Their skin is smooth and thin. Fruit color may be purple, black, yellow, white, or red, of which purple and black are the most popular.

Because of their need for a long, warm season, eggplants are usually started from transplants. Set nonhardened, blocky, 7-inch-tall plants about two weeks after the danger of frost has passed and when the daily average temperature has reached about 68 degrees F. A cool snap after planting can harden and stunt the plant. Once stunted, they seldom resume satisfactory growth. Space the plants 18 inches apart in rows 36 inches apart. You can space dwarf cultivars a bit closer.

The eggplant is a heavy feeder and responds well to soils high in organic matter. Mix some rotted manure with the soil in the hole at planting, and broadcast fertilizer to help get the plants off to a quick start. Side-dress the plants lightly when growth resumes after transplanting. A small handful of 10–10–10 fertilizer spread in a broad band about 1 foot from the base of each plant will do it. Continue to side-dress every six weeks throughout the season to push the plants and keep their growth from checking.

Water stress during flowering and fruit set can reduce yields substantially, and lack of water when fruit is mature can result in blossom-end rot. The plants need at least 1 inch of water a week during their vegetative growth phase, and up to 2 inches during fruit set.

Eggplants usually are freestanding and don't need staking. Stake them, however, if they have set a heavy fruit load or if stormy, windy weather is predicted.

There are about forty cultivars of eggplants available through U.S. seed companies. The most popular bear large, purple, oval-shaped fruit that mature seventy to eighty days after transplanting. These include 'Black Beauty', 'Early Beauty Hybrid', and 'Dusky'.

There are several other types of eggplants. Snake eggplants produce fruits averaging about 1 inch in diameter but up to 15 inches in length. Dwarf eggplants produce small, pear-shaped, purple fruits. These plants are small and weak and do not need as long a growing season to mature as the other varieties. Chinese, scarlet-fruited, or tomato eggplants are grown for their ornamental fruits. Oriental eggplants, within the botanical variety *esculentum*, produce small, elongated, slender fruits. Popular Oriental cultivars include 'Ichiban', 'Tycoon', and 'Slim Jim'.

In addition to diseases and insects, the eggplant may succumb to blossom-end rot, a physiological disorder that can be a problem under conditions of uneven moisture availability or moisture stress. This disorder is discussed in the Tomato section.

Most cultivars require two to three months to mature their fruits; however, the fruits can be eaten from the time they are about one-third grown until they are ripe. Very unripe eggplants contain the potentially poisonous alkaloid solanine, the same compound found in green potatoes, so avoid eating them too early. Fruits ready for harvest are firm, and the purple cultivars are a glossy purple. Overmature fruits become spongy and seedy, lose their gloss, and turn a bronzy green. The seeds become dark. To determine whether your fruits are ready for harvest, first look at their sheen and color. Then press your thumb into the side of a fruit. If the indentation springs back to the original shape, the fruit is immature; if it remains, the fruit is mature. The eggplant fruit bruises easily, so don't use the thumb test on every fruit, but only on those you believe are probably ripe. Continue to harvest the fruits as soon as they are ready, and the plant will bear until frost.

The fruit stem is woody and spiny, so you'll have to cut the fruits from the plant with pruning shears. Leave about 1 inch of stem and the calyx, or cap, attached to the fruit after harvest.

Eggplant fruits deteriorate rapidly at warm temperatures but suffer chilling injury below 50 degrees F. Once warmed, chilled eggplants appear pitted, exhibit surface bronzing and seed browning, and become very susceptible to rot.

What's Wrong?

Why do the leaves of my eggplants have tiny holes in them?

This is probably flea beetle damage. See chapter 16 for control measures.

All my eggplant plants wilted and died. What happened?

If you watered well and didn't hoe too deeply, you might have verticillium wilt. Rotate your crop into an area where eggplants, tomatoes, peppers, and potatoes have not grown for several years.

I set my eggplants into the garden early and they just sat there. Why?

Eggplants require a very warm growing season. Setting the plants early will not necessarily result in early fruit maturity, and if they were subjected to temperatures below 60 degrees F., they may have had their growth checked and will never resume normal growth.

Peppers

There are sweet, mild peppers and pungent, hot peppers, but all except one of those grown in the United States belong to the same species. The tabasco pepper belongs to a related species. None are related to the black pepper (*Piper nigrum*) that appears in its ground form on every table.

Peppers are perennial tropical plants that are grown as annuals in most of the United States They were gathered from the wild at least seven thousand years ago and cultivated at least two thousand years ago in their native Mexico and Central America, where most wild types are very hot. Columbus introduced chili peppers to initially skeptical Europeans in 1493 and they quickly took hold, their use spreading throughout western and southern Europe. But the fruit was not eaten as it is today—it was dried, ground, and used as a substitute for the expensive spice, black pepper.

Like other members of the nightshade family, peppers are fussy about temperature. They are more chill sensitive than tomatoes and will not tolerate prolonged periods below 50 degrees F. Nor will they set fruits at temperatures below 60 degrees F. Sweet peppers make their best vegetative growth when the average daily temperature is between 65 and 85 degrees F. but will set the most fruits when the temperature cools to about 65 degrees F. Above 85 degrees F., many fruits will be misshapen, and above 90 degrees F., the flowers will abort.

Hot peppers love hot weather. They make their best growth when daytime temperatures are above 75 degrees F. and nights are consistently above 70 degrees F. Temperatures above 90 degrees F. increase fruit set in hot peppers. Like sweet peppers, hot peppers will not set fruits when temperatures fall below 60 degrees F.

The common garden peppers are determinate, erect, bushy plants that reach heights of 1 to 3 feet. They have a shallow root system and cannot forage widely for water and nutrients. Their stems and leaves are very brittle, and breakage can become a problem when soil moisture is high or the plant has a heavy fruit load. Stake your plants when there's a chance of a severe storm or high winds.

Flower buds are formed at the stem apex and in the branch and leaf axils. Although the plant is officially day-neutral, flower buds form faster under long days and warm temperatures. The fruits form after the flowers are self-pollinated.

Because of their temperature requirements, peppers are usually transplanted in the garden two weeks after the danger of frost has passed. Set the transplants 18 inches apart in rows 30 to 36 inches apart. Larger transplants produce a larger early yield but may not give as large a total yield as slightly smaller plants. Overhardening stunts young plants and reduces yields substantially, if you get any peppers at all.

Use a liquid transplant fertilizer, and side-dress with a granular fertilizer when the plants have set several fruits. Using rotted manure or compost in the planting hole will never hurt, but peppers do not respond to manure as well as some other vegetables.

All peppers are extremely sensitive to excess soil moisture and will quickly drop their flowers and small fruits if their roots become waterlogged. Too little water increases the incidence of blossom-end rot. Pepper plants should receive 1 to 1 1/2 inches of water a week. You can apply this with a regular garden sprinkler, but wetting the plant surfaces can spread bacterial spot and Phytophthora. It's better to use a soaker hose or watering can for peppers.

Mulching is the best way to control weeds, as the pepper has a small, shallow root system. Your yield of top-quality fruits will be best with black plastic mulch. This keeps the fruits clean and warms the soil for better root and top growth. If you use organic mulch, let the soil warm up before you apply it.

There are many kinds and cultivars of peppers, and they can be categorized as follows.

Bell. Plants of this type produce large, sweet, blocky fruits up to about 4 inches wide and 4 inches long. The immature green fruits usually turn red or another color at maturity, but most are eaten green. Some common cultivars are 'Yolo Wonder', 'Keystone Giant', and 'Bell Boy'.

Pimiento. These plants produce sweet, round to slightly pointed fruit about 2 inches wide and 3 to 4 inches long. The fruits are used to stuff green olives and are eaten in salads. Cultivars include 'Pimiento' and 'Sweet Banana'.

Celestial. Plants of this type bear small fruits up to 2 inches in diameter that are borne upright on the plant. The fruits may be red, yellow, orange, or purple, and fruit color can be mixed on a single plant. The plants are grown as ornamentals, and the hot fruits are often ground for use in chili powder. Cultivars include 'Fresno Chili' and 'Celestial'.

Cayenne. Fruits from these plants are slender, curved, pointed, and from 2 to 12 inches long. They are green when immature and red when mature. Fruits of the sweet types are dried and ground to make paprika; those of the hot types are used in chili powder. Some popular cultivars are 'Anaheim' (mild), 'Hungarian Wax' (hot), and 'Jalapeño' (very hot).

Cherry. These plants produce cherry-shaped fruits that are large or small, sweet or hot, and orange or red at maturity. The plants are grown as ornamentals, and the fruits are pickled or ground for chili powder. 'Large Red Cherry' (hot) and 'Sweet Cherry' (mild) are popular for the home garden.

Tomato. Fruits of these plants resemble small, green tomatoes and are pickled immature. 'Tomato' and 'Sunnybrook' are popular cultivars.

Tabasco. These plants produce slim fruits up to 3 inches long that are very hot. They are grown as ornamentals, and the fruits are pickled or ground for use in chili powder. Some cultivars are 'Small Red Chili', 'Tabasco', and 'Coral Gem'.

The fruits of most pepper cultivars are green when immature and red when mature. This is particularly true of the open-pollinated types. Seeds of this type are relatively inexpensive to produce, and the large number of good-quality, open-pollinated cultivars forces little demand for hybrid seeds. Recently, however, consumers have been introduced to bell-type fruits that are yellow, orange, chocolate brown, or purple. Most of these are grown in greenhouses in the Netherlands and shipped to U.S. markets in the off-season. If you wish to grow these in your garden, you'll have to buy hybrid cultivars.

The hotness of pepper fruits is rated in Scoville heat units. The sweet bell types rate 0; the Anaheim, 150 to 2,500; the cayenne and jalapeño, 10,000 to 18,000; and the tabasco, around 40,000. The hotness is due to the presence of capsaicin, an alkaloid. This compound is extracted and used to produce the warmth in some topical balms. It is the irritant in mace and is an effective animal repellent as well.

Pepper plants may develop a few physiological disorders, but these should not become an overwhelming problem in your garden. Blossom-end rot can occur under very dry soil conditions and is related poor to calcium distribution in the plant (see the Tomato section). Sunscald results in off-white blotches and papery, dead skin on fruits exposed to direct sun. This often occurs when the plants have been partially defoliated by insects or severe wind.

Pepper fruits are normally harvested from 65 to 140 days after planting. If you want red bell peppers, wait for the fruit to mature before picking; otherwise, pick the fruit as soon as it has reached acceptable size, usually 3 to 4 inches in length. With varieties that are normally red, pick the peppers when they have attained their full color. Harvest all peppers by snapping the stem from the plant, but be careful—they bruise easily. High soil moisture will also make the plants especially brittle. Support the rest of the plant when you snap off the fruit, or you may break the branches.

Pepper fruits are not ready for harvest all at once. Pick the largest fruits every week to ten days. The green fruits will redden off the plant if stored above 50 degrees F., but bacterial soft rot can be a problem at those warm temperatures.

What's Wrong?

All the flowers have dropped from my pepper plants, and I have no fruits. Why?

The weather has been too cold or too hot. At temperatures much below 60 degrees F. or above 90 degrees F., peppers will naturally drop their flowers and fruits.

Late in the season, my bell pepper fruits acquire a purple cast. Why didn't the fruits turn red when they matured?

If the fruits have a purple cast, chances are they won't turn red. This dark coloration is the result of cool weather and shorter days and is common on green bell peppers near the end of the season. The fruits are perfectly edible, but your garden is running out of time.

How do I know when to pick my peppers?

This depends on the cultivar and type of pepper. When a fruit has developed the color and size you want, pick it. Bell peppers are usually picked immature, while they are still green.

Tomatoes

Ancestral, small-fruited tomatoes probably originated in the Andes mountains of Bolivia and Peru. The Aztecs and Incas developed these into the large-fruited forms we grow today.

Early European explorers carried tomato seeds to Italy, where the plant gained notice by 1544. By 1600, tomatoes had spread to France, Germany, and other European countries. The British thought the tomato was poisonous, probably because of its relationship to poisonous belladonna and mandrake. This prejudice carried over into the colonies. While the tomato is mentioned as being grown in the Carolinas and Georgia in the early 1700s, the plant was not generally cultivated in the United States until 1835, and it was not until the latter part of the nineteenth century that it came under extensive commercial cultivation.

The tomato is a heat-loving crop that requires a growing season of 60 to 120 days from transplant to ripening of fruit, depending on the cultivar. Daytime temperatures of about 70 degrees F. are best for growth. The plant stops growing at temperatures above 95 degrees F. and below 53 degrees F. and is killed with long exposure to temperatures below 50 degrees F.

Most tomato plants display one of three growth habits: indeterminate, determinate, and semideterminate. Because of the great amount of hybridizing, however, cultivars may show varying degrees of these habits.

In indeterminate plants, the central shoot continues to grow until killed by frost. The side shoots are short with few branches. Flower clusters, usually separated by three or four leaves, are produced along the length of the vine. The fruits produced on the lower clusters ripen first, followed by fruits on progressively younger clusters. The vine tends to sprawl, and the fruits ripen over a long period of time.

A determinate vine produces several flower clusters, each separated by a leaf or two, and terminates with a flower cluster at its tip. This results in many side branches. The growth of each side branch follows a pattern similar to that of the main stem, ending with the production of a flower cluster at its tip. This plant is more compact and has a more concentrated period of fruit ripening.

Semideterminate types have growth characteristics intermediate between the indeterminate and determinate. They may have several lateral flower clusters, and the main stem ends in a flower cluster as well.

Flower clusters develop directly from the stems and not in the leaf axils, as is common in most plants. The flowers are borne in groups called *inflorescences*, each having from four to twelve or more flowers. Fruits develop after pollination, but development is uneven because all flowers are not pollinated at the same time.

Pollination is best at temperatures between 60 and 70 degrees F. During the blooming period, daytime temperatures above 85 degrees F. and nighttime temperatures above 70 degrees F. or below 55 degrees F.

reduce fruit set markedly. Low humidity, drying winds, excess nitrogen, insufficient light, and drought cause flowers to drop prematurely.

Generally, only gardeners in the South are able to direct seed tomatoes. The temperature 1 inch beneath the soil's surface must be at least 55 degrees F. at seeding, and the growing season must be long enough for the cultivar to ripen fruit. Sow the seeds in clumps 18 inches apart, each containing four to six seeds. The resulting seedlings can be trained as a single plant, eliminating the need to thin. Take care not to crowd the plant clumps, since this decreases fruit set and delays ripening.

If your growing season is too short for direct seeding, you will have to use transplants. Transplants will produce the earliest tomatoes.

Good tomato sets are 6 to 8 inches tall and have stocky, pencil-thick stems with four to six true, dark green leaves. Plants properly hardened to withstand garden conditions will have a slight purpling on the stems and leaf veins.

Tomato sets that have become too tall dry out rapidly and may blow over in a wind if planted at the usual depth. Plant them deeply, or dig a small trench and lay their stems along the bottom with only the top several inches of the plant showing aboveground. Fill the trench with soil. Roots will sprout along the buried stem. When planting deeply, pinch off any leaves that would be buried to reduce the chance of rot. Don't plant tomato transplants that are in bloom or that have small fruits. These plants will be stunted and produce a poor crop.

Space plants that are to be staked 20 inches apart in rows 3 feet apart. Space caged plants 30 inches apart in rows 48 inches apart. In either case, give them plenty of room, because crowding will shade the plants and reduce the total yield.

Roots of the tomato plant can penetrate the soil to depths of 6 feet or more to bring up water and some nutrients. Most of the feeder roots are within a few inches of the soil's surface, however.

Tomatoes respond well to high fertility, but excess nitrogen delays maturity and fruit ripening and results in vinyness and an abundance of small, green fruits. Broadcast fertilizer just before planting, and side-dress the plants when they have become established and again after they have set several fruits. Don't fertilize after this, since that can cause the plants to remain vegetative and delay fruit ripening.

Tomato plants need 1 to 2 inches of water a week. Plants that suffer

Tomato sets that have become too tall and lanky should be planted deeply or trenched. Roots will form along the stem.

water stress during their early development may never recover, even if they are given adequate water thereafter. Blossoms may drop if the plants receive insufficient water during bloom, and fruits may develop blossom-end rot if there is too little water during fruit development.

Watering with sprinklers is satisfactory for tomatoes during the first half of their development, and it won't knock off the flowers. During the second half of development, however, use soaker hoses or a watering can to apply water directly to the soil, since wetting the fruit during ripening will cause them to crack and spoil.

Black plastic mulch is ideal for tomato plants; it promotes earlier maturity by warming the soil, retains soil moisture, and prevents the growth of most weeds. Straw mulch or grass clippings are also good for tomato plants, but allow the soil time to warm up before applying an organic mulch.

Because tomato plants are vines, they trail along the ground unless provided with support. Sprawling vines bear the most fruits, but they ripen later and are more susceptible to damage. If you decide to let them sprawl, apply a thick layer of straw mulch around the plants before they begin to run in order to control weeds and to keep the fruits off the ground.

Supports will increase the yield of good fruit, make picking easier, save space, and reduce the chances of stepping on vines during normal garden care. The most common method is to drive a 6-foot stake 2 feet into the ground 3 to 4 inches from the plant at transplanting. Cedar, redwood, or black locust stakes are good for their rot resistance. When plants have reached 12 to 15 inches in height, prune them to two or three stems by pinching off the side shoots as they appear in the leaf axils. Fruits on pruned plants can ripen up to fourteen days earlier than those on unpruned plants, though pruned plants won't bear as many fruits. You may prune to only one main stem, but that leaves no security for the crop should that stem be injured. Tie the stems loosely to the stakes with soft baling twine or old nylon stockings. Knot the twine tightly to the stake about 2 inches above a leaf stem, then wrap it loosely around the stem just below the leaf base. As the plant grows, make new ties about every 12 inches along the stem.

You can buy tomato cages or make them yourself from 4-foot-wide 4-by-6 inch mesh stock fencing or concrete reinforcing wire. A piece 5 feet long will make a cage 18 inches in diameter.

Vinyl-covered wire cages resist rust. These and the new plastic cages also resist heating by the sun, which can burn the tomato leaves and stems. Set the cage over the young tomato plant, and tie it to four 4-foot stakes driven into the ground. Fruits on caged plants ripen slightly later but are better shaped than those on staked plants.

Several hundred tomato cultivars are presently on the market, and more than thirty new ones are introduced each year. These vary according to vine habit; fruit color, size, and shape; season of ripening; pest

Support your tomato vines for the best fruit. Tie plants to sturdy stakes loosely with soft twine, cloth, or old nylon stockings. You can also train the vines to grow up string suspended from a taut wire.

Pruning tomato plants can be more trouble than it's worth. For those who want to try it, pinch off all suckers, which grow in the leaf axils, while they are young. When several clusters of fruit have formed, or if the plants grow too tall, pinch out their growing tips.

resistance; and the area of the country to which they are adapted. Look for cultivars that show the greatest degree of pest resistance and that grow well in your area.

Tomato cultivars can be categorized as follows.

Beefsteak. There is a 'Beefsteak' cultivar, but the term is generally applied to any large tomato that has thick, solid flesh with few seed cavities. Most of these require long seasons (about 100 days) to ripen their fruits. 'Beefmaster', 'Pink Ponderosa', and 'Beefsteak' are popular cultivars.

Container. Although any tomato plant can be grown in a container, those cultivars that produce small, red fruits less than 2 inches in diameter on plants less than 24 inches in height are best suited to this method of growing. These include 'Early Salad', 'Patio', 'Presto', 'Tiny Tim', and 'Toy Boy'.

Main crop. This type produces medium to large fruits with varying maturing times. Most cultivars commonly found in seed catalogs are of this type, including most yellow cultivars, such as 'Sunray'.

Paste. Fruits of this type contain less water and more meat and are used for paste, canning, and catsup. They are also wonderful to eat out of hand. 'Roma' and 'San Marzano' are popular.

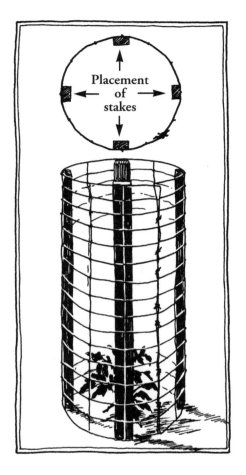
Placement of stakes

Make your own tomato cages. Wrap a 5-foot long piece of 4-by-6-inch mesh stock fencing or welded wire into a cylinder, and fasten the edges with wire. Place the cylinders over newly set plants, and fasten to four 4-foot stakes.

Salad. These are the cherry tomatoes, with fruit up to 1 ¹/₂ inches in diameter. Popular cultivars include 'Cherry', 'Pear', 'Red Cherry', and 'Basket Pak'.

White. These are actually a light yellow color and, like the yellow cultivars, are no less acid than the red. Popular ones include 'Snowball', 'White Beauty', and 'White Wonder'.

Several types of physiological disorders may affect tomatoes. Blossom-end rot is the result of tissue breakdown near the blossom end of the fruit, characterized by a sunken, dark brown, leathery spot that enlarges as the fruit matures. It is associated with a calcium deficiency in the fruit tissue that is aggravated by fluctuations in soil moisture, excessive nitrogen fertilization, and root damage. It's more commonly found on staked plants, pruned plants, and those that have been clean cultivated. Always mulch your plants, and make sure they have a constant supply of moisture.

Catfacing, a web of tan scars on the skin, is most likely to occur on early-ripening fruits. The faded blossom sticks to the developing fruit during cool, cloudy weather, causing the blossom end to become puckered and malformed.

Sunscald occurs when green fruits are exposed to the sun. This causes

There are hundreds of tomato cultivars for the home garden. Here are some popular ones. Vine types are indeterminate (I), determinate (D), or semide-terminate (SD). Cultivars may be resistant to verticillium (V), fusarium (F), nematodes (N), and cracking (C). Fruit size can be large (10 ounces), medium (6 ounces), small (3-4 ounces), paste-type, or cherry.

CULTIVAR	SEASON DAYS	VINE TYPE	RESISTANCE	SIZE
Beefmaster	80	I	V, F, N	Large
Beefsteak	90	I	—	Large
Better Boy	72	I	V, F, N	Large
Big Boy	78	I	—	Large
Big Girl	78	I	V, F	Large
Big Set	75	D	V, F, N	Large
Early Girl	62	I	V, C	Medium
Fireball	60	D	—	Small
Glamour	74	I	C	Medium
Jet Star	72	I	V, F	Medium
Marglobe	75	D	F	Medium
New Yorker	64	D	V	Medium
Ramapo	80	I	V, F	Medium
Red Cherry	65	I	—	Cherry
Redpak	71	D	V, F	Medium
Rocket	50	D	—	Small
Roma	75	D	V, F	Paste
Scotia	60	D	—	Small
Small Fry	60	D	—	Cherry
Springset	65	D	V, F	Medium
Starfire	56	D	—	Medium
Super Fantastic	70	I	V, F	Medium
Supersonic	79	SD	V, F	Large
Sunray	80	I	F	Medium
Terrific	70	I	V, F, N, C	Large
Tiny Tim	55	D	—	Cherry
Ultra Girl	56	SD	V, F, N	Medium

a light green or greenish white patch to develop on the exposed surface. It's common on plants that have been pruned or have been partially defoliated, as in the case of uncontrolled hornworm depredation.

Growth cracks occur when the fruit skin cannot stretch fast enough to accommodate swelling of the flesh. This is often the result of extreme changes in the growth rate of the fruit caused by radical moisture fluctuations and temperatures above 90 degrees F. Radial cracking begins at the stem end and radiates out over the fruit surface. Concentric cracking occurs in concentric circles around the top of the fruit. Never water the crop heavily following an extended drought, and never sprinkle water on the fruit surface while the fruit is maturing. Plant crack-resistant cultivars if you have had this problem.

Tomato fruits take about a month and a half to two months after bloom to mature and ripen, depending on temperature. The lowest temperature at which they will ripen properly is 55 degrees F.; the optimum temperature is 68 degrees F. Even a brief exposure of green fruits to a temperature of 40 degrees F. or lower will destroy the enzyme responsible for ripening. Temperatures above 80 degrees F. inhibit the development of red color, and red fruits will turn yellow-orange. Leave fruits on the vine until they are fully ripe and just begin to soften. If temperatures are expected to remain above 80 degrees F. or if frost is expected, harvest the fruits as soon as they begin to color, and ripen them indoors at about 70 degrees F.

What's Wrong?

My tomato plants look very healthy, have dark green foliage, and grow tall and bushy, but they produce very few fruits, and those fruits remain small, green, and hard and never ripen. Why?

There are several possibilities. You might be fertilizing with too much nitrogen or overwatering. Or the nights might be too hot. Pinch the terminal shoots to force extension growth to stop, and cut back on watering and fertilizing.

I planted my tomato plants in the early spring, and they took forever to begin growing. My crop is no farther ahead than my neighbor's, which was planted several weeks later. Why?

Tomato plants will not grow when night temperatures fall into the fifties or below. Therefore, planting them early will not necessarily give you an earlier crop.

Why do the blossoms on my tomato plants drop before producing fruit?

This is common when night temperatures fall into the fifties or remain in the mid-eighties and higher. You can't do much but wait for moderate nighttime temperatures.

Are yellow-fruited cultivars less acidic than the red?

Yellow, orange, and pink cultivars have exactly the same acid content as the red ones.

Sections of my plants have all stems and no leaves, and the ground beneath them is covered with greenish brown pellets. What does this mean?

You have tomato hornworms. Handpick these pests early in the morning when they are most visible. Later in the day, they move to the undersides of the foliage.

The lower sides of my fruits develop sunken, leathery areas that darken. What's wrong?

This is blossom-end rot, which technically is related to a lack of calcium, but really is more often a problem with inadequate or fluctuating soil moisture.

OKRA

Okra, a cousin of cotton, is a perennial grown as an annual. Its origin is somewhere near Ethiopia and the upper Nile region of Sudan. It was taken to Spain by invading Moors in the eighth century and eaten by the Egyptians in the twelfth century. It was brought to the New World, finding its way into Brazil by 1658 and into the United States by the early 1700s.

Okra is a tender crop that requires a warm season. It tolerates temperatures as low as 65 degrees F. and as high as 95 degrees F.; it grows best at temperatures above 85 degrees F. It's grown throughout most of the United States, but yield is poor in the short northern growing seasons. It is at its best in southern gardens, where it withstands the very hot summers better than most other vegetable plants.

Okra comes in many forms. The shrublike woody plants of the dwarf types attain heights of only about 3 feet; those of the tall types can reach 10 feet. Some types have spines, to which many gardeners are allergic. Spineless types are available and popular.

Flower buds develop in the axils of every leaf above the seven most basal leaves, and the plants begin to flower about thirty-five to sixty days after emergence. The flowers are large and beautiful—five yellow petals washed with purple at their bases—and each can bear a single pod-type fruit.

Pods can be round or ridged and short or long and pointed. Many varieties have spines. Their color also is variable, ranging from creamy white to dark green.

Okra normally flowers under short-day conditions of less than eleven hours. The flowers abort at longer day lengths. Days of this length occur from mid-October to the end of February, when the weather is much too cold for the plant in northern gardens. One popular cultivar, however, 'Clemson Spineless', is day-neutral and better adapted to colder areas.

Okra seeds have a hard coating; soaking them in water at room temperature overnight just before planting will speed germination. If you forget to soak them the night before, soak them in 110-degree F. water for two hours just before you plant. Don't let the water get much hotter than that, or you'll cook them.

Plant the seeds after all danger of frost has passed and the soil has warmed to at least 75 degrees F. The soaking will speed germination in warm soil but will only speed decay in soil that is too cold. Okra is intolerant of wet, poorly drained, or highly acidic soils.

Thin plants of the dwarf cultivars to stand 1 foot apart in rows 3 feet apart, and those of the tall cultivars to stand about 2 feet apart in rows 5 feet apart. Because even the dwarf cultivars are fairly tall, locate okra on the north side of the garden so that it won't shade the shorter vegetables.

Broadcast fertilizer before planting, and side-dress when the first pods begin to form. Don't use a high-nitrogen fertilizer on okra; this will force the plant into excessive vegetative growth at the expense of fruit production.

Spineless dwarf okra types are best for the home garden. 'Clemson Spineless' and 'Emerald' are popular cultivars.

Cut the pods from the plant when they are four to six days old and about 2 to 4 inches long. That's when their color is bright and their eating quality the best. That quality deteriorates rapidly after the seventh day, and leaving pods on the plant beyond that point will shut down flowering. If you've planted the spiny type, wear gloves and a long-sleeved shirt to prevent the spines from irritating your skin.

What's Wrong?

I planted seeds in the spring and nothing happened. Why?

If you planted too early, the seeds probably rotted, especially if you soaked them beforehand. Or your seed may have been too old.

My plants produced only a few fruits, then stopped. What happened?

You may have let some of the old fruits mature on the plant. This causes flowering to cease.

My plants look very vigorous but produce few fruits. Why?

You probably used too much nitrogen fertilizer early on, causing the plants to remain vegetative.

SWEET CORN

Corn belongs to the grass family. It's one of the few vegetables that is distinctly American. Archeological records of fossilized maize pollen show that the plant grew in Mexico at least 80,000 years ago. It was cultivated in southern Mexico at least 7,200 years ago. It's a variable plant, and the ancestors of our modern type were strange indeed, with a tassel at the tip of each ear. This staple of pre-Columbian cultures was brought to Europe by Columbus in 1493, where it was called turkey corn.

The corn of historical record is the dent corn (cow corn or field corn) grown for feed and meal. But we grow sweet corn in our gardens. The Iroquois raised sweet corn, and the colonists were quick to follow. By 1820, sweet corn had become a major crop.

It is a tropical and subtropical plant. The best temperatures for corn growth are between 70 and 85 degrees F. Growth slows at 60 degrees and 95 degrees F., and the plant will not grow at 50 degrees F. or below. The warmer the temperature, the more leaves that are produced. Corn does not grow well on hot nights, however.

The nearly complete cornstalk is telescoped back into the young seedling, so that much of the growth of the plant is simply due to elongation of the internodes, or portions of the stem between two leaves. Each cornstalk produces one to three ears and one tassel. The first ear usually forms at about the middle of the stalk and will be the biggest, since it partially suppresses the development of other ears. Tasseling begins when about seven leaves have unfolded. The tassel, the male flower, is initially retracted into the plant and may not be visible, but the reproductive process has begun, and the tassel begins to produce up to fifty thousand pollen grains for each silk. The silks are the female flowers and are each attached to one kernel on the cob. After pollination, the ears rapidly enlarge and collect sugars from the leaves. The more leaves, the more sugar can be produced.

Flowering in corn, as in many other vegetables, is controlled by day length. Long days and high temperatures favor vegetative growth; shorter days and cooler temperatures favor reproductive growth. There is great variation among cultivars in the amount of sunlight required for fruiting. Tropical cultivars will not flower in temperate regions until the days shorten to about twelve hours; they may become 19 feet tall before they flowering! This makes them winners in the tall corn contests at the county fair. Northern cultivars bred to flower under long days and cooler temperatures yield poorly when grown under the warm temperatures and short days of the South. Plant cultivars adapted to your area.

Corn seeds will not germinate when the soil temperatures are below 50 degrees F. Wait until the soil 2 inches below the surface reaches at least 55 degrees F. before you plant. The longer you can wait, the better off you'll be. At 55 degrees F., it takes three weeks for corn seeds to germinate; at 75 degrees F., four days.

Plant the seeds in short blocks rather than long rows. This will help each ear get plenty of pollen during bloom. Space the short rows 3 feet apart. Thin the plants when they are 5 inches high to stand 10 inches apart in the row; overcrowded plants produce small ears with many undeveloped kernels at their tip (poor tip fill). It's tempting to transplant the young thinned seedlings, but don't bother; corn doesn't transplant well.

You don't want all your corn to ripen at once, so plant early-, midseason-, and late-ripening cultivars at the same time, or make successive plantings of the same cultivar about ten days apart. This will spread out the harvest and give you time to enjoy your bounty.

Corn has a shallow, fibrous root system about 2 feet deep. It is moderately tolerant of soils with higher pH, but it is not tolerant of poor soils. It likes fertility. Broadcast before planting, or spade under manure and compost in the fall prior to planting. Side-dress the corn if the lower leaves begin to yellow.

Corn needs adequate water, especially during tasseling and silking, although it won't tolerate flooding. Supply at least 1 inch of water a week, or the stalks will be stunted, the silk will rot, and the ears, if you get any at all, will be late, poorly filled, and stubby. Look at the corn leaves early in the morning. If they are tightly rolled like cigars, water immediately.

There are more cultivars of sweet corn available to the home gardener than of any other vegetable. There are white and yellow cultivars, as well as bicolor, which have both white and yellow kernels. Nearly all of these are hybrids that have been selected for better disease resistance and increased sugar content. New classes of sweet corn have been recently developed. The distinctions among classes are as follows.

Sugary class (su). Also called *normal, traditional, sugar,* or *standard,* this is the sweet corn we grew up with. It contains moderate levels of sugar at harvest (10 to 15 percent), as well as a certain amount of starch, which gives it a creamy texture. The sugar is rapidly turned into starch during maturation, however, resulting in a rapid loss of quality. In other words, it goes downhill fast. 'Silver Queen', 'Butter and Sugar', and 'Golden Cross Bantam' are some popular cultivars.

Sugary-enhanced class (su se or se). Corn in this group has twice as much sugar and about the same amount of starch as the cultivars in the sugary class. The starch gives the kernels a creamy texture. The sugar is converted to starch at the same rate as in the sugary-type corn, but since this corn has more sugar to begin with, it remains sweeter longer after harvest. 'Double Treat', 'Remarkable', and 'Miracle' are popular cultivars.

Shrunken-2 class (sh2). Cultivars in this group are also called *supersweet* or *extrasweet*. They develop two to three times more sugar than the sugary cultivars, and that sugar is converted to starch much more slowly. They are terrific if you have a sweet tooth, but many people, myself included, find this corn much too sweet. And because of the lower starch content, the kernels are crunchy rather than having a creamy texture, which lessens their appeal to some people. The seeds grow poorly under cool soil conditions and water stress and must be planted later than the sugary cultivars, and the yield is lower than that of the sugary and sugary-enhanced cultivars. 'Illini Xtra Sweet', 'Sucro', and 'Dinner Time' are popular for the garden.

Augmented class. These cultivars have a combination of two different sweetness genes. They are sweeter than the sugary types but have the same creamy texture. 'Symphony' is a delightful cultivar.

ADX class. These cultivars have a combination of three sweetness genes, and their sugar level is as high as that of the supersweets. Unfortunately, there are few cultivars available. 'Pennfresh ADX' is one of them.

bt class. This abbreviation stands for *brittle*, the name of the gene that gives the sweetness to these cultivars. Their flavor and sweetness are about the same as those of the ADX cultivars. 'Hawaiian Super-Sweet' is a good cultivar.

If you have a sweet tooth, choose one of the new sweeter cultivars. If you like the good old corny taste you remember from childhood, stick with the sugary class. If you decide to try a few different kinds, good for you. Sweet corns will cross-pollinate, however, and you must isolate some of the different classes to maintain their characteristics. A super-sweet pollinated by a sugary cultivar, for example, will lose its extra sugar. Observe the following guidelines.

1. You may plant different cultivars of the same class near each other—with the exceptions noted below. For example, planting 'Miracle' and 'Double Treat' together will not influence the sugar content.

2. Isolate cultivars of Shrunken-2, bt, and ADX types from each other and from all other corn, since cross-pollination will make their kernels starchy, and pollen from these will make kernels of sugary and sugary-enhanced cultivars starchy also.

3. Isolate sugary-enhanced from sugary. Sugary pollen landing on the silks of a sugary-enhanced cultivar will cause the latter to produce the relatively low sugar levels of the sugary type. Sugary-enhanced pollen has no effect on sugary ears, however.

4. Isolate different-colored cultivars, which can also cross-pollinate. Pollen from a yellow cultivar landing on the silks of a white cultivar will

cause the kernels to which those silks are attached to become yellow, and you'll wind up with a bicolored corn. If it lands on silks of a bicolor, it will reduce the number of white kernels in the ear. Pollen from a white cultivar landing on the silks of a yellow cultivar will not change the color of the kernels, however, nor will it affect the number of yellow or white kernels in a bicolored cultivar.

When in doubt, isolate every cultivar from every other one. Do this by keeping each cultivar at least 250 feet away from another or by planting the cultivars at least fourteen days apart.

Sweet corn is affected by a number of diseases and insects, and it may succumb to a couple of physiological disorders. Poor tip fill is usually the result of poor pollination. Hot, drying winds, temperatures above 96 degrees F., and drought stress all can interfere with pollination and prevent the kernels near the tip of the ear from developing. Shriveled kernels near the tip of the ear are not a sign of poor pollination, but of nitrogen deficiency during maturation. To prevent this, provide sufficient fertilizer for good plant growth.

Quality in sweet corn means sweetness, tenderness, a creamy texture, and low starch. As the corn ear matures from the edible stage (about twenty days after pollination) to the dry mature stage, sugar converts to starch, and quality rapidly decreases. There are easy ways to gauge the maturity and quality of your corn. Peak quality will be about twenty days after silking. At this point, the silk will have begun to dry and the ears will feel plump. Pull back the husk, and crush a kernel with your finger. If clear water comes out and the kernels are small, it's in the premilk stage and not yet ready to be picked. If milk—really a milky-colored starchy sap—squirts out, the ear is ready.

Corn loses quality rapidly and can pass from the milk stage into the early dough stage in less than a week. You can still eat it in this stage, but it is noticeably less sweet and much more pasty. If it has reached the dough stage, it's ready for the compost pile or the chicken yard.

Harvest the ears by snapping them from the stalk. Corn will lose a quarter of its sugar after twenty-four hours at room temperature, so cool the ears to 32 degrees F. immediately by plunging them into ice water. Then you can store them in the refrigerator for a few days. But the best way to eat corn is to have the water boiling when you pick it!

What's Wrong?

Will removing the suckers from corn make the plants grow better?

Removing corn suckers is a waste of time. It will not increase yield.

Why do I get very few ears on my corn?

You may be having poor pollination. Plant corn in small blocks for best production. Also, it's normal for each stalk to produce only one to three ears.

The kernels are not developing at the tips of my corn ears, sometimes the entire top third of the ear. Why?

This is known as *poor tip fill,* and it's usually caused by poor pollination or bad weather during silking.

My young corn seedlings are all lying on top of the soil and the seeds are missing. What happened?

Crows probably pulled out the seedlings to get at the seeds. It's difficult to keep these pests away; pie plates and scarecrows are not very effective. The problem will disappear as the seedlings grow larger.

Why does my corn sometimes produce little ears in the tassel and little tassels in the ear?

Any climatic stress, such as long, cool springs following early periods of warm weather, will produce these abnormalities. You can't control it most of the time, so don't worry about it.

SWEET POTATOES

The sweet potato is not related to either the Irish potato or the yam. The sweet potato plant is a long, trailing vine, a perennial grown as an annual in most of the United States for its swollen, tuberous roots. Four to ten such roots are produced on each plant.

Cultivated since prehistoric times in Central America and on several South Pacific islands, the sweet potato was carried to Spain at the beginning of the sixteenth century by Columbus and other early European explorers. It was brought to the United States by the colonists, who grew it in Virginia perhaps as early as 1610 and in New England by 1764.

This plant requires a four- to five-month growing season and grows best when both days and nights are warm, with the average temperature about 75 degrees F. It stops growing at 59 degrees F. and will chill and die if subjected to 50 degrees F. or below for prolonged periods. It's best adapted to gardens from New Jersey to Texas.

The sweet potato is responsive to day length. The vines grow rampantly under long days, then flower and undergo root enlargement as the days shorten. The flowers, which resemble those of the morning glory, rarely appear in northern gardens.

Light, well-drained soils are best for growing sweet potatoes. Such soils warm faster in the spring and also produce cleaner roots. Wet soils and those high in organic matter cause the skin of the roots to crack and roughen and so become more prone to infections.

This crop is grown by vegetative propagation. Seed potatoes are planted in beds maintained at about 80 degrees F. These sprout in about six weeks, and the sprouts form roots and leaves. When the small plantlets, also called *slips, draws,* or *sprouts,* develop six to ten leaves, they are removed from the seed pieces and transplanted 15 inches apart in rows 4 feet apart. You'll do well to forgo the propagation stage and purchase slips for your garden from a reputable nursery.

The plants are voracious feeders. Broadcast fertilizer before planting, and apply at least two side-dressings during the season. Avoid using too much nitrogen, however, as that will cause excessive vinyness. High organic matter has a detrimental influence on the root, so don't apply manure to your sweet potato soil.

The roots of this plant can extend to depths of 6 feet, allowing it to withstand severe drought once it has become established. Still, provide at least 1 inch of water a week throughout the season.

There are two types of sweet potatoes: the food type, used for human consumption, and the feed type, used in industry and as animal feed. The food type is divided into soft-fleshed and firm-fleshed cultivars. The soft-fleshed roots are sweet, soft, orange, and moist and are used for baking. These cultivars are sometimes mistakenly called *yams* by grocers. The firm-fleshed cultivars have yellow skin, and white, yellow, or light orange dry flesh and are used for frying or boiling.

Popular cultivars of soft-fleshed roots include 'Centennial', 'Jasper', and 'Goldrush'; 'Nugget' and 'Yellow Jersey' are good firm-fleshed cultivars.

The plants are usually ready for harvest about 130 to 150 days after transplanting, though the roots will continue to grow as long as the vines remain green. As soon as the leaves begin to yellow and fall, cut the foliage away and carefully dig the roots. Dry soil makes digging easier. Get them all out of the ground before the soil temperature drops to 50 degrees F. The thin-skinned roots bruise easily, so handle them as little as possible.

Sweet potato roots should be cured to keep well. Pile them 2 to 3 feet high in your garden, and cover them with clear plastic for seven to ten days. Heat generated by the respiring roots and from sunlight will keep the pile temperature around 80 degrees F. Any small cuts or digging marks in the roots will cork over and heal quickly. After curing, store the roots at 55 to 60 degrees F. They will keep for two to six months, depending on the cultivar. Do not store them in the refrigerator; this would chill them and lead to decay.

VINE CROPS (CUCURBITS)

Members of this group all belong to the gourd family, Cucurbitaceae. All produce sprawling vines that require much space and should be trained onto trellises or planted near the edge of the garden and trained to grow outward onto the lawn. Some members also have bushy cultivars that are useful where garden space is limited. Side-dressing and most cultivation ceases when the vines begin to run.

Cucumbers

Like so many other vegetables, the origin of the cucumber is obscure, though scientists now believe it originated in southeast Asia at least twelve thousand years ago. We know it has been grown for its immature fruit for more than three thousand years and was carried along the ancient trade routes from India to Greece and Rome, and somewhat later into China. The Romans were so fond of cucumbers that they raised them in greenhouses in winter. Roman traders introduced the plant to other parts of Europe. It was brought to North America by the middle of the sixteenth century.

The cucumber makes its best growth in temperatures between 65 and 86 degrees F., with 82 degrees F. being ideal. Growth slows substantially above 90 degrees F. or below 60 degrees F. Below 50 degrees F. the plant chills and will eventually die.

The cucumber is a deep-rooted annual vine that can grow up to 10 feet in length. The plant displays one of three different habits of growth. Indeterminate cultivars form new shoots and extend in length during the entire season, until they die in the fall. This makes for a sprawling plant that takes up a lot of space. With determinate cultivars, a flower cluster forms at the tip of the vine and stops its extension growth. Plants of this type are not quite as sprawling as those of the indeterminate type. Compact cultivars have a bushy habit and are well suited to the small garden and containers.

Standard cucumbers are monoecious—they have male and female flowers on the same plant. You can identify the female flower by the small undeveloped fruit at its base. The first flowers to bloom are male, and early in the season under long days and high temperatures, or under stressful conditions any time of the season, you'll have more male flowers than female. As the season progresses and the days become shorter and cooler, male and female flowers will appear in about equal proportions.

Cucumber cultivars have recently been bred that produce a greater number of female flowers. Predominately female, or PF, cultivars produce far fewer male flowers than the monoecious lines. Since they produce many more female flowers, they bear more fruits, and fruit set is more concentrated, which enables all the cucumbers to ripen at about the same time. Gynoecious cultivars produce only female flowers; thus every flower on the plant is a potential fruit. These cultivars also ripen all their fruits at about the same time. Since there are no male flowers in gynoecious cultivars, the packet includes a few seeds of a PF or monoecious cultivar so that there will be male flowers for pollination.

For good cucumber seed germination and plant growth, soil temperature of at least 68 degrees F. is required, and 85 degrees F. is optimum. Plant your seeds in well-drained soil 1 to 1½ feet apart in rows 4 feet apart, or plant several seeds each in hills 3 to 4 feet apart, and thin the seedlings to two plants per hill. (The term *hill* does not mean a small mound of soil, but a single planting hole.) You can use transplants as long as you don't disturb their root systems.

Since cucumbers are vines, you can save garden space by training them onto a trellis or planting them on the edge of the garden and letting them sprawl out onto the grass.

These are fast-growing plants that require a lot of nutrients. Broadcast fertilizer before planting, and side-dress once just as the plants begin to form vines and sprawl. They respond well to rotted manure, and you can place a handful or two into each hill at planting.

Since the fruits are mostly water, these plants need large amounts—up to 2 inches a week in hot weather—for best yields. Adequate water is especially critical during bloom and fruiting. Do not wet the foliage; this will create mildew problems, especially if it's late in the day, when the leaves have no time to dry before dark. Use a soaker hose or watering can, and water in the morning only.

A cucumber or squash plant will nearly stand upright several inches off the ground just before it begins to run, or sprawl. Side-dress before the plant falls over and begins to run.

Black plastic mulch prevents weed growth, warms the soil, conserves moisture, and can increase your yield substantially. It's worth the extra expense for cucumbers. Organic mulches are satisfactory, but don't apply them until the soil has warmed. If you choose to cultivate instead, do so shallowly and often until the plants begin to run.

In addition to the different vining and flowering habits, cucumbers can be categorized as slicing or pickling types. Slicers, used mostly in salads, are generally long, slender, straight, thick skinned, and dark green. They have a relatively large seed cavity that will make them soft if pickled. 'Pacer', 'Poinsett', and 'Sweet-Slice' are particularly good monoecious cultivars; 'Dasher II', 'Gemini', and 'Slicemaster' are great gynoecious cultivars.

Picklers are light green, short, thin skinned, and warty. They have a smaller seed cavity that allows them to stay firm during the pickling process. Most newer pickling cultivars, such as 'Bounty', 'Pioneer', and 'Score', are gynoecious.

Harvest begins about fifty-five to seventy days after planting. Pick slicing fruits while they're still green and several inches long and pickling fruits at 2 to 4 inches long. Never let cucumbers ripen and yellow on the vine. Fruits in this state are seedy and tasteless, and they send signals to the plant to stop flowering. If you can't use them, pick them for the compost heap.

What's Wrong?

Many of my cucumber fruits are misshapen and fall from the vine before they're ready to be picked. Why?

This sounds like poor pollination. Perhaps you didn't have enough bees for the task, or the weather was windy, cool, or wet.

Why are my cucumbers bitter? My neighbor told me it was because I planted them near carrots.

Bitterness in cucumbers may be due to temperatures above 92 degrees F. or excessive amounts of cool, wet weather. But carrots do not cause bitterness in cucumbers.

When we returned from vacation, our cucumber plants had only a few big yellow fruits on them. They never produced any more. Why?

Vacation at a different time next year. Cucumber fruits that are allowed to mature and ripen on the vine will shut down the fruit production. Keep picking the fruits as they enlarge, and the plant will keep producing.

Melons

Although different types of melons originated in different parts of the world, all are heat-loving members of the same family, and their cultural requirements are similar.

Muskmelons probably originated in western Africa or the Middle

East—their precise center of origin is unknown. Columbus brought the first seeds to the New World in 1494, and the plants were reintroduced into North America by colonists in the 1600s. It is a muskmelon that you buy in the store, not a cantaloupe. The name was changed as a marketing ploy to increase consumption of the fruit, since "cantaloupe" sounds so much more exotic to the consumer's ear than "muskmelon." Very few true cantaloupes are grown in the United States.

Honeydews, casabas, true cantaloupes, and Persian melons belong to the same species as muskmelons, and so all readily intercross, resulting in many gradations among the different fruits. The watermelon belongs to a different genus and species that is believed to have originated in tropical Africa but supposedly was reported by the first European settlers as being grown by the Native Americans in the Illinois River Valley in the early 1600s. The mystery as to how this melon crossed the Atlantic so early may be solved by conjecturing that the "Indian melon" was truly a native citron and not a watermelon.

All melons love heat and require a long growing season, with optimum temperatures between 65 and 90 degrees F. Muskmelons do better at the lower end of this range (65 to 75 degrees F.); watermelons prefer the upper end (75 to 85 degrees F.). Because of its tropical origin, the watermelon is a bit more tolerant of high humidity.

Melon seedlings are damaged very easily. Do not disturb their root systems during transplanting. Any cultivation or frost damage to the seedling during its first week of growth will set the plant back substantially. The highly branched taproot, which in muskmelons and relatives grows about 18 to 36 inches deep and in watermelons up to 60 inches deep, supports vine growth that is at first upright. After the first six leaves have formed, the main shoot branches, and the plant falls and begins to run, meaning it forms vines and begins to sprawl.

Muskmelons are andromonoecious—they bear both perfect and male flowers. Watermelons are monoecious and bear both male and female flowers. The male flowers are the first to bloom, followed by the female flowers several days later.

Watermelon plants usually bear only one or two fruits. If more set, all will be small. Muskmelons bear several fruits per vine.

Light soils warm earlier in the spring and give melons a quick start. Melon seeds germinate at soil temperatures as low as 60 degrees F., but it's better to wait to plant until the soil has warmed to around 75 degrees F. to speed germination. Soil temperatures of 90 to 95 degrees F. are optimum for germination of all melon seeds.

Plant the seeds in hills of several seeds each. For muskmelons, space the hills 18 inches apart in the row, with 6 feet between rows; for watermelons, 30 inches apart in the row, with 8 feet between rows. A handful of rotted manure or compost in the bottom of each hole will get the plants off to a good start.

If you use transplants, they should have been grown in peat pots. Do not remove the plants from the pots, but plant the entire pot, since any damage to the root system will doom your crop.

As with other vine crops, train the melons onto trellises to save garden space, or plant them at the edge of the garden and let them sprawl onto the lawn.

Though melons are not particularly heavy feeders, they should have sufficient fertilizer to sustain uninterrupted growth throughout the season. Good vine growth is necessary to supply sugar to the fruits. Apply preplant fertilizer, and side-dress the plants just before they begin to run.

Although watermelons are more drought tolerant than muskmelons, all melons should receive 1 to $1^1/2$ inches of water a week throughout the season. Water is especially critical during fruit set and melon growth. Avoid wetting the foliage; use drip irrigation or water with a watering can. Melons are highly susceptible to both powdery and downy mildews, which destroy the leaves and cause the melons to be bitter or tasteless.

Once the melons begin to run, they will smother many of the weeds in the garden. Until that time, however, you must keep weeds from competing with the melon plants. Because melons love warm soil temperatures, they respond very well to the use of black plastic much. Using this mulch in conjunction with plastic tunnels can substantially increase both your early and total yields. You can also use organic mulches, provided the soil has warmed before you apply them, or you can cultivate.

Melons are highly susceptible to mildew and wilts. Crenshaw melons have very poor disease resistance and are grown mostly in the dry West. Some cultivars of the other melons are resistant to many of the mildews and wilts that once made melon growing so difficult. Stick to these varieties for your garden.

The icebox type of watermelons are usually small (about 10 pounds) and round. They require only about 70 to 80 days to ripen their fruits, making them perfect for northern gardens. 'Sugar Baby' and 'Yellow Baby' are two good ones. If you have a longer season (up to 130 days), try the regular size 'Crimson Sweet' or the old standby 'Charleston Gray'.

Seedless watermelons usually require a longer growing season and need to be started indoors for northern gardens. Seedless plants need to have a normal cultivar planted alongside for pollination. Under stressful conditions, such as drought, don't be surprised to find a few rudimentary seeds in these melons.

Muskmelons need about the same amount of time as watermelons to mature their fruits. Some great orange-fleshed cultivars include 'Ambrosia', 'Luscious Plus', and 'Sweet Granite'. Honeydews do best in dry climates. If you want to try them and you live in a humid climate, try 'Earli-Dew'.

Muskmelon fruits mature about six to eight weeks after pollination, watermelon ten weeks. When fully mature and at its highest sugar content, the muskmelon fruit will separate from its stem. This is called the *full slip* stage. Wait for this to occur, then pick the melons immediately.

This melon was placed on a flowerpot to avoid rot. The stem has separated from the fruit, signaling the full slip stage and time to harvest.

Honeydews and casabas do not separate when ripe, so you'll have to use other criteria to determine when to harvest. The changes that occur during ripening—the skin of the melon turns from lime green to creamy white or even golden yellow, and the blossom end softens slightly—are good indicators of ripeness.

Watermelons also do not separate, but there are many ways to tell when to harvest these fruits. First, look at the ground spot, a light area on the bottom of the fruit where it rested on the ground. This will turn from white in an immature watermelon to yellow in a ripe one. Next, examine the tendril across from the stem of the melon. The melon is usually ripe when this turns brown or black. Last, you can try thumping the melon. Unripe melons have a metallic ring when rapped; ripe melons have a dull thud. The sound varies with the time of day, however, and the technique requires a lot of practice, so you are better off using the first two methods. If you harvest discerningly, your melon will be sweet and have bright flesh.

What's Wrong?

Why are my melons bitter?

There are many causes for off flavors in melons. Cool weather during ripening will make melons bitter, and the loss of foliage due to storms or mildew will cause them to generally lack flavor.

Why do the blossoms on my watermelons drop and the plants set no fruit?

The first flowers to appear are male and cannot set fruit. In another week or two, you should see fruits beginning to form.

Each year my melon leaves dry up before the fruits are ripe. The melons are tasteless. Why?

This is caused by powdery mildew. This prevalent disease is exacerbated by the high humidity of late summer, making it a problem on this crop. Look for white powdery areas, and use a fungicide before these get too bad. If the plant has no leaves to produce sugar, the melons will taste terrible.

Pumpkins

Pumpkins, squash, and *gourds* are common terms based not in botany but in culinary uses for the fruits. Plants bearing these fruits belong to different species of the vine crop family. Most pumpkins belong to the species *Cucurbita pepo* and *C. moschata*. The term *pumpkin* refers to those thick-rinded fruits that are harvested mature and either fed to livestock or baked into pies. Their flesh is generally strong flavored and coarse textured, and they are not usually served as a vegetable with meals. Pumpkins bear some of the largest fruits of any plant, with some weighing hundreds of pounds.

The terms pumpkin and squash are based on culinary uses of the fruit. Scientifically, there is no distinction. Here are some common ones.

SPECIES	PUMPKIN	SUMMER SQUASH	WINTER SQUASH	GOURDS
pepo	Field Pie Naked- seeded Miniature	Yellow Scallop Zucchini Cocozelle	Acorn Fordhook	Gourds
maxima	Ornamental Jumbo		Hubbard Banana Delicious Buttercup Boston	Turban
moschata	Cheese Crookneck		Butternut	
mixta	Cushaw		Cushaw	

Pumpkins originated in Central America and the southwestern United States and were grown throughout North and South America before Columbus. Tribes as far north as southern Canada were familiar with pumpkins, which originally were grown for their seeds, not their flesh. Earlier explorers thought pumpkins were a type of giant melon and introduced them to Europe and Asia, where farmers found novel ways to eat them. The Italians ate the flowers deep-fried and Manchurians dried strips of pumpkin meat in the sun for later use. Early colonists brewed a beer from pumpkins, persimmons, and maple sugar.

Pumpkins are warm-season plants that grow best when the temperature is between 65 and 85 degrees F. They require 85 to 120 days to mature their fruits but are sensitive to both cold and heat and will not thrive in southern summers.

Three to eight laterals arise from the base of the pumpkin stem, then

Cucurbits bear separate male (left) *and female* (right) *flowers. Only the female bear fruit.*

the plant falls and begins to form vines that spread through the garden. Vines can reach up to 50 feet in length.

Like most other members of this family, pumpkins are monoecious, bearing separate male and female flowers. The male open first, followed by the female several days later. Also like most other family members, they are pollinated by bees. Pumpkins will not cross with cucumbers, muskmelons, or watermelons, but they will cross with other members of the same species. Such crossing will not affect the fruits produced the same year but will show up if seeds from those fruits are saved and planted the following year.

These plants do best on fertile, well-drained soil high in organic matter. A light soil warms faster in the spring and allows earlier planting. Wait for the soil to warm to at least 60 degrees F. before planting.

Plant several seeds of vining pumpkins 6 to 10 feet apart in hills. Thin to two to three plants per hill. Because of their smaller plant size, you can plant seeds of semivining types in hills 4 feet apart in rows 8 feet apart. Seeds of bush-type plants can be planted in hills 3 feet apart in rows 6 feet apart. Most pumpkin plants sprawl, and they will quickly smother the rest of your vegetables if you're not careful. Plant them at the edge of your garden and train them out onto the lawn, or train them onto trellises as you would cucumbers, but you'll have to support the heavy fruits in mesh bags. Old onion bags work well. These plants tolerate partial shade, so you might be able to relegate them to a less-desirable corner of your plot where they can roam freely.

Broadcast a complete fertilizer before you plant, and place a spadeful of compost or rotted manure into the bottom of each planting hole. Side-dress the plants just as they begin to run. Because they are a warm-season vine crop, pumpkins benefit from black plastic mulch.

These succulent, sprawling vines have large fruits made mostly of water and need at least 1 to 2 inches of water a week throughout the season. World-class mammoth pumpkins weighing nearly 1,000 pounds require 8 to 10 inches of water a week.

There are many pumpkin cultivars, in various sizes. Miniature types, including 'Munchkin' and 'Jack-Be-Little', are grown for the specialty trade. Small types bear 4- to 6-pound fruits that are used for cooking and pies. Some good cultivars include 'New England Pie' and 'Baby Pam'.

Intermediate types, such as 'Small Sugar' and 'Spookie', bear 8- to 15-pound fruits. Large types, such as 'Pankow' and 'Connecticut Field', bear 15- to 25-pound fruits. Both are used for cooking and jack-o'-lanterns.

Jumbo, or mammoth, types, such as 'Big Moon' and 'Big Max', bear fruits weighing in excess of 50 pounds. These are the ones used in exhibitions. The world-record pumpkin, weighing nearly 1,000 pounds, was raised from seeds of this type. To grow these extra-large pumpkins, remove all but a single fruit per vine, and keep the plants well supplied with water and nutrients. Then hire a bucket loader to harvest them.

Naked-seeded cultivars, such as 'Lady Godiva', are also available. These bear fruit with large, hull-less seeds.

Allow the pumpkins to mature fully on the vine. Then, before the first frost, when the vine begins to yellow and the fruit rind is hard and well colored, cut them from the vine, leaving a 2- to 4-inch handle. Pumpkins should be cured before storage. Hold them at 85 degrees F. for about ten days to allow any small cuts to cork over. Then store them in a cool, dry place (55 degrees F. and 60 percent relative humidity) for one to six months, depending on the species and condition. Allow for air circulation around all sides of the fruit.

What's Wrong?

Why do many of my blossoms fall without setting fruit?

The male flowers, which bloom first, will drop without setting fruit. Wait a couple of weeks for the female blossoms to appear. If they fall without setting fruit, you probably have too few bees for good pollination.

> **Why are so many of my fruits misshapen?**
> In most cases, this is probably due to poor pollination. With the mammoth type, the fruits will flatten under their own weight.

Squash

As with pumpkins, the name *squash* suggests the use of the fruit rather its botanical classification. Like pumpkins, squash belong to the genus *Cucurbita,* in the species *C. pepo, C.maxima, C. moschata,* and *C. mixta.* Like pumpkins, they originated in the area running from the southwestern United States to the Andes mountains in South America. Unlike pumpkins, however, squash have a mild, fine-grained flesh and are eaten as vegetables with meals. They are also sometimes baked into pies.

Although no warm-season crop will tolerate a frost, squash do better in cooler climates than cucumbers and melons. Winter squash require a long, warm growing season of 80 to 140 days; summer squash need only about 40 to 60 days to produce a crop. This is partly because summer squash are eaten immature, but winter squash must mature fully to be palatable. Dry, sunny weather is important for good pollination, though drought conditions can reduce fruit set.

Squash plants may have either viny or bushy habits. Most summer squash form bushy plants, whereas most winter squash plants are vines.

All squash are monoecious, bearing separate male and female flowers in the ratio of about three female to one male. The male flowers appear first, followed by the female in a couple of weeks. Plants within a species intercross, and certain species will cross with other species. For example, *C. moschata* will cross with *C. pepo* and *C. mixta.* Don't worry about this, however, since the cross will show up only if seeds are saved and planted the following season.

Squash plants do very well when supplied with high amounts of organic matter and moisture, so add a spadeful of rotted manure or compost to the bottom of each hill at planting. Broadcast preplant fertilizer, and side-dress vine types when the plants begin to run and bush types when the first flowers bloom. Squash are heavy feeders, so don't neglect the fertilizer.

The soil should be well drained and have warmed to at least 60 degrees F. or, better yet, to 70 to 95 degrees F. before planting. Plant seeds of bush or small vine-forming cultivars 2 feet apart in rows 5 feet apart. Plant those of the large vine cultivars at least 3 feet apart in rows 7 to 8 feet apart. Drop several seeds into each hill. Thin to two or three plants when they have formed their first leaves. You can also use transplants, but be careful not to disturb their fragile root systems.

Squash, like the other vine crops, need plenty of moisture. Wetting the foliage with sprinklers will encourage diseases, so use a watering can or soaker hose.

Cultivars with smaller vines or even bushes—more practical for the home garden—are becoming common. And the large fruit of the 'Hubbard' has been reduced through breeding to manageable size.

Summer squash come in many colors and shapes. Most common are green, yellow, and white fruits that are round and flat (patty pan), straight (straightneck), club shaped (zucchini), or curved (crookneck). Zucchini cultivars include 'Ambassador', 'Milano', and 'Zucchini Elite'. Yellow squash cultivars such as 'Dixie', 'Early Prolific Straightneck', and 'Seneca Butterbar' (actually a golden zucchini) are terrific. Crookneck squash are passing out of favor because much of the fruit is lost in trimming the crooked neck. Patty pan types include 'Patty Pan', 'Scallopini' (a zucchini–patty pan cross), and 'White Ruffles'.

Winter squash are usually green, golden, or buff and more or less globe shaped or cylindrical. There are several main types in this group. Hubbard types all have the typical shape of a Hubbard but may be blue-green or golden. They may be standard size (up to 50 pounds), such as 'Blue Hubbard', or dwarf (several pounds), such as 'Dwarf Blue Hubbard'. Acorn squash form bushy plants with acorn-shaped fruits, which may have a deep green or golden rind. 'Table Ace' and 'Table Queen' are good cultivars for the home garden. Buttercup squash actually look more like acorns than the acorn squash do, coming complete with caps like those of acorns. 'Buttercup' and the bush-type 'Sweet Mama' are home garden favorites. The familiar buff-colored butternut squash is available in a large-fruited cultivar, 'Waltham', and the somewhat smaller 'Puritan', which is just right for today's smaller families. Delicious types resemble butternut squash with long, curved necks. 'Delicious' is a standard cultivar.

Pick summer squash two to eight days after bloom (forty to sixty days after planting), when the fruit is 4 to 8 inches long and 2 inches in diameter (3 to 4 inches in diameter for scallop squash) and the rind is still soft. Summer squash grow fast, and you may have to harvest them daily. Never let the fruit mature on the vine; this signals the plant to stop flowering. Besides, mature summer squash are seedy and lousy to eat. If you can't use all the squash, and you've already inundated your neighbors with bags of zucchini, then pick the fruit and put them onto the compost pile or feed them to the hogs—just don't leave them on the plants. Be gentle when you harvest summer squash; the fruits bruise very easily.

Harvest your winter squash when they are fully mature (80 to 140 days after planting), full-size, and a deep color. Butternut fruit should have no green veins. The fruit rinds should be so hard that your fingernail cannot puncture them. Pick them before the first frost, since even the slightest freeze will damage them. Butternut types are especially sensitive to chilling in the garden at temperatures of 35 to 45 degrees F. Cut them from the vine, leaving a 2-inch piece of stem attached. Cure any squash you plan to store. Place them under cover at 80 degrees F. for ten days. This will allow any wounds to the rind to seal. Store them in a dry room at 50 degrees F. and about 60 percent relative humidity, where they will keep for several months, depending on type.

What's Wrong?

I have wonderful-looking squash vines, but few fruit. Why?
This is probably due to poor pollination. Either there were not enough bees, or there was poor weather during bloom.

My squash vines grow well, then suddenly wilt. Why?
Look for a little hole with sawdustlike material in the stem where the plant leaves the ground. If you find such a hole, made by a squash vine borer, slit the stem lengthwise with a razor blade, passing through the hole and upward along the stem, until you slice through a small worm. Then mound damp soil over the wound. The vine will send out roots in that area.

Gourds
Gourds are vine crops that are grown for their ornamental, novelty, or utilitarian value. Most originated in tropical and subtropical America.

The *Luffa* genus originated in tropical Asia and spread to China by 600 A.D.

Though many of them have edible flesh, their original use was as ladles, spoons, and water jugs or other containers.

Gourds have requirements similar to those of pumpkins and squash. They are very tender and will not grow at all when temperatures fall below 60 degrees F.

Gourds can be direct seeded to the garden 3 feet apart in rows 7 feet apart. Train them onto a trellis so that the fruits can hang freely and maintain their shape. Support the larger fruits in onion bags. Other cultural requirements are similar to those of squash.

Gourds belong to several species. Those in the genus *Cucurbita* have thick shells and are difficult to cure. Their color fades after three to four months, and they are probably not the best choice for ornaments. 'Apple', 'Crown of Thorns', and 'Spoon' are some popular cultivars. 'Turk's Turban' is also a gourd in this category, but it is sometimes listed as a winter squash. Harvest *Cucurbita* gourds after a light frost has killed the vine, and the fruits are bright and hard. Cure them for several days in a warm, dry, dark place.

Specimens of the genus *Lagenaria*, including the cultivars 'Calbash', 'Drum', and 'Swan Gourd', make the best dippers, birdhouses, and rattles. Grow them on a fence so that the fruits hang free. You can harvest immature *Lagenaria* fruits about a week after bloom and eat them like eggplant or summer squash. Or wait until after a light frost, when the fruit rinds harden, the fruits feel light, and the tendrils next to the fruit stems brown. Cure them for six months in a warm, dry room.

Gourds of the genus *Luffa*, also called vegetable sponge and dishrag gourd, are grown primarily for their fine networks of fibers used as sponges for bathing. You can harvest *Luffa* fruits when they are about 4 inches long and eat them raw like cucumbers or as a cooked vegetable. Or you can harvest them as you would mature *Lagenaria*, place them in a tub of running water, and peel them like an orange. Then squeeze the inner core to remove the seeds and flesh. Dry the remaining fibrous skeleton for use as a bathing sponge.

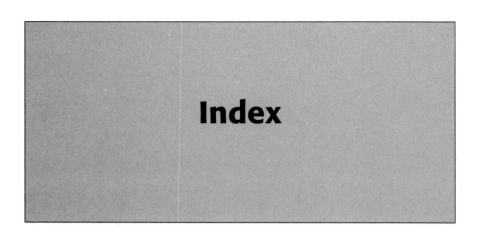

Index

Page numbers in italics indicate illustrations, tables, or charts.

Alliums, 164-72, *see also* individual
  names
Annuals, *8, see also* individual names
Aphids, *121*
Asparagus, 154-58
  pest and disease control methods
    for, *136*
  symptoms of pest damage on, *124*

Bacillus thuringiensis, 133
Beans:
  adzuki, 225
  asparagus, 224
  black-eyed peas, 224
  catjang, 224
  fava, 224
  garbanzo, 224
  garden soybeans, 224
  hyacinth, 225
  lima, 221-24
  mung, 225
  pest and disease control methods
    for, *136*
  scarlet runner, 224
  snap, 221-24
  symptoms of pest damage on, *124*
Beetles:
  Colorado potato, *120*
  cucumber, *120*
  Japanese, *120*
  Mexican bean, *121*
Beets, 202-4
  pest and disease control methods
    for, *136*
  symptoms of pest damage on, *124*
Biennials, *8, see also* individual
  names
Black salsify. *See* Scorzonera
Bolting, 13
Broccoli, 175-77

hardening off, 95
pest and disease control methods
  for, *137*
symptoms of pest damage on, *124*
Brussels sprouts, 178-79
  hardening off, 95
  pest and disease control methods
    for, *137*
  symptoms of pest damage on, *124*

Cabbage, 179-82
  hardening off, 95
  pest and disease control methods
    for, *137*
  symptoms of pest damage on, *124*
Cabbage maggot, *121*
Calcium (CA), 53
Carrots, 205-7
  pest and disease control methods
    for, 137
Cauliflower, 183-85
  hardening off, 95-96
  pest and disease control methods
    for, *137*
  symptoms of pest damage on, *124*
Celeriac, 172
Celery, 172-75
Chicory, 219-20
Chinese cabbage, 185-86
Chitting, 79-82
Chives, 164
  harvesting, *165*
Cold frames, *89*
Cole crops, 175-87, *see also* individ-
  ual names
Collards, 188
  pest and disease control methods
    for, *137*
Companion planting, 114
  pest control and, 115
Compost, 44-48
  factors that determine speed of
    decomposition, 46-47

garbage can, 47, *48*
  as mulch, 72
  pile, *45*
Cool-season crops, 5-6, 7, 154
  alliums, 164-72
  celeriac, 172
  celery, 172-75
  cole crops, 175-87
  greens, 187-94
  peas, 194-97
  perennials, 154-64
  planting dates for, *103, 108-11*
  potatoes, 197-201
  root crops, 201-14
  salad crops, 214-20
  see also individual names
Corn, sweet, 244-49
  classes of, 246-47
  pest and disease control methods
    for, *137*
  symptoms of pest damage on, *125*
Corn earworms, *121*
Cover crops, 44
  for weed control, 74
Crop protectors, 96-99
Crop rotation, 117
  for pest control, 119-20
  for weed control, 74
Cropping systems, 114
  companion planting, 114, 115
  interplanting, 114-16
  nurse cropping, 117
  relay cropping, 117
  rotation cropping, 74, 117, 119-20
  succession planting, 27, 116
  trap cropping, 116, 128-29
  vertical cropping, 116-17
Cucumbers, 251-54
  pest and disease control methods
    for, *137-38*
  symptoms of pest damage on, *125*
Cucurbits. *See* Vine crops
Cultivation, 68-71

Cutworms, *121*

Damsel bugs, 131
Dandelions, 188-89
Disease control, *136-41, see also* Pest control

Eggplant, 226-29
hardening off, 96
pest and disease control methods for, *138*
symptoms of pest damage on, *125*
Endive, 218-19
Escarole, 218
Ethylene, 149
European corn borers, *120*

Fertilizers, 55
applying, 60-61
broadcasting, 60
commercial, 55-57, 58
foliar, 14, 61
organic, 55-56, 57-58, *59*
side-dressing, 60-61
soil testing and, 58-60
starter solution, 61
Field capacity, 14
Flies:
syrphid, *132*
tachinid, *132*

Garden planning, 25-27
shape, 29
site selection, 29-34
size, 27-29
Garden problems:
causes and control of, *122-23*
see also Disease control; Pest control
Garlic, 165-66
Globe artichokes, 158-59
Gourds, 264-65
Green manure crops, 44
Greens, 187-94, *see also* individual names

Hardening off, 93-95
guidelines for, 95-96
Harvest, when to, 145-46
Hoes, 62
sharpening, *65*
see also Wheel hoes
Horseradish, 160-61
Hotbeds, *89*

Insects:
beneficial, 131-33
see also Pest control; Pests
Interplanting, 114-16

Jerusalem artichokes, 159-60

Kale, 189-90
symptoms of pest damage on, *125-26*
Kohlrabi, 186-87

Lacewings, 131, *132*
Ladybugs, 131, *132*
Leeks, *166*, 167
Lettuce, 214-18
hardening off, 96
pest and disease control methods for, *138-39*
symptoms of pest damage on, *125*
Liberty Gardens, vi
Lime, 38-39
materials, *39*

Magnesium (MG), 53
Manure, 43-44
as mulch, 72
Melons, 254-58
pest and disease control methods for, *139, 141*
symptoms of pest damage on, *126*
Micronutrients, 53-54
Mulching, 71-72
materials, 72-74
Mustard, 190-91
pest and disease control methods for, *139*
symptoms of pest damage on, *126*

New Zealand spinach, 225-26
Nitrogen (N), 49-52
Nurse cropping, 117
Nursery stock, *80-81*
Nutrients, 13-15, 49
calcium, 53
magnesium, 53
micronutrients, 53-54
nitrogen, 49-52
phosphorus, 52
potassium, 52-53
sowing indoors and, 90
sulfur, 53

Okra, 242-44
pest and disease control methods for, *139*
symptoms of pest damage on, *126*
Onions, 167-71
curing, *170*
hardening off, 96
pest and disease control methods for, *139*
sets, *168*
symptoms of pest damage on, *126*
Organic matter, 41-43
breakdown of, 42
compost, 44-48
cover crops, 44
green manure crops, 44
manure, 43-44
Oyster root. *See* Salsify

Parsnips, 208-9
Peas, 194-97
pest and disease control methods for, *139*
symptoms of pest damage on, *126*
Peppers, 229-33

hardening off, 96
pest and disease control methods for, *139-40*
symptoms of pest damage on, *126*
Perennials, 8, 154-64, *see also* individual names
Pest control:
birds and other wildlife for, 130-31
companion planting, 115
crop rotation, 119-20
fall plowing, 120
hand picking, 130
hose and soap sprays, 130
keeping plants healthy, 128
location, 128
methods for specific vegetables, *136-41*
organic methods of, 143
pathogens, 133
pesticides, 133-44
physical barriers, 129
planting times, 128
predators and parasites, 131-33
reflectors, 130
sanitation, 118-19
seed and plant quality, 121-28
trap crops, 128-29
traps, 129
see also Garden problems
Pesticides, 133-35
biological, 135
botanical, 135-42
inorganic compound, 142-44
synthetic organic compound, 142
toxicity, *134*
Pests:
common garden, *120, 121*
damage made by which, *124-27*
pH, soil, 35-36
adjusting, 36
adjusting with lime, 38-39
adjusting with sulfur, 40
adjusting with wood ashes, 39-40
influence on nutrients, *36*
range, *38*
scale, *37*
Phosphorus (P), 52
Photoperiod, 11-12
Photosynthesis, 11
Pirate bugs, 131, *132*
Pit storages, 150-53
Plant growth:
nutrients and, 13-15
phases of, 15
photoperiod and, 11-12
photosynthesis, 11
temperature and, 12-13
water and, 13-15
Plant protectors. *See* Crop protectors
Planting dates, 101-3
for fall crops, *108-11*
latest, *103*
for spring crops, *102, 104-7*
Potassium (K), 52-53
Potatoes, 197-201
pest and disease control methods f